THE CORRESPONDENCE OF
NICHOLAS BIDDLE
DEALING WITH NATIONAL AFFAIRS

THE CORRESPONDENCE OF
NICHOLAS BIDDLE

dealing with

NATIONAL AFFAIRS · 1807-1844

Edited by REGINALD C. McGRANE, Ph.D.

ASSISTANT PROFESSOR OF HISTORY IN THE UNIVERSITY OF CINCINNATI

C

BOSTON & NEW YORK
HOUGHTON MIFFLIN COMPANY
MCMXIX

TO THE MEMORY OF

MY FATHER AND MY GRANDMOTHER

I AM NOT *a Whig. I am not a Locofoco. I once belonged to a party now obsolete called the Democratic Party, a very good party until it was spoiled by Genl. Jackson. I am now only an American Citizen deeply concerned in the welfare & very anxious about the character of the country.*

NICHOLAS BIDDLE

Preface

No APOLOGY is necessary in presenting to the public the following correspondence of Nicholas Biddle, President of the Second Bank of the United States. From 1804 to 1839 he was almost constantly engaged in some official capacity with national or state administrations; and throughout his whole life, until his death in 1844, he was intimately in touch with the leading statesmen of the day. These years embrace a most eventful epoch in the history of our nation. The purchase of Louisiana, the War of 1812, the financial and commercial readjustment following the conflict, the establishment of the Second Bank of the United States, the organization and development of its power, the long struggle with President Jackson, the re-charter of the institution by the State of Pennsylvania, the panic of 1837, the Sub-Treasury and President Van Buren, the appeal of Texas for annexation, the whirlwind election of 1840, the rupture between Tyler and the Whigs, the Webster-Ashburton Treaty, and the preparation for the heated campaign of 1844 — all fall within the scope of Nicholas Biddle's life; and with all these movements the great financier was more than an interested spectator. Not only was he in close communication with those in power, but in many instances he was the center of operations; and on all occasions he displayed the sterling, stalwart qualities which have marked the Biddles of Pennsylvania one of the most distinguished families in our land.

Since their entrance into America, now more than two centuries ago, the Biddles have been active in the service of the country. Their advent was contemporaneous with that of William Penn, for the original ancestor, William Biddle, accompanied Penn to the new province. They bore their part in the privations and aspirations of the early settlers; and in the Revolution they gave their best in blood and brains to further the cause of democracy. Charles Biddle, the father of Nicholas, was, at the birth of the latter, Vice-President of the Supreme Executive Council of Pennsylvania; Edward Biddle, an uncle, was a representative from Pennsylvania in the Continental Congress of 1774, and later Speaker of the House of Representatives of Pennsylvania; Nicholas Biddle, another uncle, distinguished himself during the war while commanding the frigate *Randolph* by attacking a British gunship of double the number of guns and losing his life in the cause for which he fought. With such ancestors as these, Nicholas Biddle could not help being imbued with patriotism, loyalty, and devotion to his native land. His life, as illustrated in his correspondence, records his adherence to these lofty principles. In the following pages Nicholas Biddle, in his own words, relates his participation in the events of his period; and the editor has trespassed on the account only with such notes as might help the halting memory of the reader in uniting the broken links of the narrative. But in view of the grave deficiency of an adequate life of this distinguished man — which the editor hopes to remedy in the near future — a short sketch of his life and a brief analysis of the salient contributions to our historical knowledge disclosed in the ensuing letters, seems not inappropriate.

Nicholas Biddle was born in Philadelphia, January 8, 1786. He began his education at the academy, whence he went to the University of Pennsylvania. He was about to take his degree from the latter institution in 1799, when, owing to his extreme youth — being then but thirteen years of age — he determined to enter Princeton. In 1801, after a two-and-a-half-year course, he was graduated at the head of his class, dividing the distinction with Mr. Edward Watts of Virginia. He then commenced the study of law, and soon attracted the attention of some of the leading men in the land by his diligence and skill. He was called from the pursuit of his profession by General Armstrong, a friend of the family, when the latter was appointed Minister of the United States to France in 1804. In that year, as private secretary to the Minister, Nicholas Biddle embarked upon his public career.

From 1804 to 1807, Mr. Biddle was in Europe. As secretary to General Armstrong, he was involved in the financial transactions necessitated by the sale of Louisiana; and in this capacity he began to exhibit those phenomenal abilities which later marked him as one of the greatest financiers of his age. At the conclusion of his service with General Armstrong, he traveled extensively in Europe, visiting with particular interest Greece and England. In England he met our Minister, James Monroe, and there began the friendship between these two which continued throughout their lives. He returned home in 1807 and began the practice of law in Philadelphia. However, his innate love for literature could not be quelled, and he occupied his spare moments in editing the "Journal of Lewis and Clark," writing a great deal for periodicals on various subjects, and finally associating himself with Dennie in the editing of the *Portfolio*, one of the landmarks in American literature. Between 1810 and 1818, he served two terms in the state legislature, where he distinguished himself in his advocacy of adequate education for Pennsylvania, in behalf of the re-charter of the United States Bank, and in military legislation during the War of 1812. He was chosen a Government director of the Bank of the United States in 1819; in 1822 he was elected President of the institution. He continued in this office until 1836, when he was elected President of the new corporation organized under the laws of Pennsylvania. But until the close of his life, in 1844, he took an active interest in current events.

This brief sketch of Nicholas Biddle's life, however, fails to disclose the man or his achievements. Only a close reading of his entire correspondence can do this. When one peruses the numerous letters from such men as James Monroe, Henry Clay, Daniel Webster, John C. Calhoun, Dr. Thomas Cooper, Horace Binney, John Tyler, George McDuffie, Edward Everett, John McLean, Edward Livingston, asking and seeking advice on public questions, the manifold activities of the great financier begin to appear. Agricultural societies, literary clubs, educators, colleges, philanthropists, financiers, and public men besought his assistance and counsel. To all he showed the same courtesy and interest while carrying on his business transactions and his titanic struggle with President Jackson. From this great mass of correspondence the editor has selected only those letters pertaining to national affairs, and these naturally fall into the following groups: those relating to the long bank controversy; the re-charter of the bank by the State of Pennsylvania; the possibility of Biddle as a Presidential candidate in 1840; the panic of 1837 and the Sub-Treasury problem; additional information on the McCullough *versus* Maryland case; the election of 1840; the framing of Harrison's cabinet; the split between Tyler and the Whigs; the position of Webster in the Tyler cabinet and the reasons for his stand; and the preparations for the Presidential conflict of 1844. In all these affairs Nicholas Biddle was either the center of interest or a close observer, and his letters throw much light upon many disputed points in connection with these topics. In giving these for the first time to the general public, the editor has rigidly adhered to their original form, without changing either content or spelling. With reference to punctuation the editor has not of course tried to "modernize" it in any way, nor to interfere with it at all, except to substitute periods at ends of sentences, where the writer has simply placed a stroke. In other places the editor has stricken out some superfluous commas when they seemed to interfere with the reading of the sentence. But, generally speaking, he has done as little as seemed possible.

In the preparation of this volume the editor desires briefly to mention the great assistance he has received from a number of persons. First and foremost, he wishes to express his extreme gratitude for the courtesy and friendly coöperation at all stages of the work of the grandsons of Nicholas Biddle — Messrs. Edward and Charles Biddle. In 1913, the members of the family deposited a large portion of their grandfather's correspondence in the Library of Congress. Permission was freely granted the editor to cull from this mine of information; and later, at the home of Mr. Edward Biddle at Philadelphia, and at the old homestead at Andalusia, Mr. Charles Biddle rendered invaluable aid in placing at his disposal the intimate family collection. To both of these gentlemen he takes this opportunity of acknowledging their scholarly and hearty interest in the project. The debt which all historical students owe to Mr. Gaillard Hunt, chief of the Division of Manuscripts of the Library of Congress, and especially to his able and ever-courteous assistant, Mr. John C. Fitzpatrick, for their efficient services, have been but increased in the present instance. To his former teacher and continual counsellor, Professor William E. Dodd, of the University of Chicago, the editor is deeply indebted for reading the manuscript and offering many valuable suggestions. His former instructors and present associates, Professors Merrick Whitcomb and I. J. Cox, by their advice and daily encouragement have added to the heavy obligations which he already owes them. The editor's wife at all stages in the preparation of this volume has rendered indispensable assistance.

REGINALD C. McGRANE

University of Cincinnati

Contents

JULY 6, 1807   TO JAMES MONROE 3
                Advice on a career

JUNE 21, 1809   TO JAMES MONROE 4
                Relations of England and America

JULY 11, 1809   FROM ROBERT WALSH 6
                Characterization of the House of Representatives

AUG. 1, 1809   FROM ROBERT WALSH 6
                On Erskine's difficulties

MAY 5, 1815   FROM JAMES MONROE 7
                European conditions; a new coalition; Ferdinand VII
                in Spain; new policy for America

DEC. 24, 1815   FROM CLEMENT C. BIDDLE 9
                Suggestions for army bill

JAN. 31, 1819   TO JAMES MONROE 12
                Appointment of Biddle as Director of United States
                Bank

JAN. 8, 1820   FROM JOHN MCKIM, JR. 13
                Politics in the Bank

APRIL 11, 1820   FROM JAMES MONROE 13
                Politics in the choosing of a director in the Lexington
                Branch

OCT. 8, 1820   TO JAMES MONROE (enclosing pamphlet) 14
                Politics in Pennsylvania; pamphlet addressed to con-
                stituents

OCT. 29, 1822   TO ——— 26
                Biddle's ideas on qualifications for a President of the
                Bank

DEC. 2, 1822   FROM JOHN C. CALHOUN 28
                Calhoun offers his services to the Bank

DEC. 6, 1822   TO JOHN C. CALHOUN 29
                Reply to letter

FEB. 3, 1823   TO CAMPBELL P. WHITE 30
                Organization of exchanges

FEB. 3, 1823   TO ROBERT LENOX 31
                On administration of Bank

JAN. 5, 1824   TO DAVID SEARS 32
                Politics in the selection of a director in the Boston
                Branch

MARCH 15, 1825 TO COLONEL GEORGE GIBBS 34
                Biddle's business principles

APRIL 22, 1825   TO ISAAC LAWRENCE 34
     Policy of the Bank in the Panic of 1825

MAY 12, 1825   TO ISAAC LAWRENCE 36
     Solicitude for the prosperity of the Bank

JUNE 24, 1825   TO ROBERT LENOX 36
     Question of the dividend

JUNE 28, 1825   FROM WALTER BOWNE 37
     Rumor of attack on Bank

JAN. 23, 1826   TO JAMES LLOYD 38
     Bank and State authorities

FEB. 16, 1826   TO DANIEL WEBSTER 38
     First reference to Draft Notes

MARCH 14, 1826   TO JOHN McKIM, JR. 39
     Appointment of assistant cashiers

NOV. 23, 1826   TO GENERAL JOHN P. BOYD 40
     Selection of cashier for Branch Bank

MAY 7, 1827   TO JAMES CROMMELIEU 41
     Policy of promotion in Bank

JUNE 29, 1827   TO DANIEL WEBSTER 41
     Financial basis for selection of directors

NOV. 27, 1827   TO CAMPBELL P. WHITE 42
     Politics and the Bank

DEC. 13, 1827   FROM JOHN SERGEANT 43
     Barbour's attack on the Bank

DEC. 13, 1827   FROM EDWARD EVERETT 44
     Barbour's attack on the Bank

DEC. 16, 1827   TO CHURCHILL C. CAMBRELENG 44
     Effect of Barbour's attack on the Bank

DEC. 18, 1827   JOHN W. BARNEY TO COLT 45
     Barbour's attack on the Bank

DEC. 20, 1827   FROM ROSWELL L. COLT 46
     Barbour's attack on the Bank

DEC. 20, 1827   FROM CHURCHILL C. CAMBRELENG 46
     Barbour's attack on the Bank

DEC. 21, 1827   FROM JOSEPH GALES, JR. 46
     Barbour's attack on the Bank

DEC. 26, 1827   TO GEORGE McDUFFIE 47
     Biddle congratulates McDuffie on handling resolution

JAN. 7, 1828   TO JOHN POTTER 48
     Effect of Barbour's resolution on dividend and Bank

MAY 28, 1828   FROM HENRY CLAY 48
     Clay's alleged indebtedness to Bank

MAY 30, 1828   TO HENRY CLAY 50
     Reply to Clay's letter

JUNE 17, 1828   FROM A STOCKHOLDER 51
     On the subject of Bank dividend

Contents   xvii

Aug. 14, 1828   To Daniel Webster 52
                Suggestion of Mason's appointment as President of
                Portsmouth Branch

Sept. 22, 1828 From R. Smith 53
                Position of Dickins in Treasury; need for retention

Nov. 19, 1828   From Richard Rush 55
                On the subject of the annual report

Nov. 24, 1828   From Joseph Gales, Jr. 55
                Comments on Biddle's political views

Nov. 25, 1828   To Richard Rush 56
                Suggestions for annual report; value of the Bank to
                the nation

Dec. 2, 1828   To Daniel Webster 58
                Refuses loan to National Intelligencer

Dec. 10, 1828   From Richard Rush 59
                Analysis of his Report

Dec. 20, 1828   From George Hoffman 61
                Effect of Rush's Report; time for recharter

Dec. 22, 1828   To George Hoffman 62
                On Rush's Report

Dec. 29, 1828   To Samuel Smith 62
                Bank adverse to entering political contests

Jan. 5, 1829   From John McLean 63
                Accusations against Kentucky Branches for supposed
                political interference

Jan. 5, 1829   To Samuel Smith 65
                Protection against investigation of personal affairs in
                the Bank

Jan. 7, 1829   From Roswell L. Colt 66
                Rumors of the attitude of the Administration

Jan. 9, 1829   To John Harper 67
                Adverse to politics in Bank

Jan. 10, 1829   To John McLean 68
                Politics in Kentucky Branches

Jan. 11, 1829   To John McLean 69
                Politics in Branch; Kentucky Branches

June 23, 1829   To Josiah Nichol 72
                Bank and politics; Washington interference

July 6, 1829   To Robert Lenox 72
                Portsmouth affair

July 7, 1829   From Robert Lenox 73
                Portsmouth affair

Aug. 14, 1829   From Walter Dun 73
                Politics in Kentucky Branches

Aug. 28, 1829   To General Thomas Cadwalader 75
                Portsmouth Branch

Contents

SEPT. 16, 1829   TO ASBURY DICKINS 75
Newspaper attacks on Bank; no politics in Bank
Portsmouth affair

SEPT. 30, 1829   TO ASBURY DICKINS 77
On Ingham correspondence

OCT. 16, 1829   FROM WILLIAM B. LEWIS 79
Views of Jackson on politics in Bank

OCT. 21, 1829   TO WILLIAM B. LEWIS 80
Jackson and continued opposition to Bank

OCT. 21, 1829   FROM MATTHEW L. BEVAN 81
Alleged satisfaction of Jackson toward Bank

OCT. 26, 1829   FROM SAMUEL JAUDON 82
Jaudon's conference with Jackson

NOV. 9, 1829   EXTRACT FROM WILLIAM B. LEWIS TO HENRY TOLAND . 84
Alleged satisfaction of Jackson toward Bank

NOV. 11, 1829   FROM THE SAME TO THE SAME 85
Alleged satisfaction of Jackson toward Bank

NOV. 15, 1829   FROM WILLIAM B. LEWIS 85
On candidacy of Toland for Speaker of the House

NOV. 22, 1829   TO GEORGE HOFFMAN 87
Need for balancing of political parties in Branches

DEC. 10, 1829   FROM ALEXANDER HAMILTON 88
Jackson's message of 1829; advice against attempted
renewal of charter

DEC. 12, 1829   TO ALEXANDER HAMILTON 91
No idea of renewal of charter

DEC. 15, 1829   TO GEORGE HOFFMAN 91
On President's message of 1829

DEC. 17, 1829   TO NATHANIEL SILSBEE 92
Effect of President's message on stockholders

   MEMORANDUM (in Biddle's handwriting) 93
Account of Biddle's interview with Jackson

JAN. 2, 1830   TO SAMUEL SMITH 94
On President's message of 1829

JAN. 9, 1830   TO JOHN POTTER 95
Gales's and Seaton's relations with the Bank

JAN. 18, 1830   TO JOHN MCKIM, JR. 96
Biddle's views of the effect of the President's message
on Bank

MAY 3, 1830   FROM WILLIAM B. LEWIS 97
Suggests names for directors

MAY 8, 1830   TO WILLIAM B. LEWIS 99
Anxiety regarding President's views

MAY 21, 1830   FROM CHARLES A. DAVIS 101
Van Buren's alleged connection with President's
message

Contents

MAY 25, 1830   FROM WILLIAM B. LEWIS 103
     President Jackson's attitude toward Bank

JUNE 10, 1830 (?)   FROM ROSWELL L. COLT 104
     Van Buren's connection with President's message

JUNE 14, 1830   FROM HENRY CLAY 105
     Connection between Southern politics and attack on
     Bank

JULY 20, 1830   FROM JOSIAH NICHOL 106
     Jackson's visit to Nashville

AUG. 3, 1830   TO JOSIAH NICHOL 107
     Biddle's intrigue with Nichol

SEPT. 11, 1830   FROM HENRY CLAY 110
     Advice against attempt for re-charter

OCT. 30, 1830   —— TO COLONEL HUNTER 114
     Advises against re-charter

OCT. 31, 1830   TO WILLIAM B. LEWIS 114
     Business versus politics in Louisville Branch

NOV. 3, 1830   TO HENRY CLAY 115
     Adverse to an attempt to renewal of charter

DEC. 9, 1830   FROM JOSEPH HEMPHILL 116
     Effect of President's message on renewal

DEC. 9, 1830   FROM JOSEPH HEMPHILL 117
     Advises secrecy of plan for renewal

DEC. 13, 1830   FROM ROBERT SMITH 117
     Alleged views of Jackson on charter; need for modifica-
     tion

DEC. 14, 1830   TO JOSEPH HEMPHILL 118
     Determined on renewal

DEC. 16, 1830   FROM JOHN NORVALL 120
     Political aspect of Congress on renewal

DEC. 19, 1830   FROM JOHN NORVALL 121
     Political aspect of Congress on renewal

DEC. 20, 1830   TO MR. ROBINSON 122
     Supposed public opinion on recharter; need for knowl-
     edge on subject

JAN. 29, 1831   FROM ROSWELL L. COLT 122
     Political relations of Van Buren and Calhoun

FEB. 8, 1831   TO WILLIAM B. LAWRENCE 123
     Employment of newspapers in Bank struggle

FEB. 10, 1831   TO JOSEPH HEMPHILL 124
     Consideration of Duff Green's application for a loan

FEB. 28, 1831   TO ENOCH PARSONS 152
     True policy of Bank in struggle

MARCH 2, 1831   TO JOSEPH GALES 125
     Employment of newspapers in Bank struggles

MAY 4, 1831   TO JAMES HUNTER 126
     Justification for use of press

JUNE 29, 1831   To J. HARPER 127
                 Blair's connection with Bank

OCT. 19, 1831   MEMORANDUM BY BIDDLE 128
                 Biddle's relation with McLane

NOV. 11, 1831   FROM JOHN TILFORD 135
                 Position of Clay on renewal

NOV. 21, 1831   To NATHANIEL SILSBEE 135
                 Preparations for re-charter; selecting directors

DEC. 6, 1831   FROM EDWARD SHIPPEN 136
                 Jackson's view of re-charter; suggested modifications

DEC. 7, 1831   FROM SAMUEL SMITH 138
                 Position of McLane and Smith on renewal

DEC. 11, 1831   FROM ROBERT GIBBES 139
                 Friends of Jackson on Bank

DEC. 12, 1831   FROM C. F. MERCER 140
                 Advises re-charter

DEC. 15, 1831   FROM HENRY CLAY 142
                 Advises re-charter

DEC. 17, 1831   FROM SAMUEL SMITH 143
                 Clay urges renewal of the charter

DEC. 18, 1831   FROM DANIEL WEBSTER 145
                 Webster urges Biddle to come to Washington

DEC. 20, 1831   To ASBURY DICKINS 146
                 On McLane's report

DEC. 20, 1831   FROM THOMAS CADWALADER 146
                 Arrival of Cadwalader; first views

DEC. 21, 1831   FROM THOMAS CADWALADER 147
                 McLane's impressions as to vote; Cadwalader's impressions

DEC. 22, 1831   FROM THOMAS CADWALADER 151
                 McDuffie's views on re-charter; Cadwalader's impressions

DEC. 23, 1831   FROM THOMAS CADWALADER 152
                 Further impressions of Cadwalader

DEC. 23, 1831   To THOMAS CADWALADER 154
                 Influence of McDuffie's opinion on Biddle

DEC. 24, 1831   To THOMAS CADWALADER 154
                 Influence of McDuffie's opinion on Biddle

DEC. 25, 1831   FROM THOMAS CADWALADER 155
                 Further impressions of Cadwalader

DEC. 26, 1831   FROM THOMAS CADWALADER 158
                 Further impressions of Cadwalader

DEC. 26, 1831   FROM THOMAS CADWALADER 160
                 Further impressions of Cadwalader; P. R. Livingston's views

JAN. 4, 1832   To SAMUEL SMITH 161
                 Biddle's reasons for re-charter

Contents

JAN. 5, 1832   FROM LOUIS McLANE 165
         Opinions on renewal of the charter

JAN. 8, 1832 (?)   FROM DANIEL WEBSTER 169
         Views on memorial

JAN. 10, 1832   FROM JOHN CONNELL 169
         J. Q. Adams's views on re-charter

JAN. 16, 1832   TO GARDINER GREENE 170
         Attitude of Philadelphia on re-charter

JAN. 25, 1832   TO HORACE BINNEY 170
         Amount of bonus to be expected

FEB. 2, 1832   FROM CHARLES JARED INGERSOLL 171
         Jackson's views on Bank in general

FEB. 6, 1832   TO HORACE BINNEY 172
         Dallas and Pennsylvania interests

FEB. 6, 1832   TO CHARLES JARED INGERSOLL 174
         Dallas and proposed *coup d'état*

FEB. 9, 1832   FROM CHARLES JARED INGERSOLL 174
         Livingston's views on Jackson's idea of modification
         of charter

FEB. 10, 1832   TO GEORGE McDUFFIE 178
         McDuffie begins the struggle for renewal

FEB. 11, 1832   TO CHARLES JARED INGERSOLL 179
         Bank if forced determines on war; attitude toward
         President

FEB. 13, 1832   TO CHARLES JARED INGERSOLL 181
         Suggestions for relieving controversy

FEB. 21, 1832   FROM CHARLES JARED INGERSOLL 183
         Attitude of Cabinet on re-charter

FEB. 23, 1832   FROM CHARLES JARED INGERSOLL 184
         Government's plan for modification of charter

FEB. 25, 1832   TO CHARLES JARED INGERSOLL 185
         Agreement to President's modifications

FEB. 26, 1832   TO CHARLES JARED INGERSOLL 186
         Agreement to President's modifications

MARCH 1, 1832   FROM CHARLES JARED INGERSOLL 187
         On Root's resolutions in Congress; attitude of Presi-
         dent

MARCH 6, 1832   FROM CHARLES JARED INGERSOLL 188
         Effect of McDuffie's attack on Bank

MAY 11, 1832   TO JOHN G. WATMOUGH 190
         Use of press for Bank

MAY 30, 1832   TO THOMAS CADWALADER 191
         Account of visit to Washington

JUNE 5, 1832   TO THOMAS CADWALADER 191
         Results of Biddle's visit

JULY 3, 1832   TO THOMAS CADWALADER 192
         Re-charter passed Senate

JULY 5, 1832   DANIEL WEBSTER TO THOMAS CADWALADER . . . 193
                  Benefit of Biddle's visit to Washington

JULY 10, 1832   FROM W. CREIGHTON 193
                  Jackson's veto

JULY 12, 1832   FROM WILLIAM BUCKNOR 194
                  Effect of veto on stock

JULY 13, 1832   TO WILLIAM G. BUCKNOR 194
                  Policy of Bank in coming election

AUG. 1, 1832   TO HENRY CLAY 196
                  Effect of veto; faith in Clay

SEPT. 20, 1832   BANK OF THE UNITED STATES TO JOHN S. BIDDLE . . 197
                  Receipt of Bill

SEPT. 26, 1832   TO JOHN TILFORD 197
                  Circulating Webster's speech

NOV. 21, 1832   TO JOHN RATHBONE, JR. 198
                  No contraction of loans resulting from veto

DEC. 8, 1832   FROM ROSWELL L. COLT (?) 199
                  Suggests curtailment of loans

JAN. 18, 1833   FROM CHARLES JARED INGERSOLL 200
                  Rumors of Jackson's new plan

MARCH 2, 1833   FROM JOHN SERGEANT 200
                  Alliance of South and West against Jackson

MARCH 23, 1833   FROM JOHN G. WATMOUGH 202
                  Van Buren and removal of deposits

APRIL 8, 1833   TO DANIEL WEBSTER 202
                  Question of removal of deposits; Bank determines on
                  war

APRIL 10, 1833   FROM HENRY CLAY 202
                  Clay and Webster on Compromise Tariff

APRIL 10, 1833   TO DANIEL WEBSTER 205
                  McLane's visit to New York; removal of deposits

APRIL 13, 1833   FROM ROBERT W. GIBBES 205
                  Views of Cabinet on removal of deposits

APRIL 16, 1833   TO J. S. BARBOUR 207
                  Bank view of origin of Government's position

APRIL 27, 1833   FROM THOMAS COOPER 208
                  Volunteers services to Bank

MAY 6, 1833   TO THOMAS COOPER 209
                  Analysis of causes of Government's position

JULY 11, 1833   TO J. S. BARBOUR 210
                  Analysis of Government's position; opinion of Gouge

JULY 12, 1833   FROM THOMAS COOPER 211
                  Appointment of W. J. Duane

JULY 30, 1833   TO ROBERT LENOX 212
                  Confidence in Duane; policy toward State Banks

JULY 30, 1833   TO SAMUEL SWARTWOUT 213
                  Attempts to justify Bank to Duane

Contents

JULY 31, 1833   To THOMAS COOPER 213
Confidence in Duane

AUG. 13, 1833   To DANIEL WEBSTER 214
Instructions to Branches on temporary curtailment

AUG. 16, 1833   To THOMAS COOPER 215
Woodbury on position of Government toward Bank

OCT. 1, 1833   To ROBERT LENOX 215
Policy of Bank after removal of deposits

OCT. 29, 1833   FROM DANIEL WEBSTER 216
Question of policy of the Bank

NOV. 23, 1833   FROM SAMUEL SWARTWOUT 217
Rejects appointment as director; financial stringency
in market

DEC. 21, 1833   FROM DANIEL WEBSTER 218
Question of professional services

DEC. 21, 1833   FROM HENRY CLAY 218
Suggestions for Bank policy

JAN. 27, 1834   To WILLIAM APPLETON 219
Bank determines on curtailment

FEB. 2, 1834   FROM HENRY CLAY 220
Advices against struggle for re-charter

FEB. 4, 1834   FROM HORACE BINNEY 220
Webster suggests moderation in reductions

FEB. 8, 1834   To JOHN G. WATMOUGH 221
Bank determined to fight

FEB. 21, 1834   To JOSEPH HOPKINSON 221
Bank determined to fight

FEB. 27, 1834   FROM JOHN SERGEANT 222
President Jackson informed of distress; Cabinet
meetings

MARCH 1, 1834   To SAMUEL BRECK 224
Effect of Governor Wolf's message

MARCH 11, 1834   To CHARLES HAMMOND 225
Justification for policy of curtailment

MARCH 11, 1834   To SAMUEL JAUDON 226
Need for a charter

MARCH 18, 1834   FROM JAMES WATSON WEBB 227
Bank must adopt firm position

APRIL 2, 1834   To S. H. SMITH 227
Bank determined on curtailment

APRIL 11, 1834   To S. H. SMITH 229
Bank determined on curtailment

MAY 1, 1834   FROM THOMAS COOPER 230
Politics in Congress regarding Bank

MAY 9, 1834   To JOHN S. SMITH 231
True course of Bank in struggle

June 4, 1834   To R. M. Blatchford 233
     Policy toward State Banks and nation at large

June 12, 1834   To Solomon Etting 234
     Policy toward State Banks

June 14, 1834   To Alexander Porter 235
     House on Clay's resolution

July 4, 1834   To William Appleton 237
     Financial statement of Bank; attitude toward Whig
     interference

July 7, 1834   From R. Fisher 241
     Attitude of commercial classes on Bank struggle

July 9, 1834   To James Watson Webb 243
     Abandonment of policy of curtailments

Sept. 14, 1834   Alexander Hamilton to John Woodworth . . 244
     Albany Regency and the farmers

Oct. 30, 1834   To Silas M. Stilwell 244
     Refusal to interfere in N.Y. politics

Nov. 13, 1834   From Roswell L. Colt 245
     Suggestions for State Charter

Jan. 7, 1835   To —— 246
     Outline of proposed charter from State of Pennsyl-
     vania

May 9, 1835   From Daniel Webster (?) 250
     Van Buren and election of 1836

May 12, 1835   From Daniel Webster (?) 251
     On Presidential election of 1836

May 13, 1835   To D. Sprigg 252
     Placing officers of the Bank

June 3, 1835   From Edward Everett 253
     National election of 1836

Aug. 6, 1835   To John Huske 253
     Placing officers of the Bank and preparing to close
     up business

Aug. 11, 1835   To Herman Cope 255
     National politics of 1836

Nov. 16, 1835   From John Norris 256
     Desire of New York for charter

Dec. 4, 1835   From Jasper Harding 257
     Intriguing with committee at Harrisburg

Dec. 6, 1835   From Charles A. Davis 257
     New York anxiety about re-charter

Dec. 12, 1835   From William B. Reed 258
     Use of canals, railroads, and turnpikes in struggle for
     re-charter

Jan. 15, 1836   To William B. Reed 261
     Dictating to committee at Harrisburg

Contents

Jan. 15, 1836	To Joseph McIlvaine	. 261
	Similar instructions to chargé	
Jan. 18, 1836	From John B. Wallace	. 262
	Information on politics at Harrisburg	
Jan. 19, 1836	From John B. Wallace	. 263
	Bill introduced in Legislature	
Jan. 31, 1836	To Joseph McIlvaine	. 263
	Instructions to McIlvaine on Bank struggle	
Feb. 5, 1836	From Charles S. Baker	. 264
	Preparing for a struggle in the Senate	
Feb. 6, 1836	From John McKim, Jr.	. 265
	Maryland's proposal for charter	
Feb. 10, 1836	From Samuel R. Wood	. 265
	Description of Krebs affair	
March 17, 1836	From J. R. Ingersoll	. 268
	Application for Branches	
April 9, 1836	From Stephen F. Austin	. 269
	Texas sinking loan	
March 20, 1837	To Edward R. Biddle	. 271
	Conditions in financial market	
April 29, 1837	From Thomas Cooper	. 272
	Proposal of candidacy for President of the United States	
May 6, 1837	From Joel R. Poinsett	. 273
	Condition of money market; seeks advice	
May 8, 1837	To Joel R. Poinsett	. 274
	Desire for amity with government	
May 8, 1837	To Joel R. Poinsett	. 274
	Outlines relief for government	
May 8, 1837	To General Robert Patterson	. 276
	Seeks aid for his plan with Government	
May 8, 1837	From General Robert Patterson	. 277
	Van Buren's position in financial crisis	
May 8, 1837	To Thomas Cooper	. 277
	On subject of Presidential candidacy	
May 14, 1837	From Thomas Cooper	. 278
	Candidacy of Biddle for the Presidency	
May 24, 1837	From Thomas Cooper	. 280
	Candidacy of Biddle for Presidency; political aspect on eve of special session	
July 1, 1837	From Thomas Cooper	. 281
	Candidacy of Biddle	
July 14, 1837	To John Rathbone, Jr.	. 282
	Policy of Bank on eve of special session; rumor of Sub-Treasury	
Aug. 21, 1837	From B. W. Leigh	. 283
	Judge Marshall and Bank shares	

AUG. 24, 1837   TO B. W. LEIGH 285
     Judge Marshall and Bank shares

AUG. 25, 1837   TO B. W. LEIGH 287
     Judge Marshall and Bank stock

AUG. 28, 1837   FROM B. W. LEIGH 287
     Judge Marshall and the sale of Bank stock

SEPT. 4, 1837   B. W. LEIGH TO BIDDLE 288
     Judge Marshall and the disposal of shares held by his wife

SEPT. 7, 1837   TO B. W. LEIGH 289
     Judge Marshall and Bank stock

SEPT. 9, 1837   FROM SILAS M. STILWELL 290
     Effect of President's message; the "Conservatives"

SEPT. 9, 1837   FROM CHARLES AUGUST DAVIS 290
     Van Buren and the Loco Foco party

SEPT. 13, 1837   FROM B. W. LEIGH 291
     On republishing correspondence in Philadelphia and
     New York newspapers

SEPT. 15, 1837   TO B. W. LEIGH 291
     On republishing correspondence in Philadelphia and
     New York

SEPT. 15, 1837   TO CHARLES KING 291
     On vindication of Judge Marshall

SEPT. 19, 1837   FROM E. R. BIDDLE 292
     Request for money

SEPT. 20, 1837   TO E. R. BIDDLE 292
     Reply to request for money

SEPT. 27, 1837   FROM CHARLES AUGUST DAVIS 292
     Effects of President's message; Loco Foco principles

OCT. 20, 1837   FROM THOMAS COOPER 293
     Attitude of South on Sub-Treasury; candidacy of
     Biddle for President

NOV. 6, 1837   TO E. R. BIDDLE 294
     On subject of Texas loan

NOV. 7, 1837   FROM E. R. BIDDLE 295
     On subject of Texas loan

NOV. 11, 1837   FROM E. R. BIDDLE 295
     On Texas loan

NOV. 24, 1837   FROM E. R. BIDDLE 296
     On Texas loan

DEC. 16, 1837   FROM THOMAS COOPER 296
     On candidacy of Biddle for President

JAN. 20, 1838   FROM M. NEWKIRK 297
     Political outlook of Sub-Treasury

JAN. 28, 1838   FROM D. A. SMITH 298
     Prospects of the Sub-Treasury

FEB. 3, 1838   TO HENRY CLAY 299
     Getting instructions for Pennsylvania Senators; Sub-
     Treasury Bill

FEB. 5, 1838	FROM HENRY CLAY 300
	Question of instructions for Buchanan
FEB. 6, 1838	FROM HENRY CLAY 300
	Instructions for Buchanan
FEB. 7, 1838	FROM C. S. BAKER 301
	Instructions for Buchanan
FEB. 1838 (?)	FROM DANIEL WEBSTER 301
	Efforts of Van Buren on Sub-Treasury
FEB. 8, 1838	FROM CHARLES S. BAKER 302
	Struggle at Harrisburg over instructions to Buchanan
FEB. 9, 1838	FROM CHARLES S. BAKER 302
	Struggle at Harrisburg over instructions to Buchanan
FEB. 14, 1838	FROM CHARLES S. BAKER 303
	Struggle at Harrisburg over instructions to Buchanan
FEB. 16, 1838	FROM CHARLES S. BAKER 304
	Passage of resolution instructing Buchanan
FEB. 20, 1838	FROM HENRY CLAY 304
	Effect of instructions to Buchanan
APRIL 28, 1838	FROM JOHN SERGEANT 305
	Policy of Calhoun on Sub-Treasury
APRIL 30, 1838	TO JOHN FORSYTH 307
	Suggestions to the Government for reconciliation
MAY 30, 1838	FROM HENRY CLAY 309
	Repeal of Specie Circular passes Senate
MAY 30, 1838	—— TO ROSWELL L. COLT 310
	On subject of repeal of Specie Circular
MAY 31, 1838	TO SAMUEL JAUDON 311
	On subject of repeal of Specie Circular; Biddle's delight
JUNE 9, 1838	TO SAMUEL JAUDON 313
	On repeal of Specie Circular; defeat of Sub-Treasury
JUNE 15, 1838	TO JOHN SERGEANT 313
	Defeating the Sub-Treasury Bill
JUNE 23, 1838	TO SAMUEL JAUDON 314
	On Specie Circular and the Sub-Treasury Bill
JUNE 29, 1838	TO SAMUEL JAUDON 314
	Defeat of the Sub-Treasury Bill; repeal of the Specie Circular
JULY 3, 1838	TO THADDEUS STEVENS 315
	Advances toward the Administration
JULY 11, 1838	TO JOEL R. POINSETT 316
	Advances toward the Administration
JULY 13, 1838	TO THOMAS COOPER 316
	Defeat of the Administration
JULY 31, 1838	TO R. M. BLATCHFORD 317
	Control of press on defeat of Administration

AUG. 1, 1838   FROM R. M. BLATCHFORD 317
     Control of press on defeat of Administration

AUG. 3, 1838   TO SAMUEL JAUDON 318
     Culmination of Bank war

AUG. 11, 1838   FROM B—— 321
     Attitude of Van Buren on politics of nation

AUG. 14, 1838   FROM THOMAS COOPER 323
     Candidacy of Biddle for Presidency

AUG. 15, 1838   TO SAMUEL JAUDON 324
     Attitude of Bank toward Government

SEPT. 6, 1838   TO DANIEL WEBSTER 325
     On Texas affair

SEPT. 7, 1838   TO HENRY CLAY 326
     On Texas affair

SEPT. 10, 1838   FROM DANIEL WEBSTER 328
     On Texas affair

SEPT. 14, 1838   FROM HENRY CLAY 330
     On Texas affair

OCT. 1, 1838   FROM THOMAS COOPER 333
     Suggestion of Biddle for Cabinet position

OCT. 31, 1838   TO E. C. BIDDLE 334
     Relation of Government and Bank

NOV. 27, 1838   TO JOHN FORSYTH 335
     Suggestion for President's message

NOV. 29, 1838   FROM JOHN FORSYTH 336
     Reply to Biddle's suggestions for President's message
     PERSONAL CARD TO BIDDLE FROM PRESIDENT VAN BUREN 337

DEC. 13, 1840   TO DANIEL WEBSTER 337
     Seeks ambassadorship to Austria

DEC. 24, 1840   FROM DANIEL WEBSTER 339
     On ambassadorship to Austria

DEC. 30, 1840   TO DANIEL WEBSTER 339
     On subject of Secretary of the Treasury in Cabinet

JAN. 21, 1841   FROM R. M. BLATCHFORD 340
     On subject of the Sub-Treasury

FEB. 2, 1841   TO DANIEL WEBSTER 341
     On President's inaugural

FEB. 4, 1841   FROM DANIEL WEBSTER 341
     On President's inaugural

APRIL 10, 1841   FROM CHARLES AUGUST DAVIS 342
     Death of President Harrison

AUG. 19, 1842   TO JOHN TYLER 342
     President Tyler and the Tariff Bill

AUG. 25, 1842   FROM JOHN TYLER 343
     President Tyler and the Tariff Bill

FEB. 27, 1843   TO DANIEL WEBSTER 344
     Advice to Daniel Webster

Contents xxix

MARCH 2, 1843   FROM D.(ANIEL) W.(EBSTER) 345
       Webster's position in the Cabinet

MARCH 11, 1843   FROM D.(ANIEL) W.(EBSTER) 345
       Webster's decision on Cabinet position

MARCH 4, 1843   TO JOHN TYLER 346
       On need of retaining Webster in Cabinet

APRIL 5, 1843   MEMORANDUM OF BIDDLE TO DANIEL WEBSTER . . 348
       Suggestion of retreat for Webster

APRIL 24, 1843   —— TO C. B. PENROSE 351
       Suggestion to retain Webster in Cabinet

JAN. 9, 1844   TO JOSEPH GALES 352
       On politics of the day; Webster and Clay

JAN. 9, 1844   TO DANIEL WEBSTER 352
       On politics of the day

APPENDIX 355

INDEX 361

Illustrations

NICHOLAS BIDDLE . . . .   *Frontispiece*
    From the portrait by Rembrandt Peale

NICHOLAS BIDDLE 12
    From a miniature by B. Trott

NICHOLAS BIDDLE 192
    From a miniature by Henry Inman

BIDDLE'S HOME AT ANDALUSIA 342

THE CORRESPONDENCE OF
NICHOLAS BIDDLE
DEALING WITH NATIONAL AFFAIRS

THE CORRESPONDENCE
OF NICHOLAS BIDDLE

BIDDLE TO JAMES MONROE

London July 6th 1807

Dear Sir

The observations you made in our walk yesterday were of so interesting a nature, that I hope you will excuse my recurring to the subject of them. About to enter on a scene where I may not be permitted long to remain merely a spectator, & in which all my success will be influenced by my first steps, I feel a natural anxiety to prescribe a course of conduct which may become the rule of my political life. The violence of party [1] which disgraces our country is indeed discouraging to one who feels no disposition to become the follower of any sect, or to mingle political animosities with the intercourse of society. But I have sometimes thought that the interests of the nation might be advanced without join-

[1] In 1806 James Monroe with Pinkney negotiated a treaty with England; and on October 29, 1807, he left England. On his return to America he "drew up an elaborate defense of his diplomatic conduct in England in a letter to Madison, which covers ten folio pages of the State papers. The enthusiasm with which he might have been received immediately after the Louisiana Purchase was dampened by his failure in the English negotiations. Politicians were already discussing the presidential succession, the Republican party being divided in their preferences for Madison and Monroe. Jefferson endeavored to remain neutral; Wirt was in favor of Madison; at length the legislature of Virginia settled the choice by pronouncing in favor of the latter. Monroe's friends acquiesced. Soon afterwards Madison was placed and Monroe, after a brief interval, was reëlected to the post of governor." Gilman, Daniel C., *James Monroe* (Boston, 1898), pp. 105, 106.

ing those who think themselves exclusively its friends, and that even the intemperance of party would respect a manly independence founded on honor & maintained with firmness without descending to adopt the prejudices or to be guided by the passions of others. You Sir more than any other character with whom it has been my happiness to be acquainted have passed thro' all the stages of political advancement honorable for yourself & useful to your country. From you therefore I am particularly desirous of receiving advice which would be useful to a person who like myself has a profession the pursuit of which is a primary object, but who from many motives aspires to any political distinction which may be acquired & preserved by honorable means.

The kindness & confidence with which you have hitherto favored me as they are a principle inducement will I trust be at the same time the apology for this trouble.

BIDDLE TO JAMES MONROE

Philadᵃ June 21. 1809

Dʳ Sir

It is so long since I have had the pleasure of hearing from you that I take the liberty of asking news of yourself & the family. I should indeed before this have acknowledged your kind letter, but there is you know a tranquil, one might say a happy uniformity which gives to American life but little variety of incidents, & it would be superfluous I trust to repeat the assurances of my respect & esteem. My young friend Mʳ Walsh [1] whom you may recollect in London has

---

[1] In 1819 Walsh established the *National Gazette* and remained the editor until 1836 when he sold it to William Fry. Walsh was for a time a writer for *Dennie's Portfolio* of which Biddle was an associate editor for a number of years. Cf. sketch

just returned in the Pacific. With regard to our affairs, he left Mr Pinkney [1] under a strong impression that the modification of the Orders in Council was all that England meant to concede to this country. He had no idea of the more enlarged arrangement which has been made, or is expected at Washington. It seems singular that whilst negociating in London the ulterior views of the British government should have been concealed from him, & it would be unfortunate if in a matter of such consequence there should be any misapprehension. But the declaration of Mr Erskine [2] appear[s] full & explicit. M^r M's observation of the pressure of the embargo rather confirms the opinion that we have only revealed the dangerous secret of our impotence — yet the experiment tho' dear may perhaps be valuable, since nations like men should learn to estimate their comparative value. All England is so much occupied with the Duke of York [3] that this new war in Austria has attracted very little attention, & excited no expectation of success. Lord Holland still remains in Spain. Mr Burr was ordered to leave England, not as was stated at the requisition of the Spanish minister but from a belief that he was travelling over England for the purpose of collecting information which might render him afterwards acceptable to the French gov^t. He had been at Edinburgh & the gov^t understanding his intention of going to Ireland sent orders there to prevent his landing. . . .

of life in Hudson, Frederic, *Journalism in the United States, 1690–1872* (New York, 1873), p. 322.

[1] William Pinkney, Minister to England.

[2] D. M. Erskine, British Minister to the United States. Erskine's difficulties are discussed in full in Channing, Edward, *The Jeffersonian System* (New York, 1907), pp. 233–236.

[3] For the life and habits of the Duke of York, cf. Walpole, Spencer, *A History of England since 1815* (New York, 1912), vol. I, pp. 131, 137, 283, 308.

ROBERT WALSH TO BIDDLE

Baltimore July 11th 1809

My Dear Friend

... I proceeded to our Capitol two days after my arrival here, in order to fulfill my mission & was greeted with all the courtesy I could wish. Fortunately the House had not terminated its sittings & accordingly afforded me an opportunity of forming some judgment of its character. I attended two long debates & could [have] desired to have you at my side at the time. Never most assuredly was there exhibited a more disgusting caricature of legislation. I did not expect to find much wisdom among them, but was truly surprised to discover that the affairs of any nation could by any possibility be managed by men such as the members of the House of Representatives. I had several meetings with the President and Secretary of State [1] & saw much reason to be satisfied with the intentions of both. I can not venture to give an opinion as to their talents. In my conferences with the President, I discovered a feeling towards England much more conciliatory than his former policies entitled me to expect.

ROBERT WALSH TO BIDDLE

Baltimore August 1st 1809

My Dear Biddle

... I had some conversation with Mr Erskine on his way to your city; but not on his return to Washington. As I never entertained a doubt concerning the fate of his arrangements, I was not a little surprized at the satisfaction and confidence which he manifested on that subject. If our admin-

[1] Robert Smith of Maryland.

istration were admitted to a view of his instructions, they must have foreseen the result & were in my opinion highly censurable for acquiescing in so extraordinary an assumption of authority on the part of the Minister. Mr Madison, to whom I communicated my apprehensions, seemed perfectly sure of the validity of the whole negociation. There must be still some lurking fallacy in this business — I confess that the whole is a mystery to me. Whoever has been in England or has attended to the management of affairs in that country, must at once see the impossibility of a collusion between the ministry & their envoy — or of perfidy in the former. Neither could escape the sagacity of the opposition — & no ministry could expect to weather the storm which the exposure of so detestable a fraud would collect over their heads. It may, moreover, be easily shewn, that no views whatever of public or private utility could be answered by such a proceeding; or could have been in the contemplation of sensible men. I regret, therefore, that any federalist should countenance an idea every way unjust and eminently injurious to the good cause among ourselves.

JAMES MONROE [1] TO BIDDLE

(*Confidential*)   Washington May 5, 1815
My dear Sir

I have yours of the 28 ulto. and am much gratified to find that we agree in every circumstance as to the dangers with which we are menac'd by the late events in France,[2] and the precautions we ought to take to avoid them. It would I

[1] Secretary of State and of War in the Cabinet of President Madison, 1814–1815.

[2] For the last years of Napoleon's career cf. Rose, J. H., *Life of Napoleon I* (New York, 1902), chs. 37–41.

think be improper to suffer our squadron to sail for the Mediteranean or to disband our army, untill we saw more distinctly what were likely to be the consequences of those events, especially as to the U States. It is probable, or rather certain, that Boniparte will claim to the Rhine; and that will produce a war with England, if she can form such a combination of force as promises to make head against him. If Austria is on his side I should not be surprised if there should be a general acquiescence in his restoration, provided all France is in his favor(?), as circumstances indicate. The British nation must be fatigued with the war in Europe, with that with the U States, and its disasterous termination at N. Orl: Their finances are embarrassed. Repose has been caught at with avidity, and the mortification must be extreme when it is seen that the prospect of it is snatched from them, and that a new struggle is to be encountered, more burthensome perhaps than that through which they have already passed, to place them at the point at which they lately stood, if it is (?) even practicable. It is equally doubtful, whether, as Russia may have relinquished her claims on Poland, she can be brought to bear on France, and without her aid, the attempt of England & Prussia would be a desperate one. I think it is not improbable that Spain will be neutralized, by events at home. Ferd.[1] has cut off the heads of many of those who fought for his restoration; reinstated the inquisition, and revolted the feelings of the whole nation. The contest for him was a kind of revolutionary mov'ment; it was certainly a national one, in which a species of popular gov^t. ruled. He has put himself

---

[1] Ferdinand VII of Spain. For a discussion of the events of this reign consult Seignobos, Charles, *A Political History of Europe* (trans. by S. M. Macvane, New York, 1899), pp. 289-291.

against that gov^t., and against that mov'ment. The restoration of Bonaparte by the will of the nation, operating as it were by free suffrage, will revive revolutionary feelings in France, which may extend to Spain, under the existing circumstances there. If however Bonaparte takes to the Rhine, & Egld declares war, she may strike at us as in the former wars. This is the moment when we may fix our entring in such a struggle, sho^d. it occur; for on the part which we now act, it may depend, whether we shall [have] pass'd successfully thro it, possessed of the firmness & gallantry displayed in the late war, or made their exertions in vain. If we take a decisive tone at once, we may & probably shall command the respect of both parties. If we hesitate, we shall [be] as sure of their contempt. . . .

CLEMENT C. BIDDLE [1] TO BIDDLE

Philad^a. 24. Decr. 1815.

My dear Nicholas,

Your letter of the 20. inst. for which, permit me to thank you, was rec^d. yesterday. I shall avail myself of your kind intimations respecting the letters, and forward them to you by the first private hand.

I cannot but exceedingly regret the failure of your bill for an immediate *levy* of a regular State force, satisfied, as I am, of the insufficiency of *any scheme by voluntary enlistment,* of obtaining the men (independent of their proper organization, and discipline fit for service) before the middle of the ensuing summer, — if even by that time. My opinion is formed from

[1] Clement C. Biddle, a cousin of Nicholas Biddle and a son of Clement Biddle of Revolutionary fame. Commanded the Pennsylvania Regiment of Light Infantry Volunteers in 1812–1814, afterwards distinguished in civil life.

my own experience in the recruiting service, when we were abundantly supplied with funds, — and from conversations which I have recently had with the officer (col. Clemson) now superintending that service in this district.

From a perusal of the Bill, which is now before you, the following objections objections have presented themselves to me. Sect. 1st Line 4th. In lieu of a Regiment say a Battalion of Artillery, which will conform to the organization of the U.S. Artillery: they having no Regiments, but twelve Battalions of four companies each, commanded by a Lieut. Col. or Major. This will give a large proportion of Artillery for four Regts. of Infantry, viz. one tenth of the Infry. General Scott says *one twentieth* is sufficient. Sect. 2d. line 6th after the organization of a Regt. let that of the Battalion of Artillery come according to the U.S. viz. Four Companies — Field of Staff, — 1 Lieut. Col. 1 Adjut. 1 Quarter Master, 1 Pay Master, the Surgeon, the surgeon's mate, 1 Sergeant Major, 1 Quarter Master Sergeant and 2 Principal musicians. Line 9th. The U.S. organization of a Company of Artillery is much better than that of the Bill: it is 1 captain, 1 first Lieut. *2* second lieut's (*one of which is Conductor of Military Stores, and has charge, and is responsible, for the ordnance &c &c.*) 1 third lieut. 1 quarter master sergeant, 5 sergeants, *8 corporals*, 4 musicians and *100 privates*. Line 11th. The number of Non Commissioned officers and privates of a company of Riflemen should be the same as that of Infantry. It is in the U.S. service — the five officers are quite sufficient for the command of ninety men, and a company, which when full had but *sixty eight* men, wd not generally have in the field above forty, which are too few, particularly where there are so many company officers. There is an additional reason for increasing the strength of the Rifle corps, to wit, in the French and most of the European services, the *Tiraileurs* or Light Infantry bear to the Infantry of the Line, at least the proportion of *one* to *three*, whereas even after this augmentation, they w^d in this Bill only bear the proportion of *one* to *four*, and without it of *one* to *six*, only half that of the French, when our Country requires a greater proportion. Sect. 3 Line 5th. In order to make this enumeration complete *Brigade Majors* sh^d be added, and besides *Assistants* and *Deputies*, there sh^d be *Assistant Deputies*, there being officers with that title in the U.S. service. This section seems to imply that in the U.S. service the Adjutant & Inspector Generals must be taken from the line of officers, which is not the case, and they are frequently taken from Citizens, as in the cases of Col^s. Duane, Drayton, Powell & others. The U.S. regulations require their *Assistants* to be taken from the line of officers. Also in the Quarter Master's Department in the U.S. service, none of the officers *can* be taken from the line of officers. According to the U.S. regulations Six Regiments should make *three* Brigades.

Should there not be an additional section giving the officers rank over all officers of the militia and Volunteers of the same grade?

It may be observed that wherever this Bill differs from the organization of the U.S. army as to the number of officers, non-commissioned officers and privates in a Reg^t or comp^y it is defective, as great attention has been paid to that subject in the U.S. service, and many alterations made before the present organization was adopted.

In lieu of the six companies of artillery which it is proposed to strike out, let there be *four* troops of Dragoons, formed into a *Squadron* under a major, organized as in the U.S. service, which will then *complete* the formation of a "Legion," which this Bill contemplates. A *Small* corps of Cavalry will be much wanted.

Excuse the irregularity with which the foregoing remarks are drawn up, & beleive me with perfect esteem & regard

BIDDLE TO JAMES MONROE

Phil^a. Jany. 31. 1819

My dear sir,

I have received by this day's mail your letter of the 29th announcing your having nominated me one of the Directors of the Bank of the U.S. I need not say that I consider this rememberance a proof of that uniform kindness & friendship on your part which I value so highly, and as such I beg you to accept my thanks for it. I have however little concern with Banks & have hitherto declined sharing in the management of the institution when it was proposed to me by the stockholders. Yet I am unwilling to avoid any duty by which you think I can be of service.

The truth is, that with all its faults, the Bank is of vital importance to the finances of the gov^t and an object of great interest to the community. That it has been perverted to selfish purposes cannot be doubted — that it may — & must — be renovated is equally certain. But they who undertake to reform abuses & particularly of that description, must encounter much hostility & submit to much labor. To these, the hope of being useful can alone reconcile me — and if I should undertake the task I shall endeavor to persevere till the character of the institution is reestablished.

Nicholas Biddle

From a miniature by B. Trott

JOHN McKIM JR.[1] TO BIDDLE

Baltimore Jan.[y] 8th 1820

Dear Sir

M[r] Riggin, who was nominated by me, and Elected one of the Republican Directors of the Branch here, having Resigned, M[r] Alex[r] M[c]Kim was nominated last Tuesday to fill the Vacancy. I am sure no man in Baltimore would give more satisfaction to the Citizens of this place than he Would, if Elected, and at the same time the Board here would have an opportunity of making him their President, If they chose.

I now wish you to attend to this Election, as you know that the Republicans are one short of their number, and the necessity of giving us our Share of the Direction, as we do hold more then the half of the Stock, and it having been Policy to divide the two Party, in the direction, Since the Bank was Established.[2]

I know that you can Manage this in your usual good, & Handsome manner, which has often gave me great Pleasure.

JAMES MONROE TO BIDDLE

Washington April 11. 1820

Dear Sir

. . . A representation has I understand been made to the directors of the national bank respecting a change in the Direction of the branch in Lexington K[y]., which it is thought

---

[1] Director of the Bank, 1835–1836. A trusted adviser at Baltimore along with Robert Oliver and R. L. Colt.

[2] This letter shows how solicitous the Bank men were to keep the political parties absolutely balanced even before Biddle entered upon his presidency. The later correspondence will show Biddle's policy on this most crucial question of the administration.

will produce a good effect there, & promote the general interest of the institution. Being well acquainted with the leading
characters of that State, and my attention being drawn to
the subject last summer, as I passed through it, at the particular request of some residing there, in whom I have the
highest confidence, I enclose you a note of several, who I think
very deserving of the appointment. The effect which may be
produced, by a judicious selection of persons, for that trust, in
conciliating the public opinion to the institution, you will
fully appreciate. I make this communication to you in confidence, & am . . .

BIDDLE TO JAMES MONROE

Andalusia October 8. 1820.

My dear Sir,

You will I am sure feel some interest in the inclosed
paper which I have thought it advisable to publish in order
to correct some deeply rooted prejudices against some of the
measures of the last war. Having never taken any formal notice of them till now, I believed that after so long a time it
was right to state distinctly what it was I had really done, to
excite the violence of that period. As far as I can learn, its effect upon fair & liberal minds has been such as I could wish.
Nevertheless it will not contribute at all to my election
which will be decided by very different considerations. According to the unfortunate system of nomination prevailing
here, it is always in the power of a cabal to take from the
people all share in the real business of an election. Thus for
instance I was originally nominated by both sections of the
Republican party — by a Committee of the friends of M^r
Findlay & a Committee of the friends of Mr Heister. But the

latter were so anxious to secure his election, that finding the federalists unwilling [to] vote for their candidate Mr Heister unless Mr Heister's friends in return would vote for the federal members of Congress, they reassembled & in order to secure the federal votes for Mr Heister gave up their Congress ticket altho' it had been formally agreed upon & published. My support therefore will be from one section only of the republicans — the other at the head of whom is Duane opposing my election, not as he himself avowed to a friend of mine from any personal hostility to me, but because I was well disposed to the administration of the general gov^t. Another very efficient motive with that individual is that my nomination excluded his own son. Such are the springs which move our election. The district is in truth a perfect chaos of small factions & as I have shunned all participation in their intrigues I do not anticipate the slightest chance of being elected. The only object of any importance is to rally the sound part of the population against the decided hostility to the general gov^t which animates some of the demagogues — & that I think can be accomplished. Will you present my best respects to Mrs Monroe . . .

The opposition is formed of a union of the federalists with the friends of Mr Heister. The latter consist of two divisions, one willing to sacrifice every thing for Mr Heister, the other at the head of whom is Duane, in addition to the same motive are stimulated by the pleasure of opposing one whom they know to be friendly to the administration of the general gov^t. This reason is distinctly avowed by their leader who at the same time professes to have no personal hostility to me. Such are the secret springs which will control the election.

*To the Electors of the City and County of Philadelphia,
and the County of Delaware.*

I understand that many estimable persons among you, retain unkind feelings toward me from a belief that during the late war, I proposed to establish in Pennsylvania the French system of military conscription. This reproach was widely circulated at that period. But I was then too anxious about the defence of the country, to care about defending myself, and I therefore never in any way noticed it, presuming that when the violence of party passions should subside, men would return to more just and liberal sentiments. I should still persevere in the same silence, but I think it due to those gentlemen, who have done me the honor to connect my name with the approaching election for members of congress, to remove an impression which may be injurious. If then it be true, that there is any individual, who forgetting the dangers of the war, remembers only its prejudices, he will perhaps find in the following statement, some reason to think that he has been unjust to me.

The assertion is, that I proposed to introduce the French system of conscription.

The fact is, that I never proposed any thing resembling the French conscription;— that what I did propose, was a system practised in Pennsylvania, long before the French conscription was in existence;— and that the very design and effect of it was to avoid a conscription, that is a militia draft which is in principle, very nearly the same mode of levying troops.

A few words will make this evident. The French system of conscription is this. All the men between twenty and twenty-five years of age, are divided into classes. When a class is

called into service, each man of the class must find a substitute or march, or what to the mass of the citizens is
precisely the same thing, pay sixteen dollars a month. The
nature of the two services is of course different, from the
peculiar circumstances, and the different forms of government
in the two countries; but as mere modes of military levy
they are evidently similar.

Now what I have proposed was this. Every twenty-two
men above eighteen years of age, were to furnish a soldier to
serve for the defence of the state, during twelve months. If
they did not, the proper officer was to provide one, and divide the expense among the twenty-two. But before doing
this, such of the twenty-two as were liable to military duty
drew lots. If the person on whom the lot fell consented to
serve, he received a contribution of two hundred dollars from
his neighbors. If he did not, the price of a substitute should
exceed two hundred dollars, he was to pay the excess, which
was limited to two hundred dollars more.

All this might be a good or a bad system, but one thing at
least is clear, that it is totally unlike the French system, and
much less like the French conscription than our own militia
law, which it was intended to supercede.

But in fact, the mode of raising a military force at that
time, was not a question of general policy, but of immediate
expediency — not how to frame a permanent system, but how
to provide against a sudden emergency. It was necessary to
raise within ten weeks, that is between the middle of January, before which no law could pass, and the month of April,
when Philadelphia might be assailed, an adequate force for
its protection. To procure these troops by voluntary enlist-
ments, was utterly hopeless; for the United States army had,

during more than two years, gleaned every idler in the state; and even had there been time, the commonwealth had neither land to promise, nor bounty money to pay to recruits. To rely exclusively on occasional drafts of militia, hastily levied at every fresh alarm, was to entrust the fate of the city to a system the most oppressive to the citizen, the most expensive to the community, and the least efficient against the enemy. Believing then the voluntary enlistment too slow and too dear, and the militia draft too weak and too burdensome, I proposed that which promised to be at once prompt, equal, and efficient. I thought then, and I think still, that it had many decided advantages over the other plans. The first, and the most important was, that by it, and by it alone could nine thousand well officered men be brought into the field in six weeks, without any demand on the state treasury — the second was, that being chiefly composed of substitutes who would probably reinlist, the force could be retained as long as it should be wanted — the third was, that it was much more favourable to the poorer citizens, than the militia law. By that law, if a militia man leaves home, neither he nor his family receive any indemnity; and if he stays at home, he pays for a years delinquency, one hundred and ninety-two dollars. By the proposed bill, if he left home he received two hundred dollars; if he staid at home he paid, except in an extraordinary case, only the twenty-second part of the price of a substitute.

Instead moreover of being a dangerous novelty, it had all the merit of successful experience. It was an old Pennsylvania plan. In the year 1780, a law passed dividing the people into classes, each of which was to furnish a man to serve in the army of the United States during the war, and a delinquent class was to pay fifteen pounds specie or current money, equivalent, which was one thousand one hundred and twenty-five pounds currency.

A second act, passed in 1781, by which, if a class was delinquent, a substitute was to be procured without limitation of price, at the expense of the class.

A comparison of the levy of 1780, with that of 1815, will show how little reason Philadelphia would have had to complain of the latter. By the law of 1780, the city and county of Philadelphia was bound to furnish eight hundred and ninety-five men, to serve in the United States army during the war. By the proposed law, the city and county, with perhaps three times the population, and twenty times the wealth of 1780, would have been bound to furnish, for its own exclusive defence during one year, about one thousand, or eleven hundred men.

Let me now ask any fair and candid man, in what part of this proposed measure is there any thing unjust or oppressive — any thing which violates the rights, or wounds the interests of a single individual — if it be not milder than the militia law — more practicable than an enlistment system — and unless the city was prepared to submit quietly to shame and pillage, what mode of organizing resistance could be more immediate, energetic and just? But supposing it not to be the best plan, supposing it to be a wrong plan. That would be a fit reason for preferring some other, but it surely is not a fair subject of reproach against the proposer, who could not possibly have had any personal or selfish motive, and who, if he erred, could have been mislead only by mistaken zeal. So unwilling indeed was I, that any mere pride of opinion on my part should interfere with the public service, that I at the same time, supported and voted for an enlistment bill, under an impression that the few who could be raised by it, would be at least so much gained for our defence — and when my own proposal was lost in the house of representatives, was one of a committee who immediately proposed a bill for raising volunteers, on which the senate were engaged the day when peace was announced.

I proposed and supported these measures from a conviction, that the state of the country demanded a vigorous effort to save it, and I should have consented to any thing which would call forth its resources without being very fastidious as to forms. And truly if eight thousand men were willing to come from the interior to our assistance, it did seem to be a matter of utter insignificance to the citizens of Philadelphia, whether they came out of classes of twenty-two, or classes of any other number. That they came at all — that they came well armed — well officered and well paid — might, I think, have satisfied the most scrupulous, and furnished an apology at least for the system which brought them.

I have now finished the original purpose of this note, but the subject induces me to add a few words on the general measures of that time.

In the autumn of 1814, I was elected to represent this district in the senate. You all remember the condition of the country. Washington had been taken — Baltimore attacked — a large British fleet and army were on the coast, able suddenly to strike any assailable point. Against this danger, Philadelphia was totally unprepared. She relied on the general government, until the failure of the military proposals in congress announced to the states, that they must provide for their own safety. From that moment it became my duty to secure the means of defending the capital. It was manifest that unless a force could be collected before the navigation of the Delaware opened, Philadelphia was at the mercy of the enemy. We wanted then a naval defence — we wanted a stationary land force, in aid of the militia — we wanted arms — we wanted money. That none of these were neglected, will be seen by the legislative journals of that day, which I cite, because they offer a simple and unquestionable statement of facts.

Extract the Senate Journal, 1814–15, p. 104. January 4th, 1815.

"A motion was made by Mr. Biddle and Mr. Lowrie, and read as follows. *Resolved*, that a committee be appointed to inquire into the expediency of raising by drafts from the militia, a corps of eight thousand men, to serve during twelve months for the defence of Pennsylvania and the adjoining states, with leave to report by bill or otherwise. *Resolved*, that the same committee be instructed to inquire into the expediency of procuring one or more steam frigates, steam batteries, or other means of defence for the protection of the shores of Delaware, with leave to report by bill or otherwise. *Resolved*, that the same committee be instructed to inquire into the expediency of borrowing a sum not exceeding one million of dollars, to be employed solely for the defence of this state — with leave to report by bill or otherwise.

"On motion, said resolutions were severally read, considered, and adopted, and ordered that Mr. Biddle, Mr. Lowrie, Mr. Forster, Mr. Frailey and Mr. Beale, be a committee for the purpose expressed in said resolutions."

In two days — January 6th, 1815. Page 110.

"Mr. Biddle from the committee appointed for the purpose on the fourth instant, reported an act to raise a military force for the defence of this commonwealth." This passed the senate on the 14th of January.

On the 13th January — Page 128.

"Mr. Biddle from the committee appointed for the purpose on the fourth instant reported a bill entitled an act to authorize a loan of one million of dollars, for the defence of this commonwealth." The loan was to be at seven per cent, and to be applied exclusively "to defray any expenses which may be incurred in military or naval preparations for the defence of this commonwealth."

On investigation it appeared that the steam frigates could not be built in time, and that the approach to the city might be adequately defended, by strengthening the United States flotilla in the Delaware. It consisted of twenty-seven boats and vessels, but such was the desperate state of the recruiting service, that this armament had only about one fifth of its complement; and a large part of its crew were to be discharged in April. The commander was requested to state distinctly, what number of men would render his flotilla perfectly efficient, and what bounties would procure them. He did so, but, that in a service so important nothing should be left to hazard, the number of men as well as the bounties, were increased beyond his estimates.

Accordingly, January 25th, 1815:

"Mr. Biddle read in his place, and on permission presented to the chair a bill, entitled 'An act granting additional emoluments to seamen, employed in the defence of this commonwealth.'" This bill passed February 1st.

Of arms the state possessed enough to equip the new levies, (Senate Journal, p. 21,) but that every thing which promised to be useful, might be pressed into the public service.

"On motion of Mr. Biddle and Mr. Graham, the following resolution was twice read, considered, and adopted. Resolved, That a committee be appointed to inquire into the nature and advantages of Chamber's repeating guns, and the expediency of employing them in the service of the state." Senate Journal, p. 46.

Page 67. "Mr. Biddle, from the committee appointed on the 15th, to inquire into the nature and advantages of Chamber's repeating guns, made report as follows," &c. &c. Concluding with a resolution to purchase fifty swivels, and to have five hundred muskets altered to the new plan.

These documents prove that, within a few days after the duty of protecting the capital, devolved on the legislature, an efficient system of defence was proposed and passed in the Senate; a system, which before the month of April, would have placed between Philadelphia and its enemy, a strong flotilla, capable of being speedily reinforced, by all the naval resources of the city; and a well officered army in aid of the local militia; a system, which would have shielded the city from all danger and all alarm during the war.

Of the energy and patriotism of those gentlemen, from the interior, who co-operated with me, and who, although remote from the capital, readily and zealously took their share in its defence, I can never speak nor feel too warmly. Nor did I permit myself to question the motives of those who opposed any of these measures. I knew them too well, not to ascribe their opposition to a fair and honourable difference of opinion. But I also had some right to a liberal construction of my own views. In executing the duties assigned to me, I had endeavoured to do what was useful, not what was agreeable; and never having sought to please, not to have pleased, would have been a subject neither of surprise, nor mortification. But I could not easily anticipate, that after a laborious and anxious struggle to provide for the defence of my own native city against foreign enemies, after securing the aid of patriotic men from the country, willing to partake in the expense and the dangers of that defence, I should become an object of denunciation in that very city; should have been put under a sort of political proscription, avowedly for my activity in striving to protect it.

There was about the same time another measure, to which from my share in it, it may be well to advert. When Massachusetts and Connecticut proposed to Pennsylvania, the changes in the constitution, originally projected at the convention of Hartford,[1] it appeared to me after very deliberate examination that their inevitable effect would be to loosen the whole structure of the confederation, and that they were therefore more dangerous to the country than the foreign armies which threatened it. The discussion of these proposals had in every quarter, inflamed to their utmost violence the feelings of the community. I thought then that Pennsylvania, neutral in its position, yet embracing nearly all the interests on which these changes

[1] For a full discussion of Biddle's activities during the War of 1812 and the results of the Congressional election of 1820 cf. sketch of life by Conrad, R. T., in *National Portrait Gallery of Distinguished Americans* (by James B. Longacre and James Herring, Philadelphia, 1839), vol. III, pp. 8–10.

would operate, might usefully interpose its calm strength between the passions of its neighbours, and by a course of mingled decision and gentleness, reclaim them to milder feelings towards each other. The report on the amendments was hastily drawn in the midst of other occupations, and much of it written on the road to Harrisburgh. It of course has no pretension as to form. But if my recollection does not deceive me, its general tone was fair and impartial, it imputed no unworthy motives, it contained no phrase which could wound even any member of that convention, it discussed the proposals with candor, nor was there the slightest departure from that courtesy, which among independent states, is at once the proof and the security of mutual respect. Yet this paper it seems has been the subject or the pretext of much censure upon its author.

Of all these things I have never complained. I do not now complain. Their singularity has much oftener tempted me to smile at finding myself reproached not by the men of the country, for calling them from their homes, but by the men of the city, because in suddenly raising nine thousand soldiers for its defence, I had been guilty of arranging them into classes of twenty-two. It is right however, to say that if during the war I persevered in these measures in opposition to prejudices, which I saw were estranging from me many honest and amiable citizens, and if I have suffered nearly six years to pass without any effort to remove them, my silence has proceeded rather from a disregard of what was merely personal to myself, than from any insensibility to the good will of the community. I do not feel and I will not affect any such indifference. I have lived long enough to know that the kindly feelings of those

who surround us, are among our best and safest enjoyments.
But even that good will may be too dearly purchased, and
I am quite sure that the applause of others, could never
console me for the loss of my own esteem. That I should
have forfeited irretrievably, if at a season of great national
disaster, when not merely the safety, but the honor of the
state was menaced, when all the free institutions of this
country were rocking to their foundations, I should from
any spirit of faction, or the despicable dread of being what
is called unpopular, have shrunk from any one duty of the
station in which your confidence had placed me.[1]

NICHOLAS BIDDLE.

BIDDLE TO ——[2]

And[a]. Oct[r]. 29. 1822

Dear Sir,

I have received your letter of the 26th inst. in relation to the Presidency of the Bank, and shall cheerfully
give as you request such views of the subject as my service
in the Bank & my acquaintance with the community may
suggest.

If the Bank were in a prosperous situation with an efficient Direction & a full complement of experienced officers
the President might, be as so many Presidents, are, a gentleman of high character to do the honors of the Bank with-

---

[1] For a discussion of the Hartford Convention consult Babcock, K. C., *The
Rise of American Nationality* (New York, 1907), pp. 161–166.

[2] This letter, although it has no definite address, is undoubtedly written to
one of the directors of the Bank. The Biddle Correspondence contains a number
of letters from different members of the board urging Biddle to present his views
on the qualifications of a President and subtly hinted the desirability of his ap-
pearing as a candidate; and it is evidently in reply to one of these requests that
the above letter was drafted.

out much attention to its business. But you well know that the Bank of the U.S. is deficient in these respects and the next President must have such a decided influence over its management as very materially to affect its future fortunes. He should if possible therefore unite in his person these qualifications, talent for business — standing with the gov^t. & residence in Phil^a.

1*st*. I say *talent* for business rather than what is commonly called a man of business — for without meaning at all to disparage the knowledge of details which men of business are presumed to possess I am quite satisfied from what I have myself seen at the Bank that the mere men of business are by no means the most efficient in the administration. The fact is that the misfortunes of the Bank which grew principally out of the injudicious extension of the Western Branches [1] were actually occasioned by the men of business & their errors were precisely the faults into which the men of business were most likely to fall. They trusted the Western people with money — as they trusted them with goods — and suffered themselves to be deluded by the visions & currencies of equalizing exchanges more & liberal habits of thinking would have easily dispelled because without intending reflections, there are not in the Bank such a set of officers as there should be — & the personal inspection of a President is therefore the more necessary.

2. He should be known to, & stand well with the Gov^t — not an active partizan — not even a party man — but a man in whom the gov^t would confide. I am far from think-

---

[1] On the administration of Langdon Cheves, cf. Catterall, R. C. H., *The Second Bank of the United States* (1903), chap. III.

ing that the govᵗ should have any direct or indirect influence over the Bank — on the contrary the less of it which exists the better for both. But the govᵗ is a great stockholder and a great customer — and as the govᵗ Directors cannot exercise the same degree of concert & previous communication as the rest of the Directors & stockholders do. It would be not unwise to consult to a certain extent the feelings of the govᵗ where the great interests of the Bank may depend so much on its countenance & protection.

3. His being a Philadelphian tho' not an essential is yet a desirable circumstance. The Bank has by a combination of circumstances become so odious in Philᵃ., that it is exceedingly difficult as you well know to procure a competent Direction. There are certainly all the materials of an excellent Board, if they would consent to rally round any one individual — and the character of the Bank will wholly depend on the local Board, the Distant Directors are in fact from the very nature of things rather ornamental than useful. Now I fear that a stranger would not easily obtain the aid of such a Board as ought to be collected. If yet such is the importance of that circumstance that I am not sure whether the wisest plan would not be first to make a list of 20 Directors & the best names of the City & then see under what President 15 or 16 of them would consent to serve — and name him accordingly. . . .

JOHN C. CALHOUN TO BIDDLE

Washington 2 Decb 1822

Dear Sir,

Feeling as I do deep solicitude in the prosperity of the Bank, I have been very much gratified with your nomination to the Presidency of that institution and most sincerely hope, that you may be elected.

. . . If at any time, I can render aid to the institution, it will afford me much pleasure, and should you be elected, of which there can be no reasonable doubt, the pleasure would be still farther advanced by cooperating, as with the present President, with one for whom I have so great an esteem.

BIDDLE TO JOHN C. CALHOUN

Phil^a. Decr 6, 1822

Dear Sir,

I had the pleasure last night of receiving your letter of the 2^d inst, & thank you with great cordiality for the friendly dispositions which dictated it. The course which I have hitherto prescribed to myself, has been neither to seek nor to shun a situation of so much responsibility, but if I am called to share in the administration of the Bank, I shall bring to its service at least a laborious & zealous devotion to its interests. This unfortunate institution has from its birth been condemned to struggle with the most perplexing difficulties, yet even with all its embarrassments it has sustained the national currency & rescued the country from the dominition of irresponsible banks, & their depreciated circulation. The time has perhaps arrived when it may combine its own & the country's security with a more enlarged development of its resources and a wider extension of its sphere of usefulness. To this object to which my own exertions shall be anxiously directed. I have long known and appreciated the manly & decisive services which you have rendered to the same cause — & if I should see any occasion in which the Bank may avail itself of your assistance I shall ask it with the same frankness & sincerity with which I now assure you of the great personal respect & esteem of

BIDDLE TO CAMPBELL P. WHITE [1]

(*Private*)   Bank of the U.S.
                                                        Feb. 3, 1823
Sir,

Your letter of the 2^d. inst: has just reached me. Our mutual friend M^r. Colt [2] has already apprized me of the advantage which I might expect from your confidential communication, & your letter satisfies me that he has not overrated the value of them. I beg you to believe that I shall always be gratified at hearing from you whenever any thing occurs which you deem interesting and that I am perfectly prepared always to reciprocate your confidence.

It is my anxious desire to see your Office at the head of the business of N. York, and for that purpose not to suffer itself to be encumbered with state Bank balances, nor with more debts from Southern Offices than necessarily grow out of the receipt of their paper and a profitable and accommodating exchange business. The practice here is this. Every morning the Clerks from this Bank and the State Banks meet and inter change the notes received respectively on the preceeding day. The Balances are Struct accordingly — but no Bank ever calculates on its Balance

---

[1] Merchant and Congressman of New York.

[2] Roswell L. Colt. A director of the Baltimore Branch from 1816 to 1819. Colt was undoubtedly the closest financial adviser of Biddle and one to whom the latter always referred in time of trouble. He was in touch with all the financial conditions of the country and the correspondence shows that Nicholas Biddle frequently followed his advice on political as well as financial affairs.

remaining for any length of time & whenever it grows a little too large, no Bank ever hesitates to send for ten or fifteen or twenty thousand dollars from its debtor. We had the other day a draft for $25,000 — from one of our City Banks which was paid as cheerfully & with as little sensation as if it had been a check for $25. Whenever there is a draft from an individual for Specie to any amount the State Banks are made to pay it if their Balances allow it. Thus it goes round — no one complains and every one is Satisfied. In truth, it is only when these balances accumulate & remain for any length of time that they become oppressive to both parties and excite mutual ill will. You have now a fine oportunity of establishing and maintaining your preeminence and I hope anxiously that it will not be lost. The other subjects of your letter will receive an early attention, but my occupations this morning allow me time only to acknowledge the receipt of it thus briefly & to add that I am

BIDDLE TO ROBERT LENOX [1]

Bank of the United States
Feby. 3, 1823

Sir,

. . . The view which I have of the true policy of the Bank is this. We have had enough & more than enough of banking in the interior. We have been crippled & almost destroyed by it. It is time to concenter our business — to bank where there is some use & some profit in it, and therefore (while anxious to do business in the interior the mo-

---

[1] Robert Lenox, one of the foremost merchants of New York, was a trusted adviser of Biddle. Cf. Life in Wilson, James G., *Memorial History of New York* (New York, 1893), vol. IV, p. 417.

ment there is clear prospect of doing it usefully & safely) to make at present the large commercial Cities the principal scene of our operations. With this impression my object is to give to the Office at New York the command of the business of N. York — to make it the first banking institution there. To this it is entitled from its Capital its resources, and the character of its Direction. But it never can have the power which it ought to possess, if it suffers itself to be crowded out of its proper sphere by the State Banks & to be constantly preyed upon by them. It would be desirable too that it should keep its means as much as possible to itself — except what may be necessary for profitable exchange operations, & as far as possible avoid having large balances from Southern Offices. . . .

BIDDLE TO DAVID SEARS [1]

Philada Jany 5th 1824

My Dear Sir

The frequent experience which we have had of your liberality and your attachment to the interest of the Bank, has induced us to take a liberty which I persuade myself you will not disapprove. Since the Presidency of the Office at Boston has passed out of the political family where it has been so long, there has been a feeling of disquiet at the circumstance, increased by the political cast of a great majority of the Board. These are considerations, which situated as we are we cannot wholly overlook, that they shall never be permitted to interfere with more important matters. Still in the effort to attract towards the Bank the good

---

[1] Sears, David, a wealthy Bostonian. Winsor, Justin, *A Memorial History of Boston* (Boston, 1883), vol. IV, p. 657.

wishes of the country at large it is desirable whenever a safe opportunity presents itself, of assuaging feelings which may hereafter grow into hostility, to take advantage of it. During the present year our two directors from your state are both of the same political denomination and as the President of the Office is now of that section also it is thought well to give to their political opponents, if indeed they can be so called, a larger share in the administration. This we have done by substituting M[r] Crowninshield,[1] for M[r]. Mason.[2] To the latter's gentleman his seat at this Board is I presume an object of indifference, as his high standing and character place him beyond the reach of wishing a mere compliment, and his occupations prevent his personal attendance. M[r] Crowninshield is a gentleman of character, a large Stockholder, and he will now visit us necessarily twice a year. Under these circumstances, Gen[l] Cadwalader[3] and myself have thought it was for the interest of the Bank to make the change, and we have relied on the good feelings of yourself and M[r] Mason to understand, and appreciate our motives. To that gentleman, whom I have not the pleasure of knowing personally, I trust you will be good enough to explain the reasons of this change, which in

[1] A rich merchant and literary man of Boston. Cf. sketch of life in Winsor, Justin, *A Memorial History of Boston*, vol. IV, p. 293.

[2] A great lawyer, formerly senator from New Hampshire. Dean of Harvard Law School. *Ibid.*, vol. IV, p. 598.

[3] Soldier and lawyer. Brigadier-General of volunteers in Mexican War. Placed in command of Baltimore during the semi-revolt at the time of the Civil War. In 1862 commissioned Major-General and one of the board to revise military laws and regulations in the United States. One of Biddle's most trusted advisers. Cf. Appleton, *Cyclopædia*, and Simpson, Henry, *The Lives of Eminent Philadelphians* (Philadelphia, 1859), pp. 168–170. For Cadwalader's relations with President Jackson, cf. Bassett, J.S., *The Life of Andrew Jackson* (New York, 1911), vol. II, pp. 404, 590, 591, 617.

truth has been occasioned by our perfect conviction, that in the endeavor to reconcile conflicting interests we have some right to claim and are sure of receiving, the indulgence of such gentlemen as Mr Mason and yourself.

BIDDLE TO COLONEL GEORGE GIBBS [1]

Phila. March 15, 1825

My dear Sir,

I have just received your favor of the 14th inst. and regret much that it will not be in my power to negotiate the note you have forwarded, which is therefore returned to you herewith. Since my connection with the Bank I have been obliged to make it an invariable rule not to be a borrower from the Bank itself — and not to be an indorser on notes discounted either there or in other institutions. To this I have on principle adhered, to the prejudice of my own interest, from a conviction that situated as I am, it was in all respects proper. I should feel more unwilling to act on it upon the present occasion if I did not know that it would not incommode you as you will find no difficulty in making the arrangement elsewhere. . . .

BIDDLE TO ISAAC LAWRENCE ESQR. [2]

Bank of the United States
April 22nd 1825.

Sir

Allow me again to invite your attention to the subject of turning the balances with the State Banks, in your

---

[1] Literary man. Cf. Wilson, *op. cit.*, vol. IV, p. 417.

[2] President of Branch of United States Bank in New York. Cf. Lamb, Mrs. Martha J., *History of the City of New York* (New York, 1881), vol. II, p. 520.

favor by bringing your discounts within your income. In the midst of the speculations [1] which are abroad, combined with the demands for specie, prudence requires that we should keep within reasonable limits, and that under all circumstances, and at all hazards the Bank should keep itself secure and strong. Since the 18th of March when I wrote to you on the subject of your ability to do business paper falling due on or about the 1st of July, your discounts have increased about $700,000, a fair addition to your business which would be attended with no inconvenience did not an extraordinary demand for Specie which has arisen render the extension more hazardous by exposing you to calls for Specie against which every consideration of prudence requires you to guard. It is no doubt very unpleasant and even painful to decline good business paper, but you have already by so large an increase of your discounts contributed your full share to the public accomodation — and beyond a certain limit the convenience of the customers of the Bank however desirable it may be to promote it is only a secondary consideration when there is the slightest risk that by pushing the spirit of accomodation as to require a sudden reduction, which would more than over balance the facilities to a few individuals which had occasioned it. In the present state of the office the true course I think is, to turn over as quietly as possible to the other Banks, any demand which you cannot supply — to let the diminution of your discounts, and the public revenue as it accumulates turn the scale in your favor with the other

---

[1] The first great test of Biddle's policy as President of the Bank came during the crisis of 1825; and largely owing to his foresight and policy, as shown in the above letter, the institution and the nation were able to weather the storm. For a complete discussion of this topic, cf. Catterall, *op. cit.*, pp. 106–108.

Banks, and then not to make sudden or very rigid demands on them for Specie when you feel satisfied that you can claim your balances the moment they are wanted. By pursuing such a system you will I hope soon be able to regain your ascendency over the State institutions without risk or inconvenience.

BIDDLE TO ISAAC LAWRENCE

Bank of the United States
May 12th 1825

Dear Sir

I again observe with pleasure your proceedings of yesterday. Everything will go as we could wish if we have but the firmness to withstand the solicitations of persons whose wants or whose interest overcome every other consideration. Our first duty is to take care of the Bank, and at the present moment of wild and exaggerated speculation if we suffer ourselves to be borne away by the current, if we do not on the contrary, like sober and prudent men, resist alike the entreaties or the clamors of individuals we shall betray our trust. You are doing now perfectly well. Let us not by the hope of doing better or getting more business risk the prosperity and safety of the institution. . . .

BIDDLE TO ROBERT LENOX

Phila. June 24, 1825

Dear Sir,

. . . The truth is simply this. The Bank is doing very well. During my connection of six years with it, I have never seen its affairs in so satisfactory a state, as at the present moment. It will have certainly have earned during the last six months more than three per cent. But then I am clearly of opinion that we should never advance our rate of dividend, till we are perfectly satisfied that we will never have occasion to diminish it. In Jany. 1823, we began without one dollar in our pockets — and we have been trying ever since to accumulate a fund in reserve, so as to equalize our dividends. You may be very sure of two things: in the first place that no determination with regard to the next Dividend has been generally formed, & in the second place that whatever that Dividend may be the succeeding dividend will be at least as much. . . .

WALTER BOWNE [1] TO BIDDLE

(*Privat*)   New York June 28, 1825
Dear Sir

     . . . A foolish report has been going about that a combination of persons who have obtained an influence in several of our local moneyd institutions have commenced an arrangement to attack the U S B, obtain votes and effect a change in the direction the thing in my mind is altogether preposterous — that is as to success one favorite argument with them to weak stockholders is a promise of better dividends.

     P.S. some increase of div'd. at this time in the opinion of many of our best friends will most materially subserve the best interest of the Bank.[2]

---

[1] Mayor of New York 1828–1833. A descendant of the well-known and highly estimable Quaker family of the Bownes of Flushing, Long Island. Engaged in the hardware business. Wilson, *op. cit.*, vol. III, p. 338.

[2] A combination had been formed to remove Biddle on account of his refusal to increase the dividends. However, the affair came to nothing, but Biddle finally agreed to pay $2\frac{3}{4}$ per cent.

BIDDLE TO JAMES LLOYD

Jan.ʸ 23, 1826

My dear Sir,

. . . If there be any one principle upon which we have acted, with the most fastidious care, it is, to treat the State authorities with the greatest respect, and in all our intercourse with them to blend the utmost perseverance in asserting the rights of the Bank, with the utmost courtesy to all who opposed them. . . .

BIDDLE TO DANIEL WEBSTER

Philadelphia Feby. 16, 1826

My dear Sir,

. . . I have no doubt that we could at once give to the Southern & Western sections of the country two or three millions of sound & useful circulating medium if we could sign that amount of 5 & 10 dollars. But to make two millions of five dollar notes, it would be necessary to sign my name 400,000 times, which, to a person whose time is & must be absorbed during the day by the duties of his station, is wholly impracticable. The application for this purpose was made to Congress some years ago, but it was accompanied by a request that Congress would alter the Charter so as to prevent the universal receivability of the notes. This I am satisfied from experience, as I was at the time from theory, is not desirable; & all that the Bank now wants is, that it may carry into execution a purpose useful alike to itself & to the community, by assisting in the diffusion of a wholesome currency. I wish therefore to consult you as to the best mode of presenting that subject to Congress. I have been for three years past so anxious to keep the Bank out of view in the political world & bring it down to its true business character as a Counting House, that I have been very reluctant to apply to Congress for anything. . . . I believe it to stand better with Congress than it did some time ago, but the political odour of sanctity is very evanescent & if our purpose can be obtained without bringing on two weeks debate upon the constitutionality of the Bank, the usurpations of the Supreme Court, & omni scibile & quibusdem aliis, it would be a great satisfaction. . . . [1]

BIDDLE TO JOHN McKIM, JR. ESQ.

Philadª. March 14ᵗʰ 1826

My dear Sir,

. . . With regard to our late arrangements, they are simply these. It has been impossible hitherto while the officers of the Bank were so fully occupied with local duties to know as much as was necessary of a great many matters of the highest importance. For instance we have nearly two millions of real estate besides Banking houses, & we have about nine millions of old & new suspended debts. You know how apt real estate & bad debts are to suffer for the want of looking after after. We therefore appointed an officer here to take care of those two concerns. Again, we have never had a sufficient knowledge of the accounts between the officers. It was thus that West the Cashier of New Orleans was enabled to defraud the Bank of $20,000 — we wish to examine these accounts, & we wish also to have our

---

[1] This is the earliest mention of one of Biddle's most important innovations. Draft notes were adopted in 1827 and were first issued in June, 1827. Cf. Catterall, *op. cit.*, p. 119.

Exchange business particularly well managed. We have therefore appointed another Officer for those two purposes. With a view to attract gentlemen of first rate abilities, as the salaries are low ($2500 for one & $2,200 for the other) we have called them not Clerks but Assistant Cashiers. . . .

BIDDLE TO GENERAL JOHN P. BOYD [1]

Philad^a. Nov 23d 1826

My Dear Sir,

I have had the pleasure of receiving your letter of the 18th inst which revived a great many agreeable recollections. In regard to the establishment of a Branch at Portland nothing is as yet decided but should it take place the policy of the Bank has been in the appointment of confidential Officers to live at a distance and to execute such important trusts to take in preference Officers brought up in the Bank under our own eye whose character & conduct are known to us and afford the best guarantee of their capacity to carry into effect the system of the Bank with which they are familiar. I have long been satisfied that this is the true policy of the Bank and I think it will be pursued in case a Branch is established at Portland. The observation applies of course only to the Cashier. The other Officers are appointed by the Directors of the Branch. This is all that I can say at present and although it would be more agreeable to me personally to offer to your nephew more favorable prospects yet this candid explanation is due to you.[2]

[1] A free lance and soldier of fortune. Cf. Appleton, *Cyclopædia*.

[2] This letter shows Biddle's insistence upon promotion by merit rather than through political influence.

BIDDLE TO JAMES CROMMELIEU [1]

Phila^a. May 7, 1827

Dear Sir,

... With a view to secure the best talents in its service & to reward the meritorious officers, the rule of the Bank is that whenever any vacancy occurs it is filled by promotion, & the person last introduced takes his place at the foot of the list, & is gradually advanced if found deserving. The salary of the Officers on their first entrance into the Bank is seven hundred dollars ($700) a year. A comparatively small compensation, but as it is known to lead to more lucrative situations, it is sufficient to attract to the service of the Bank a great number of applicants of respectability. When a vacancy takes place a selection is made from these by a ballot at the Board — in which I of course participate as one of the members merely. At present there is no vacancy. It is impossible however to say how soon there may be one — and if you think it desirable after what I have stated to come into the Bank I would recommend this course. ...

BIDDLE TO DANIEL WEBSTER ESQR

Bank of the United States
June 29th 1827

(*private*)

My Dear Sir

In consequence of your letter I wrote to the proper source suggesting the gentleman mentioned by you and have this morning an answer of which the following is an extract.

"In regard to the appointment of Mr —— it is well known

[1] Cashier of Brooklyn Bank. *American Almanac, 1836–1837*, p. 14.

"here that he is in embarrassed circumstances and his notes
"now in the Bank are considered discounted on one name,
"which however is unquestionably good. Repeated efforts
"have been made to obtain an additional name, in which we
"have failed. It is with much inconvenience he meets even
"his check of 10 per cent and his note for $3330 has recently
"passed the Board for the same amount (now under protest)
"on condition of his paying 20% on the next renewal. Under
"these circumstances however happy I should otherwise be
"to have him attached to the Board, I cannot at present con-
"sistently recommend him for a Director." This presents a
strong case. Obliged as we are to look at the pecuniary side of
men's characters, to be in embarrassed circumstances and to
be even under protest, are deemed disqualifications for sitting
at the Board which must decide on his own applications for
loans. It is probable that you are not aware of these facts and
I mention the subject thus early, so that in case you wish to
make any further remarks on it, they may be in time for the
election on the 11th of next month. I will only add that as the
letter to me is in the most entire confidence, you will consider it in the same manner. I should particularly regret that
your correspondent knew the source of the objection as
it might excite personal hostility towards a very worthy
man. . . .

BIDDLE TO CAMPBELL P. WHITE ESQR.

Bank of the United States
Nov\[r]. 27, 1827

Dear Sir

. . . I thank you for the suggestion in regard to the
political character of the Board These are considerations

which tho' secondary are not to be overlooked and while I would not go out of the way to seek for that object among persons entirely equal in other respects, it would due weight.[1]

JOHN SERGEANT [2] TO BIDDLE

Washington Decr. 13, 1827

Dear Sir,

Tomorrow's paper will give you a resolution introduced to day by M^r. Barbour, and the remarks with which he accompanied it, instructing the Comm^ee. of Ways and Means to enquire into the expediency of selling the Gov^ts. stock in the Bank. It ought to have been decided at once, and I think might have been, but before I could get the floor, a motion was made to lay it on the table which supersedes debate. I believe it will be rejected. In the mean time, however, it will do some mischief, and, if considered as the beginning of an attack, lead to permanent distrust in the stability of the institution which will somewhat enfeeble it. The motion will have the effect, too, of putting the Bank among the topics to be handled by those who are seeking popularity. I am sorry for it.

I have never heard a word about our cause, from which I am afraid there was nothing pleasant to say.

---

[1] The Bank was not impervious to the need of political balance as indicated in the above.

[2] Representative from Pennsylvania. Sergeant was one of the closest friends of Biddle and one upon whom the latter often relied in political controversies. For a full discussion of Barbour's attack, cf. *Cong. Debates*, vol. IV, pt. I, pp. 815, 843, 854, 858.

EDWARD EVERETT [1] TO BIDDLE

H. of Representatives
13 Dec^r. '27

My dear Sir,

A proposition was this day submitted by Mr. P. P. Barbour [2] to sell the bank stock of the United States, or rather to make such sale the subject of Enquiry by the Com^t of Ways & Means. The proposition was ably opposed by Messers McDuffie [3] & Gorham, [4] and was laid on the table. Mr. Barbour will probably bring it up again. Pray let me know (in addition to the obvious considerations on this matter ably Stated by Mr Gorham) what you would wish to have Said about it.

BIDDLE TO CHURCHILL C. CAMBRELENG [5]

Phila. Decr. 16, 1827

Dear Sir,

. . . I wish Mr Barbour had introduced his motion at some other time for just now it is particularly inconvenient. I need not tell the Chairman of the Com. of Commerce that for the last four or five months the course of trade and exchange has carried off a great part of the specie fund of the country & that the Banks may probably be obliged to defend themselves by diminishing their accomodations to the Community which is you know the ultimate remedy. But it is

[1] Representative from Massachusetts.
[2] Representative from Virginia.
[3] George McDuffie (1788–1851). One of the most brilliant of South Carolina leaders. For life, cf. O'Neall, *Bench and Bar of South Carolina*, vol. II, pp. 463–468.
[4] Representative from Massachusetts.
[5] Representative from New York.

sometimes a severe one. We have been striving to avoid it by very large sales of bills which yet do not supply the demand. Just at this moment it happened very luckily that the quotations of the Bank Stock in England were such as to show that remittance of it would be as good as specie calculating the present rate of exchange & the price of £5.10 in London. Accordingly large remittance of Stocks were contemplated the effect of which would have been, besides the profit to our citizens to furnish an amount of exchange which would relieve by so much the pressure on the Banks by specie. I think that a million of dollars would have taken that direction in a week or two & would have afforded real relief. The proposal to sell 7 millions of course destroys all chance of a sale in England at present prices. Nor is this all. For if the foreign Stockholders should take the alarm & throw their stock into the market here it would create a new demand for exchange to remit the proceeds, & thus increase the pressure on the Banks. Whatever be the decision of Congress it is desirable that it should be soon made.

JOHN W. BARNEY [1] TO COLT

Washington December 18th 1827

My Dear Sir

Mr Barbour's resolution has been so generally reprobated by every intelligent member of the House, that I doubt whether he would willingly consent to have it called up again, but as you are of opinion that it is desirable to have it finally disposed of I will as soon as he returns from Virginia press a decision on the subject.

[1] Representative from Maryland, 1825–1829.

ROSWELL L. COLT TO BIDDLE

Bal. 20 De 1827

Dear Biddle

I send You a Letter I have rec^d from Barney on the subject of Barbours resolution — to day a Member called on me to whom I had written about it. he said that Cale Drayton, & M^r McDuffie both assured him the moment Barbour returned they would have it called up & finally disposed of. Mr Sargent who has gone to Harrisburg requested to have it suspended until his return, but that since the Public mind was so agitated they should not wait but act on it at once & probably its fate would be decided to day.

CHURCHILL C. CAMBRELENG TO BIDDLE

Wash^n. 20 Decr. 1827

Dear Sir,

I hope you will not let Mr Barbour resolution disturb you.

It will be put at rest by a large majority — the debate will be of service to the Bank.

JOSEPH GALES, JR,[1] TO BIDDLE

Washington, Dec. 21. 1827

Dear Sir

I beg leave to congratulate you and the country on the decisive & overwhelming defeat of Mr P. P. Barbour's motion directly proposing a sale of the U.S. Bank Shares.

As it has thus terminated, it is fortunate that it was made, and made from so really respectable & disinterested a Source.

[1] Co-editor of *National Intelligencer* with his brother-in-law William W. Seaton.

I consider this vote as definitively settling, in advance of its agitation, the question of the renewal of the charter, as well as the subordinate question to which it [is] more immediately related. All my fear, now is that the Stock will again, as once it has before, mount too rapidly; a consequence of the late decision which I trust, if it appear probable, the Mother Bank will occasionally check by throwing into Market portions of the Stock which it holds itself or can control.

BIDDLE TO GEORGE MCDUFFIE

Phil^a. Decr. 26. 1827

Dear Sir,

Whilst the resolution of Mr Barbour was under consideration I forbore to intrude on you with any observation in regard to it, because I was aware that I could add nothing either to your knowledge of the subject or your disposition to do it ample justice. The decision of the question leaves me at liberty to enjoy the pleasure which I cannot refrain from indulging — of expressing the high gratification felt throughout the community at the great promptness & ability which have distinguished your course on this occasion. They who are directly interested in the result have naturally strong sentiments of gratification to one who has averted from them a great calamity; but there is a more numerous & impartial class of spectators of public affairs who are delighted in recognizing among our public men, enlarged & statesmanlike views of the great interests of the country, unbiased by local & sectional prejudices. To such of these you have given unmingled satisfaction — and you have added largely to the number of your fellow citizens who will watch your advancement with the most friendly solicitude. I know that you do not require the stimulous of applause to do your full duty to the country; but no public man need be indifferent to public gratitude if it be earned by public services, — and this you may well receive, because it is well deserved. I tell You that no one has been more sensible of the value of this exertion of your abilities not merely to the institution but to the country than

BIDDLE TO JOHN POTTER [1]

Phil^a. Jany 7, 1828

Dear Sir

... We might, you perceive, have increased the dividend, but we did not like, after the recent proceedings in Congress to have the air of straining our profits for the sake of appearances — and thought it better to stop far within our limits. This course I think you would approve.

The motion of Mr Barbour has, we think been serviceable to the Bank. ...

HENRY CLAY [2] TO BIDDLE

(*Private*)   Wash n. 28^t. May 1828

My dear Sir

You may have observed in the Telegraph of the 20^t. inst. an article, taken from a K. paper, in which a formidable array of my mortgages and debts is made with a view of making me out a bankrupt. Among the mortgages are two, one to the Bank of the U.S. to secure payment of $22,000, and the other to J. Harper Cash^r. &c to secure payment of $1666:66.

---

[1] Trusted adviser of Biddle with Robert Patterson at Charleston. In 1824 moved to Princeton, New Jersey. Cf. Hageman, John F., *History of Princeton* (Philadelphia, 1879), vol. I, pp. 313, 314.

[2] Secretary of State in the Cabinet of John Quincy Adams.

The latter is wholly discharged. Of the former debt all is paid but about $4000 to meet which there is deposited with the Lexington office paper payable to me, and which becomes due this fall. I have every reason to anticipate its punctual payment, and thus the entire extinction of the mortgage. The truth is that my private affairs, materially affected by a responsibility I incurred about ten years ago, as indorcer, have been in a state of progressive improvement since, and now stand better than they have done during any portion of that time. They are such that, if I were to die tomorrow, my resources are abundant to meet all my engagements, and to leave my family comfortable.

I have thought it might be benefitial to me if you would cause a paragraph to be unveiled, in some paper in your City, making concisely the above statement in regard to the two mortgages, or simply saying that a small balance only is due on the large mortgage which paper is in deposit to meet this fall, and that the small one is discharged. It would be no more than an act of justice to add that, in all my relations with the bank, I have practised the greatest fidelity to my engagements; and that whilst most of your Western debtors have been allowed to pay off their debts in property, no such easement was ever extended or asked by me. I presume the returns from the office at Lexington are such as to admit of the insertion of such a paragraph which might be signed by yourself or Mr. McIlvaine,[1] or be pub-

[1] Assistant Cashier of the Bank. McIlvaine was a special friend of Biddle and often rendered him very valuable services. It was largely owing to his management that the Bank of the United States secured its charter as a State Bank from Pennsylvania in 1836. Cf. sketch of his life in Scharf, J. H., and Westcott, Thompson, *History of Philadelphia, 1609–1884* (Philadelphia, 1884), vol. II, p. 1545; and Martin, J. H., *Bench and Bar of Philadelphia* (Philadelphia, 1883), p. 84.

lished as upon the authority of the Bank, without any signature.

I do not owe any bank in existence a cent, except the small balance due to the Lex^n. office. Instead of being indebted to the Bank of K. (which is one of my enumerated creditors) subsequent to the date and after the payment of my mortgage to that institution, it became indebted to me to the amount of $10000 for which I actually sued it.

I hope you will excuse the trouble I give you, and believe me, with great respect,

BIDDLE TO HENRY CLAY

Phil^a. May 30, 1828

My Dear Sir

I had this morning the pleasure of receiving your favor of yesterday during the session of the Board from which I was not released in time to answer it by the return of the mail I need not say that it will afford me great satisfaction to assist in refuting the injurious representations of your affairs, — which I remember to have seen without reading, as I should have read without believing them. I began by ascertaining from the records of the Bank the accuracy of your statement — but as the returns from the offices represent only the debts of the parties, and not the paper which they deposit for collection, I cannot speak on that subject with as much distinctness as I am able to do in regard to the reduction of your debt and your fidelity in complying with your engagements to the Bank. On reflection I think it better not to publish a formal certificate, but to introduce the testimony of the Bank in a manner less direct tho' equally authoritative. With the reason of this, I need not trouble you — tho' I do not doubt that you would concur with me. You will also I hope agree in the opinion that the fittest channel now for such a communication is Mr Walsh. The relation in which he stands to the present contest will under his agency [be] more independent, and he will give a pungency & force to the contradiction which will probably secure to it a wider circulation than it could obtain through any other of our papers. I have accordingly given to him a statement which he will embody in a paragraph for tomorrow's gazette. You and he I believe do not always agree in the upper regions of politics — but I regret to see estrangements among those whom I esteem — & on this occasion he will do you justice frankly & cordially. I trust you will be satisfied with the manner in which the subject will be presented & believe me very truly [1]

A STOCKHOLDER TO BIDDLE

Baltimore 17 June 1828

Sir

You are doubtless aware of the opposition to your administration of the affairs of the Bank over which you preside, which has recently manifested itself in your City, New York and elsewhere. The Stockholders are under the impression that your object is to keep in check the State Banks, and to regulate the Currency of the Country *at their cost*. This they say may not be inconvenient to you, while you receive the salary of President of the Bank, but it does not suit them. The most effectual method for you to put down the Opposition, is to give a dividend equal to what is usually

[1] The accusation was refuted in the *National Gazette*, May 31, 1828. However, it is worth recalling that if Clay was in good financial standing at this time it was not his general condition.

given by the State banks in your City and elsewhere. If it should not be deemed advisable to give 3½ p Cent, you may give something by way of surplus. Every individual can loan his own money in his own way to produce 6 p cent, and if the National Bank, with all of its advantages — cannot divide more, the Stockholders will not care much about the renewal of its charter — 7½ pcent p annum, is a moderate dividend. It is what the Stockholders expect and every man in the Nation will sanction

BIDDLE TO DANIEL WEBSTER ESQR.

(*private*)   Bank of the U States
                                                            Augt. 14, 1828

My dear Sir

I thank you for your favor of the 9th inst. in regard to the Portsmouth office which we have this day arranged aggreeably to your recommendation. The only departure from it is that we have fixed the salary at $800 & the professional compensation at $1,200 — instead of making each $1,000. This was done so as to preserve the symmetry of our system of compensation to the Presidents of Offices of similar Capital to that of Portsmouth, and not to make any invidious distinctions between them. To Mr Mason [2] the form is I presume indifferent.

It remains now to secure his election.

You know that the Parent Board indicated their preference of a President by placing him at the head of the list — and this is usually decisive — but the election is actually with

[2] Jeremiah Mason had led the attack upon the establishment of the Bank in 1816; yet, through the instrumentality of Webster, as illustrated above, he was chosen President of the Portsmouth Branch.

the Board of the Office, and altho' I have no reason to suppose that there will be any difficulty, yet [it] is always so much easier, if possible, to prevent them to overcome obstacles, that I wish you would take upon yourself to promote his election by any communication which you may deem judicious with the Board of the Office, whose names are subjoined. I enclose Mr Mason's letter to you.[1]

R. SMITH[2] TO BIDDLE

Private & confidential   Offc B U States
Washington Sept. 22[d] 1828

Dear Sir

M[r]. Asbury Dickins,[3] who has had an accommodation of about $2500 in this office, has been lately called upon by our Board, either to reduce this debt by curtailments, or to give additional security therefore. This demand has placed M[r]. Dickins in a very unpleasant situation, & he will not be able to comply with the call, unless at very great inconvenience to himself & to his family, & without being unjust to his other creditors. In a confidential conversation with him, I have learned that there are pressing claims hanging over him to the amount of about $2500, & that every dollar which he can spare from the economical support of his family, & from the interest on his debts in this office, is applied to the liquidation of his debts. If, in addition to the sum already loaned to him, the Bank would lend him $2,500, he would

[1] This letter clearly demonstrates Webster's connection with the disputed Portsmouth selection.

[2] Cashier of Branch at Washington, D.C.

[3] Chief Clerk in Treasury Department; after resignation of Samuel D. Ingham, March 6, 1829, Dickins was Secretary of the Treasury *ad interim*, June 21, 1831, to August 8, 1831.

pay off the claims pressing upon him, & would leave a standing order to be filed in the Treasury, & to be recognised by the
Secretary, to pay us $1,000 annually out of his salary, until
his whole debt should be paid off. The security which he could
give would not be adequate to cover this sum; but if he
lived, and continued in office, the Bank would be sure to
receive the whole amount of his debt.

There are other considerations of a delicate nature, which
would induce me [to] accede to this proposition. They cannot
be communicated to the Board of Directors, perhaps, but
must readily occur to you. Mr Dickins fills the confidential
station in the Treasury, which has the management of the
Bank accounts. He has already evinced the most friendly
disposition towards the Bank, & has in many instances, to
my certain knowledge, rendered services materially important to its interests. I do not say, nor do I believe, that he has
in a single instance, gone contrary to his duty to the Treasury; but I know that it is very important to have the person filling his station, well disposed to the Bank, as the view
which may be taken of the subjects referred to him, may be
materially affected by the feelings by which he is governed.
The report on the subjects of Government deposits in the
Bank, made to the Senate last winter by Genl. Smith,[1]
was in a great measure made from materials furnished by
Mr Dickins, from suggestions obtained from me. This of
course, must not be talked of, nor should I have mentioned
it, but to illustrate the idea of M^r. Dickins usefulness. Such
is my opinion of the services rendered by him, I should
think it good policy to give up entirely, the whole $5000,
sooner than not to retain his friendly disposition. . . .

[1] Senator from Maryland, 1822–1833.

RICHARD RUSH [1] TO BIDDLE

private and confidential.   Washington Nov: 19, 1828

My dear sir.

... I am about setting down to the preparation of my annual report, always a work of importance, but the materials for which, as you well know, cannot be got in, until just before congress assembles. I must prepare it, too, amidst the inevitable interruptions of daily business, drawing me aside. The receipts for the current year are likely, I think, to exceed by a million and a half (perhaps more) my estimate of them this time last year.

It is my present intention to take some notice of your Bank. This has never yet been done, as far as I recollect, as a voluntary duty by the secretary of the treasury in his annual reports. But if these reports are to consist of nothing but an account current of the receipts of the year, set off in ruled lines and columns, any copying clerk in the department might annually save the secretary the trouble of drawing them up.

Please to consider this communication as confidential, and believe me dear Sir,

JOSEPH GALES, JR., TO BIDDLE

Philadelphia, Nov. 24, 1828

2 P.M.

Dear Sir:

Since I had the pleasure of seeing you, I have received from the Post Office the enclosed Letter, which, as I find I

[1] Secretary of the Treasury. Barbour's attack was instrumental in bringing about this reference to the Bank in the Secretary's report.

shall not have my business letter ready before Bank closes, I send specially to you.

Since seeing you I have by mere accident learned that, in the last contest for the Presidency,[1] you have been of the opinion opposed to that which we have felt it to be our duty to maintain. I think it proper to say, that my belief was, until otherwise informed, that if you had inclined to either side, it was in favor of the present Administration. I advert to the fact for no other purpose than to say that I did not speak so *freely* as I did, during our interviews, with the remotest apprehension that anything falling from me in allusion to the contest could be unpleasant to you. I wish not to be considered as one who disregards the common rules of good society. As for the rest, having conversed with you as I would with my most intimate political friend, I am satisfied to leave it to your determination whether I am either as violent or as bad a man as my political enemies would make me out to be.

BIDDLE TO RICHARD RUSH

(*private*)   Phila. Nov 25, 1828
My dear Sir

     . . . I am very much obliged to you for the intimation of your purpose of mentioning the Bank in your next report. Independant of the pleasure of seeing its usefulness recognized from so high a source, it may perhaps be useful with regard to others who have hitherto not been so well disposed

---

[1] This letter is highly significant as it shows that Gales was surprised that Biddle did not warmly support Adams. If this was true, can it be possible that Biddle was favorably disposed to Jackson? Parton and von Holst both cite Jackson's interest in the Bank in 1821 and 1828; while Catterall claims that Biddle had been warned in 1828 by McIlvaine of the incoming President's hostility. However, it seems from this letter that Biddle's friends thought he was not opposed to Jackson.

& who now seemed destined to have an influence hereafter over that subject. so far as respects the country I am perfectly satisfied from as intimate a knowledge as I possess of any subject, that [but] for the presence of the Bank the currency of the country would in two months time relapse into confusion, & that the public revenue, becoming of unequal value at every part of the Union would be subject to loss & delay & expence in making transfers which would be incalculable injurious. It occurs to me — & I therefore venture the suggestion — that the subject might be appropriately introduced at that part of the report, which will naturally state the amount of debt extinguished during the last four years. It would then be satisfactory to add, that the whole of this amount, in addition to the ordinary receipts & disbursements, after being collected in various quarters of this extensive country are transferred to the several points where the public debt is payable, & actually disbursed for that purpose without the delay of amount, or the expense of a dollar — or the slightest risk — the Bank being responsible for the conduct of the agents — while in England, the Gov^t pay more than a million of dollars annually for the management of its debt by the Bank of England. What is scarcely less important is, that from the arrangements made by the Bank for these payments, the inconvenience of a great accumulation of money in the vaults of the Gov^t followed by an immediate distribution of it is entirely obviated. The Bank as the period of payment approaches, anticipates in the form of discounts the disbursement of a considerable portion of the Stock — and the rest becomes absorbed in the mass of its operations so that many millions are paid on a given day, without the slightest previous pressure, or any consciousness on the part of the community of such an operation, which unless skilfully made, may produce inconvenient shocks & fluctuations. . . .

BIDDLE TO DANIEL WEBSTER

Philad Dec 2. 1828

My dear Sir

I rec^d this morning your favor of the 29th ulto — which did not reach me until the Committee to whom Mr Gales' application was referred had decided upon it & their report was adopted by the Board today.

I have, indeed we all have, very favorable dispositions towards Mr Gales, & would gladly assist him if it could be done with propriety. But it would be wrong for us to consider the matter in any other than a pecuniary light or to treat it on any other than simple business principles. The value of his paper & the advantage of its continuance are considerations entirely foreign to us — and the very circumstance that but for the B. U. S. any newspaper would be discontinued, or that the Bank had gone out of its way in order to sustain any newspaper either in administration or in opposition would be a subject of reproach & what alone makes reproach uncomfortable of just reproach to the Bank. I have striven to keep the Bank straight & neutral in this conflict of parties, & I shall endeavor to persevere in that course. If then the support of the Nat^l Int^r. offers no adequate temptation to hazard the property of the Bank, the loan is on business principles not a proper one. The responsibilities of the party now amount to a little above $50,000: for this the Bank has it is conceived just enough & no more to make the debt secure, & all the other means of the parties are already pledged for other debts. The only chance there of any accession of means is in the contingency of their receiving the appointment of printers to the next Congress — a contingency which a politician may regard as surrounded by different degrees of probability but which to a Banker seems an unsteady basis for a loan of $15,000. I am very sorry that we were obliged to decline but really saw no other course, unless we were ready in all impartiality, to furnish the means for a newspaper under the next administration. I have written thus freely because I thought it would interest you to know the fate of his application & the reason of it.

RICHARD RUSH TO BIDDLE

private   Washington December 10, 1828
Dear sir,

I beg leave to enclose you a copy of my annual report. In framing it on this occasion, I have had reference to its making a good impression abroad, satisfied that [if] it should have this effect, in any degree, it will render it but the more valuable at home. Hence in the part about the debt, as well indeed as in other parts, I have been somewhat more elementary, or rather, I should say, explanatory, than would be necessary for home readers alone. I had written out the first sketch of the whole, including the part about the bank, before I was favored with your letter of the 25th of November, and had anticipated some of its suggestions. Others that it contained, and that I also found in your late letter to Mr Dickins, I adopted, and now make you my acknowledgments for them. At the time the Bank was attacked last winter, for so it was in effect, I took my determination not to leave the Department without placing on record my testimony to its vast value to the nation. It will be called an extra-official, volunteer, thing on my part, and other comments made; all of which I shall set at naught. The finances of the state are the state. So said Burke. Every thing that can be brought to bear upon the wealth and prosperity of the nation,— commerce, manufactures, agriculture, the shipping interest, the currency, banks, the coin, tariffs, Internal works — legislation as it may affect all or any of these topics, are open, so I hold it, to the scrutiny or recommendations of a secretary of the treasury, in his annual reports to the national Legislature. He may review in them, if he pleases, the financial systems of any part of the world, past or present, and ought to, if by it he can help our own. True he must be responsible to his own character for the manner in which he may do all this, and more, for everything is open to him. His scope is boundless. I have at least desired to give to the law under which the annual report is made, an enlarged interpretation. I would lift up its dignity, as well as its importance, leaving it for others, more able, who are to come after me, to improve to great national benefits my mere conception of the duties which it imposes. . . .

You have probably as much or more to fear for the Bank, from New York, as from Virginia, and with even less excuse. In Virginia, there are still constitutional scruples. In New York, none. But the frog of Wall Street, puffs himself into the Ox of Lombard street, and will not have you abuse him. Hinc ille lacrymæ. . . .

It is my intention to send copies of my report abroad. I shall take care that it reaches the hands not only of such persons as Mr Huskisson,[1] Mr Peel [2] and Lord Aberdeen,[3]

[1] At this time Secretary of State for War in the Wellington Ministry.
[2] Later Prime Minister of England, December, 1834, 1841–1846.
[3] At this time Secretary of State for Foreign Affairs in the Wellington Ministry.

but also some of those capitalists and bankers who can make the pecuniary world heave, in both hemispheres, by holding up a finger, at the Royal or stock exchange.

GEORGE HOFFMAN [1] TO BIDDLE

Baltimore Decem 20th 1828

My dear Sir

. . . You appear to be going on so smoothly and satisfactorily in the management and operations of the Bank that no room or need of remark or advice is necessary, and this here to fore much abused and unpopular Bank may now be hoped, and said to stand so well with the public, or of all well informed communities and experienced men, that its enemies may become its friends. I hope we may so find it when we go forward for a renewal of its charter. Mr Rush has at least come out, and has done his duty well. It has given me surprise that he, and indeed the President, as also former Secretaries of the Treasury have not usually said something of *the truth* of this matter in their reports.

I would think well of an application for a new Charter some time (years) before the expiration of the present, and would choose a tranquil fortunate session to make it in, an early application is reasonable & proper, as a Machine of its extent, and Loans should know its course, and have ample time to its closure if necessary. I cannot doubt a renewal will be had — the *terms* may give you difficulty and trouble. I have read with great dissatisfaction the assertions ensinuations and threats of Duff Green in his Telegraph of the 4th Instant. does M[r] Clay owe the Bank now a large sum? This

---

[1] One of the directors of the Baltimore and Ohio Railroad. Scharf, J. T., *The Chronicles of Baltimore* (Baltimore, 1874), pp. 377, 447.

enflated flimsy Editor does mischief and may do more if not
put right, his paper circulates extensively and has done a good
deal for the cause of Gen¹ Jackson, I should be very sorry to
imagine the next administration would in any way be influenced by such a paper. Yet I know a Gentleman here a popular
leading Jackson man a representative to our Legislature, and
whose family own a large amount of Stock B. U. S. declare he
would sell out his Stock on reading Duff Greens paper. . . .

BIDDLE TO GEORGE HOFFMAN

Philadᵃ Dec 22. 1828

My dear Sir

. . . I do not incline to fear anything for the Bank
from the change of Administration. Mr Rush's excellent
report sets the seal upon that question, & I should think that
no administration would venture to set the monied concerns
of the country afloat as they once were. When we see who is
to be our new Secy of the Treasy, we can consider seriously
the application for a renewal. . . .

BIDDLE TO SAMUEL SMITH

Philadᵃ Dec 29. 1828

Dear Sir

. . . 3. — You ask "whether any of the branches, in
any way whatever, except the individual votes of the Directors, interfered in the late contest."

Most certainly not — in the slightest degree. There is no
one principle better understood by every officer in the Bank,
than that, he must abstain from politics, and I have not seen
nor heard of any one of them in any part of the Union, who
has been engaged in this controversy. I remarked the other

day a story of a person [1] in Cincinnati who was arrested for rent, & it was supposed that the agent of the Bank had done it to prevent his going to the Senate & making a Senator of the U.S. friendly to Gen[l] Jackson. I do not consider it possible that he should have had any such design, but the subject is under investigation, & if he shall be found to have abused the power of the bank to such an unworthy purpose, he shall certainly never have an opportunity of repeating it. The course of the Bank is very clear and straight on that point. We believe that the prosperity of the Bank & its usefulness to the country depend on its being entirely free from the control of the Officers of the Gov[t], a control fatal to every Bank, which it ever influenced. In order to preserve that independence it must never connect itself with any administration — & never become a partizan of any set of politicians. In this respect I believe all the officers of the institution have been exemplary. The truth is that with us, it is considered that we have no concern in politics. Dean Swift, said you know, that money is neither, whig nor tory, and we say with equal truth, that the Bank is neither Jackson man nor an Adams man, it is only a Bank. . . .

JOHN McLEAN [2] TO BIDDLE

Confidential   Washington
                                                  5 Jan[y]. 1829
Dear Sir,

The enclosed lists of names have been handed to me by Col Johnson [3] of Kentucky, with a request that I would

[1] A Mr. Mack of Cincinnati.
[2] Postmaster-General under J. Q. Adams; later Associate Justice of the Supreme Court.
[3] R. M. Johnson, Vice-President under Van Buren.

submit them to you, as recommended by himself, and renewal of the delegation from Kentucky, for the appointment of Directors of the Branches of the United States bank, at Lexington and Louisville. The members of Congress from Kentucky favourable to the new Administration, are under the impression, that during the late elections in that State, great facilities, by the state banks, were given to those persons, who were favourable to the re-election of Mr Adams, whilst almost all accomodation was withheld from the other side of the contest. This impression may have arisen, perhaps, from the fact, that the Directors were favourable to the Administration, and on that account injustice may have been done them. It is to be expected, where party spirit has no limit, that jealousies of every kind will be cherished against political opponents, and by this means, the fairest course of conduct, may be grossly misrepresented. But, where the impression of unfairness exists, the effect on society and on our institutions may be deeply injurious, without any substantial foundation. It would therefore seem to be sound policy, to guard against every appearance of Wrong. And it is submitted with great deference, whether it would not be advisable to make the selection of Directors for the branches in Kentucky, from both political parties, where persons can be found belonging to both, who are equally competent and entitled to the public confidence.

Being friendly to the Bank myself, I should regret to see a political crusade got up against it. Some, I know are ready to engage in this course, but I wish there number may be small.

I have no doubt, you will agree with me, that every monied institution should remain free from political connections, and that every just measure, which may be calculated to preserve it free from party influence, should be adopted.[1]

BIDDLE TO SAMUEL SMITH

Phil^a. Jany 5. 1829

Dear Sir

I have had the pleasure of receiving your letter of the 2^d inst, in which you mention your being about to make a favorable report on the nomination of Directors of the B. U. S. but wished previously to know "what amount of accommodation had been granted to each by way of discount." I feel some regret at declining to answer any inquiry of yours — and as you know have given full & frank information on every topic connected with the administration of the Bank. But a question involving the private affairs of my colleagues is of a totally different character. The account which any individual keeps with the Bank is a private concern between him & the Bank of which it would be a violation of confidence to speak. The information sought moreover would be useless unless its tendency was to show that the individual had borrowed too much — a fact which would tend to prove not merely the want of personal independence on the part of the borrower, but also fix on the Board of Directors the imputation of suffering him to borrow too much — to neither of which could I with propriety give countenance without a departure from that course of delicacy in regard to the private concerns of individuals which I think due equally to them & to myself. My feeling on that subject

---

[1] A discussion of the charges against the Kentucky Branches can be found in Sen. Doc., No. 17, 23d Cong., 2d Sess., Report of the Committee on Finance with Documents.

is very strong. I have for instance been a director of the Bank for nine years — I have been its presiding officer for six years. I have never borrowed a dollar from the Bank [1] & trust that I never shall. And yet if it were made a question whether I had borrowed one dollar or one million of dollars I would not answer the enquiry, to be made President of the U.S. because it goes to establish an inquisition into the private affairs of individuals which is equally unjust & invidious. I do not think myself at liberty therefore to state any thing with regard to those who keep their accounts in the Bank. . . .

P.S. We have just made a dividend of 3½ per cent with a surplus on our last six months business of more than $100,000 so that the operations of the year close with a dividend of 7 per cent & a surplus of profits of $224,000.

ROSWELL L. COLT TO BIDDLE

Paterson 7 January 1829

Dear Biddle

I saw a friend in New York who is intimate with Cambreleng & speaking about the Presidents message, he told me that three months ago Cambreleng advised him to sell out his Bank Shares — for that the Administration were hostile to the Bank that the Bank had not meet the public estimation, by producing an uniform currency & that its charter would not be renewed & that the Gov^t would creat a new Bank a National one to be located at Washington

---

[1] Protection against the personal affairs of the Bank was the keynote of Biddle's administration. At all times the President refused to allow investigation of the internal workings of the institution until the Bank war broke out in all its fury. Then, in order to show that the Bank had nothing to conceal, he allowed it to take place. But, as a rule, he gave the inquisitor little assistance with the result that the latter was overwhelmed with a mass of abstract data.

with Branches only in such States as should pass a law author-
ising it & made use of very Similar objections to the Bank — as
those introduced into the message — from which he infers that
Van Beuren was consulted on that part of the message. . . .

BIDDLE TO JOHN HARPER [1]

Bank of the U States
Jany 9, 1829

(*private*)

Dear Sir

The annexed list has been sent to me from Washington, as containing the views of several members of Congress
from Kentucky in regard to a proper direction for your Office.
It is accompanied by an expression of opinion on their part—
not to me directly, but thro' a common friend — that during
the elections in Kentucky, great facilities were given by the
Branches in that State, to persons favorable to the reelection
of Mr Adams, whilst almost all accommodation was withheld
from the other side of the contest. I will not believe for a moment that this is not a mistake. The officers of the Bank have
hitherto so studiously avoided all interference in politics,
that I think it scarcely possible that any gentlemen connected with it, should so far forget their duty as to become
partizans, or abuse their delicate trusts to the unworthy purpose of advancing any political object. The statement is however made, and the nomination subjoined is I presume intended to prevent the recurrence of similar favoritism in
future by an union of parties in the Board. As you are about
to forward a new list, I will state to you precisely my views
on that subject.

Politics should be rigorously excluded from the adminis-

---

[1] Cashier of Branch at Lexington, Kentucky.

tration of the Bank. In selecting Directors, the first considerations [should be] integrity, independence, & knowledge of
business. No man should be shunned, & no man should be
sought on account of his political opinions merely. Nevertheless in a community where broad political divisions prevail,
we must not be wholly insensible to them — we must not
exclude, nor even seem to exclude, any one particular denomination of politicians; but where both present candidates of
equal merits, we should take them from both parties. But
still the first question is, their qualifications, distinct from
their political opinions. I would not however be disposed to
act on any regular system of equally uniting both parties
because the inevitable effect of it would be to force upon us
inferior men, merely because they were politicians. I have
myself an extreme unwillingness to blend politics with the
concerns of the Bank. Nearly all its misfortunes may be
traced to this cause, & in your section of the country we
have surely had a melancholy experience of the hazard of
lending to politicians. Since you have been relieved from
them, your affairs have prospered, and you are doing so
well that I do not wish to disturb your progress by an infusion of politics. But at the same time, we must avoid the
odium, which would naturally & justly attach to the exclusion of any party from its proper share in the government
& the loans of the Bank. . . .

BIDDLE TO JOHN McLEAN

(*Confidential*)   Phila. Jany. 10, 1829
My dear Sir,

There is one topic in my letter to you of this day, on
which I did not wish to enlarge lest it might appear invidious,

but which is very fruitful of admonition. The truth is, that almost all the misfortunes of the Bank of the United States, are traceable, directly or indirectly, to politics. In Kentucky the losses were in a great measure incurred by loans to prominent politicians of all sides whose influence procured them undue facilities which ended, as frequently happens, in such cases, by ruining them as well as cripling the Branches. These things have made us sensitive on that point, & unwilling to see any great political influence introduced, which might lead to a recurrence of similar misfortunes.

BIDDLE TO JOHN McLEAN

Bank of the U. States.
Jany. 11, 1829.

My dear Sir—

I thank you very sincerely for your favor of the 5th inst. with its inclosures. . . .

On the general question, I concur entirely in your views, which are, in fact, those which prevail in the administration of the Bank. Our theory is, that the Bank should studiously abstain from all interference in politics, & there is not an officer of the Institution who does not know that his standing & his place too, depend on his strict observance of this principle. I believe also that they have hitherto been faithful to it. I have never heard of any suspicion even, that any officer of the Bank has intermeddled with politics, except on one occasion, and that suspicion, I am satisfied after inquiry, was without foundation.[1]

In regard to Directors, the first considerations undoubtedly are, integrity, independence & knowledge of business.

[1] **Cf.** letter of Biddle to George Hoffman, November 22, 1829.

No man should be excluded, no man should be sought, merely on account of his political sentiments. Nevertheless, in a community where broad political distinctions prevail, we must not be insensible to them,—we must not reject, nor even seem to reject, any denomination of politicians, & where we have the means of selecting persons equally competent from all parties, their political opinions ought not to be overlooked. Still, however, in choosing Directors, who borrow themselves & who lend to others, the funds belonging to the Gov^t. and to the Stockholders, their personal independence, & their fitness for that particular duty must be the primary inquiry— their political preferences only a secondary concern. The great hazard of any *system* of equal division of parties at a Board is, that it almost inevitably forces upon you incompetent or inferior persons, in order to adjust the numerical balance of Directors. For instance, the Board at Nashville naturally consists of the political friends of General Jackson — that at Boston, of the friends of Mr Adams (tho', such is the fate of politicians, I am not so sure of that *now*) and this is not from any principle of political selection or exclusion, but because the best agents for managing monied concerns, happened to be on that side — just as the best lawyer or the best merchant of these places, would probably be in favor of their respective candidates — but if, with a view to redress this inequality, we were to introduce incompetent persons, the Bank might sustain serious injury.

In the Branches we naturally look to the confidential officers of the Bank (the Cashier who is appointed by the Parent Board, and the President of the Branch) to nominate suitable persons to fill the vacancies as they occur by rotation, and if, after inquiring from other independent sources, we see no reason to distrust their judgment, we generally lean to their nomination. This is the safest general practice, because if we at a distance place in the Direction gentlemen without knowing their precise pecuniary situation, we may introduce individuals who have already borrowed too much, or wish to borrow too much, or who have needy friends whose claims they may urge successfully while sitting at the Board, when they might otherwise be resisted. In regard to the Branches in Kentucky, they have met with enormous losses — not less perhaps than $600,000 — and a great portion of this not on business loans, the legitimate object of Banking, but on accomodation paper which should never have found its way into the Branches. This melancholy experience has induced us to give a more commercial & business-like character to their transactions, and they have naturally fallen into the hands of business men, who have managed their affairs very well. These Branches were never in so sound & prosperous a state as at this moment — never did business so usefully to the community & so profitably to the Bank. Being perfectly satisfied with their progress, & perceiving that the set of gentlemen in the Direction are nearly the same who have been there for four or five years, I have not examined their relation to the political parties which have grown up principally since they were first introduced into the Boards. I was not even aware, until I received your letter, of any political preponderance either way, in the Directions of the Branches, nor did I suppose it possible that they would abuse their trusts to any political object. . . .

BIDDLE TO JOSIAH NICHOL ESQ.[1]

Bank of the United States
June 23rd 1829

Dear Sir

. . . We are obliged to receive and glad to receive nominations from any respectable quarter, & always treat them with respect — but you must not suspect that any particular consideration is given to nominations from Washington. With Washington, in its character as the seat of Gov^t, the Bank has no concern. It has in fact nothing to do with the Gov^t, except that in administering the national finances, it will give its aid cordially and sincerely to every administration. But with no administration will it have any political connexion. Nor would the influence of the President and all the Departments put together be sufficient to appoint a single Director who was not considered qualified for his trust. This independence forms the point of honor with the Bank. You must not, therefore, believe for a moment, that any influence from any quarter could interfere with the regular course of our nominations or prevent our consulting you and our friends in Nashville on a subject of so much importance as the choice of those to whom the prosperity of the Bank is entrusted.[2]

BIDDLE TO ROBERT LENOX

Phil^a. July 6th. 1829

My dear Sir,

. . . I intended when I saw you to ask you to procure for me some information. The Office at Portsmouth [3] had

---

[1] President of the Nashville Branch. Woodbridge, J. (editor), *History of Nashville* (Nashville, 1890), p. 283.

[2] Cf., however, Biddle's later conversation with Major Lewis; Biddle to Lewis, May 3, 1830.

[3] This is the opening of the celebrated Portsmouth affair. Biddle had al-

got into a very bad way and great losses will be sustained there. In order however to repair them as much as possible we placed at the head of it M^r. Jeremiah Mason, who has been very busy and very useful in securing our old bad debts and preventing new ones. This operation you know, is not a pleasant one — & has raised against Mr Mason a number of enemies who complain loudly. Such complaints are generally ill founded, & we are disposed to receive them with great distrust. At the same time it is proper not to disregard them and I should like to know from an authentic source whether there is any foundation for them. . . .

ROBERT LENOX TO BIDDLE

New York 7 t July 1829

My Dear Sir

Your favor of the 6th inst is before me. I have long been aware of the existance of the uneasiness which prevails in Portsmouth. I knew it would exist as long ago as when I was there last Summer and at the time the appointment was made and the *Salary* fixed — any man that would do his duty under the Circumstances that exist, would be unpopular; but as the old saying is, "one man may Steal a Sheep while another dare not look over the fence." . . .

WALTER DUN TO BIDDLE

Lexington Ky. August 14th, 1829

Dear Sir

In a confidential conversation with John Tilford [1] Esqr. a few days ago, I learned that a charge of partiality had

ready written to Levi Woodbury, later Secretary of the Treasury, in reply to charges against Mason and it was to follow up this complaint that he now wrote to Lenox.

[1] Major John Tilford, President of the Northern Bank of Kentucky. A close

been made against the Cashier and directory of the Branch of the United States Bank, at this place, in the administration of the business of the office: of discounting more freely the paper of the friends of the administration than that of their political opponents, and thereby permitting political feelings to influence them in loaning the money of the Bank.

I was, as you know, appointed, last winter, a director of that office; and I am the only one, in the direction, who was in favor of the election, and who is friendly to the administration, of General Jackson. Since my appointment I have been pretty punctual in my attendance at the meetings of the board; and I am happy to be able to say that, since my attendance there, the charge of partiality is entirely groundless: in no single instance have the political opinions of applicants for discounts, ever been mentioned by any gentleman in the direction; the solvency and punctuality, of the drawers and endorsers of offered paper, are the only questions that have been discussed there. In cases, too, of indulgence, the directors, in granting or refusing them, have been influenced by reasons affecting the interest of the Bank, and not by political considerations. I can say more: from the character of the paper which became due after my appointment, but which was discounted before, I am certain that equal impartiality governed the board at the time it was discounted.

So far, then, as my observation extends, no charge can be more unfounded; nor can I believe, from my acquaintance with the gentlemen in the direction, and particularly with Mr. Tilford the President, and Mr Harper the Cashier, that the charge was ever true. With the greatest respect I am,

friend of R. M. Johnson of Kentucky, later Vice-President under Van Buren. Cf. Johnson MSS. in Library of Congress.

BIDDLE TO GENERAL THOMAS CADWALADER

On board the Steam Boat off
Point Judith
Augt. 28, 1829

My dear Sir,

. . . I can now say with the utmost confidence that the whole is a paltry intrigue got up by a combination of small bankrupts & smaller Demagogues — that if the choice were to be made again, we ought to choose Mr Mason — and that to have him out or not to support him fully would be to suffer ourselves to be tramped down by the merest rabble. . . .

BIDDLE TO A. DICKINS

(*Private*)   Philada: Septr. 16, 1829

My dear Sir

I received yesterday your favor of the 13th instant, & thank you for its suggestions, which are, I am sure dictated by great kindness. But I cannot go to Washington at present. I find here a state of things which I really think I had no reason to anticipate. No man, not the noisiest partizan in the country has taken more pains to make the financial operations of the administration useful to the country & creditable to themselves. And what is the return. Constant abuse of the Bank from the press which is the official organ of that Administration — during my absence the Secretary at War [1] makes a most extraordinary notation of its rights — and now I have on my table an official communication of the views of the Administration as to the manner in which the Bank ought to choose & remove its Officers. For the two first I

[1] John H. Eaton of Tennessee.

care nothing, except so far as they may indicate the disposition to condemn & to encroach, but the last cannot be passed without notice. It is regarded generally by the Board as showing a determination to injure the independence of the Bank, on a point where it is peculiarly sensitive as well from duty as from honor, & accordingly they think that it should be resisted at all hazards. And so it shall be. I have sent today to the Secretary their unanimous views on the subject, in which none of the members concur more heartily than the friends of the Administration.[1]

I regret all this exceedingly. You know my indifference to Party & how well disposed I was to act cordially with the present Administration — & particularly with your new Secretary. But having done my duty to them, I will not give way an inch in what concerns the independence of the Bank, to please all the Administrations past, present or future.[2]

The bigots of the last reproached me with nothing for them — the bigots of the present will be annoyed that the Bank will not support them. Be it so, I care nothing for either class of partizans & mean to disregard both.

The Portsmouth affair I found after an examination of six days, to be a very small intrigue to supplant an honest & excellent officer, who was of course continued in his place.

Having by my official letter of to day, satisfied my sense of duty by rejecting all interference in the concerns of the Bank, I have no further feeling on the occasion, & shall in any event take care that as far as I am concerned the relations of the Bank with the Treasury shall be as kindly as heretofore.

[1] The correspondence between Biddle and Secretary Ingham is fully discussed. Bassett, *op. cit.*, vol. II, pp. 594–597.

[2] Dickins later claimed that Ingham was innocent of the inception of the attack.

Phil[a]. Septr. 30th. 1829

My dear Sir

The mail of this morning brought me your favor of the 28th inst. the business part of which was immediately arranged.

I regret, my dear Sir, this controversy as much as you can & would gladly have shunned it, but believing that it is safer for the country to have no Bank than to have it subject to political influences, it was impossible not to resist these pretensions from so many quarters to interfere in its administration. In doing this I am not conscious of having gone beyond the limits of a necessary self defence; and no one would regret more than I would, if I thought you right in believing that the Board had persisted in imputing to M[r] Ingham [1] a purpose which he has disavowed. But what the Board imputed to him & what has he disavowed? He has in so many words, sent to the Board the views of the administration as to the mode in which they ought to choose and dismiss their officers saying that it is his "high public duty" to communicate it & their "very high obligation" to conform to it. All that the Board have answered is, that he had no right to give advice — and that if he had, the advice is bad. They have never imputed to him a design to acquire undue influence — they have only said that his theory would lead to it. They have never imputed to him a connexion with the movements of other people — they have only cited these movements in illustration of the danger of his theory. I hope

---

[1] Secretary of the Treasury for President Jackson. Resigned when the Cabinet was broken up presumably on account of Mrs. Eaton.

most sincerely that he has no such connexion & would be the first to render justice to him whenever an opportunity occurs. For really he ought not, and I am sure will not ascribe to us the least unkindness toward him. To show you the temper in which this whole matter has been conducted, I will mention a simple fact. The only political character in the Board is M^r. Sergeant and he was a member of the Committee to whom M^r. Inghams first letter was referred. But so fearful was I lest any political bias should interfere, that I would not communicate with M^r. Sergeant— nor was he consulted until during my absence his professional opinion was asked about the removal of the Pension Office, he being the standing counsel of the Bank. Moreover of the five gentlemen composing that Committee, two were the political friends of Genl. Jackson. All our predispositions therefore were kindly, and it was not until the feelings & the spirit of the Board were wounded, that they were compelled to vindicate the independence of the Institution.

Having done this, all feeling has subsided & it will remain for the Secretary himself to restore the relations of the Bank & the Treasury to their former friendly footing. He has only to say that we have misapprehended him — that he did not claim a right to interfere with the concerns of the Bank — and had nothing to do with the movement, of these other people — and I should immediately say, as I have no doubt the Board would say, that the explanation was very agreeable — that we regretted any misapprehension, and any expression on the part of the Board which might be considered as applying to a supposed design to interfere would of course be inapplicable on the present occasion. This I think he might do with great propriety and I am sure that he would be met in the most friendly temper. He ought to do it, because I think he began this whole business. My impression is that he would have done well to say in answer to Mr Woodbury that he should apply to the Bank and not to the Treasury there being a peculiar awkwardness in any interference on the part of the Sec^y. Not having done so he has become inevitably blended with these other movements of a parcel of intriguers, all participation in which, he owes it to himself to disclaim. No one will be better pleased than I shall be at his doing so. I had intended on my return from the North to explain to the Sec^y the whole machinery of this cabal of which he was to have been made the unconscious instrument & to put him on his guard against similar machinations in future. But the tone of his second letter made me abstain from any thing which might be misconstrued into an acknowledgement that he was entitled to any such explanations. . . .

WILLIAM B. LEWIS [1] TO BIDDLE

Washington Octr. 16th 1829

D. Sir,

　　Your letter of the 14th Inst. inclosing one from Mr Dun of Lexington, was received by the mail of yesterday morning. I have not the pleasure of being personally acquainted with Mr Dun, but am told by those who know him, that he is a highly reputable gentleman. His letter, as requested, has been shown to the President who, with compliments, desires me to express to you his thanks for the information it contains. He certainly has been led to believe, from the complaints of his friends, during the *pendency* of the presidential election, that the Lexington Branch in

[1] A member of the Kitchen Cabinet and a close friend of President Jackson.

disbursing its golden favours, in the way of discounts, had manifested great partiality. It is gratifying to him however, he says, to learn that probably there was no just cause for those complaints, or at least, that they probably had been much exaggerated. He requests me to say, that he has too much confidence in you to believe, for a moment, that you should knowingly tolerate such conduct in the Branches of your Bank; but from the complaints which are still made with regard to some of them, particularly the one at New Orleans, he thinks it not improbable that party feeling may yet have some influence upon their operations. He hopes this may not be the case, but an inquiry into the cause of those complaints, and a removal of the ground if there be any for them, is an object, he thinks, worthy the attention of the Parent Bank. The President thinks, as you do, that the Bank of the U. States should recognise *no* party; and that, in all its operations, it should have an eye *single* to the interest of the Stockholders and the good of the country. . . .

BIDDLE TO WILLIAM B. LEWIS

Phil^a. Octr. 21st, 1829

Dear Sir

Your favor of the 16th. inst. was very acceptable as it satisfied me of what I could never permit myself to doubt, that the views of the President were in perfect accordance with those of the Bank in regard to the exclusion of party feelings from its administration. The fact is that among the Directors, it is considered not simply a duty, but a point of honor, not to yield to party spirit — and they would anxiously & zealously prevent, or punish it should it occur on the part of any of their Officers.

I cannot give you a stronger proof of that disposition than this letter will afford. You remark in your favor of the 16th inst. that complaint, had reached the President of political feelings shown in the direction of the Branch at New Orleans. The Cashier of that Branch is here & on the point of sailing for New Orleans. But I have instructed him to go immediately to Washington, to satisfy the President, which I think he can readily do, that the statements he has heard, are erroneous, and at any rate to hear precisely what the allegations are in order that on his arrival at New Orleans he may furnish the necessary refutation of them. It is the purpose of this letter to request that you will have the goodness to put M[r] Jaudon [1] in the way of attaining this object. He is a gentleman of high character and capacity — inferior to no other Officer in the Bank & with very few equals in the country for intelligence and knowledge of business.

It will afford me great pleasure to see you when you visit Philad[a]. & in the mean time I remain

MATTHEW L. BEVAN [2] TO BIDDLE

Private   Washington City Oct[r] 21[t] 1829
My dear Sir

. . . I cannot withhold a moment the pleasure it give me in saying that the result of my visit is most satisfactory, in as much as the President expressed himself in the most clear and decided manner friendly to the Bank "that it was a blessing to the Country administered as it was, diffusing a healthfull circulation, sustaining the general credit without

[1] Samuel Jaudon, Cashier of the Bank and trusted friend of Biddle.
[2] Later President of the Bank of the United States of Pennsylvania.

partiallity or political bias " that he entertained a high regard for its excellent President (I use his own words) who
with the Board of the Parent Bank possess'd his entire
confidence and indeed his thanks for the readiness and
cordiality with which they seemed to meet views of the
Government — he said it was true many complaints had
been made of partiality in the Branches in Kentucky and
New Orleans, but further added if these complaints have
any Just foundation, he was persuaded the Parent board
knew nothing of them, and if they did would not sanction
them. . . .

SAMUEL JAUDON TO BIDDLE

Philadelphia, Octr 26th 1829

Dr Sir,

Agreeably to your instructions, I proceeded on Thursday last to Washington City, for the purpose of inquiring
into the reports which had reached the Government of the
exercise at the Office in New Orleans of a political influence
unfavorable to the present Administration. In this visit, I
had the good fortune to be accompanied by John Hagan,
Esquire, one of the Directors of our Office, and a personal as
well as political friend of the President.

Immediately after our arrival there on Friday morning, we
called on Major Lewis, to whom I handed your letter, which
introduced a free and full conversation. In reply to my inquiries he stated, that letters had been received from New
Orleans containing accusations, in *general terms*, that the
Board of the Office there were actuated in the performance
of their duties by political feelings hostile to the Administration, but that no *specific charges* had as yet been made. I re-

marked, that we could only meet general accusations by general denials, and that I did deny in the most unqualified manner that there was the least ground for the charge; that I could appeal confidently to the Books of the Office to shew that no paper had been rejected but upon sufficient commercial grounds; that if any specific charges should be preferred, I should be able to give the most convincing proofs that our Board had acted only on the strictest Banking principles without the least reference to party views or partialities — and that I knew that I should be fully borne out in these assertions by those of our present as well as former Directors who are the personal and political friends of the President. These statements, and others which I urged of a similar nature, were unhesitatingly seconded and confirmed by Mr Hagan. Major Lewis expressed himself perfectly satisfied, and promised to communicate to the President your letter and our representations; and he invited us to call upon the President in the evening.

We accordingly did call, and were received by the President in the most friendly manner. After conversing for some time upon general subjects, the President remarked, that some letters had been received from New Orleans containing charges against the Office there of the perversion of its influence to party purposes, but that he was pleased to find from your letter to Major Lewis, and from the assurances of Mr. Hagan and myself, that there was no foundation for these charges; that party feelings, he knew, often blinded the judgment, and led us to imagine faults where none existed, and that men were particularly apt to make a charge of the kind alluded to against a Bank which, with however good reason, withheld from them its favors; that he was entirely convinced that no hostility to his administration was exercised by the Board of the Parent Bank, and that in reference to yourself particularly he had the most unbounded confidence in the purity of your intentions; that the support which you had given to the financial operations of the Government was of the most gratifying as well as effectual kind, and that he wished for nothing from the Bank but its cordial and liberal cooperation in matters of this nature. He should have been satisfied, he said, by your letter alone of the want of any foundation for the accusations against the Office at New Orleans; and from my unqualified denials as well as my readiness to meet the charges, and from the testimony of Mr Hagan, not the least doubt remained on his mind. He appeared to be much gratified, that we should have paid this visit with the sole view of obliterating unfounded impressions, evincing as it did the wish of the Bank to remove all obstacles to the most perfect good understanding.

Throughout our interview, which lasted for an hour, the tone and manner of the President were of the most mild and friendly character, and both Mr Hagan and myself took our leave under the full conviction that we had to the extent of our wishes accomplished the object of our visit. I do not pretend, to have given you the precise language of the President, tho' I have followed it as far as my recollection serves.

EXTRACT FROM WILLIAM B. LEWIS TO HENRY TOLAND

Washington Novr. 9, 1829

Say to Mr Biddle the President is much gratified with the report I have made him upon the subject of his Bank, all things with regard to it will be well.

FROM THE SAME TO THE SAME

Novr. 11, 1829

If you see Mr Biddle say to him the President would be glad to see his proposition for sinking or paying off the three per cent Stock.[1] He had better write to me when his leisure will permit & I will submit it to the General. I think we will find the *old fellow* will do justice to the Bank in his message for the handsome manner in which it assisted the Gov^t in paying the last instalment of the National debt.[2]

WILLIAM B. LEWIS TO BIDDLE

Washington Novr. 15th 1829

D. Sir,

I wrote last evening to Mr H. Toland [3] informing him that some of his friends here were anxious that he should be run for the appointment of Clerk to the House of Representatives in Congress. I think, if he will consent to serve, he can be elected, and he should not, it seems to me object to it. I wish you would see and advise with him on this subject. There is a very large majority of the members of the next Congress in favour of the present Administration, and I am sure there can be no wish on *their* part to reelect Mr Clark(e)[4] nor do I believe the opposition members have any partiality for him. If Toland will consent to let his friends place his name before the House, *you* can serve him very efficiently, I have no doubt, by speaking to *Webster* and enlisting him and other New England members in his behalf. I am sure

---

[1] For a discussion of this topic, cf. Catterall, *op. cit.*, pp. 146, 151, 269–273.
[2] This extract is in Biddle's own handwriting.
[3] Representative from Pennsylvania.
[4] Matthew St. Clair Clarke of Pennsylvania.

they can have no predelections in favour of Clark, and with a little pains could be got to vote for Toland. Mr Ingham for particular reasons will support Mr Clark, and such of the Penn^a. delegation as are under his influence (Dr Sutherland [1] and two or three others) will vote for him; but I have no doubt, a decided majority would support our friend. It will be well to see Mr Hemphill,[2] and converse with him upon the subject, and if he should be favourably disposed, get him to write to his friends — particularly Judge Wilkins[3] of Pittsburgh, and old Mr Ross. You will have a fine opportunity of seeing your Eastern friends (I mean such as you can venture to speak to) as they pass thro' Phil^a. on their way to Congress, and enlisting them in the support of Toland.

I have taken the liberty, my dear sir, of writing to you upon this subject, because I know you feel, as I do, a deep interest in the welfare of Mr Toland, and will most cheerfully aid in whatever may tend to his benefit. Should he be appointed Clerk to the House it may lead to results still more important to him — it may ultimately be the means of relieving him from his pecuniary embarrassments.

I intimated in my letter to him, of last night, that should he consent to be a candidate, it might be well to let it be announced in one of your papers &c. On reflection I am inclined to think it would be best to say nothing about it in the papers — instead of that course it would be better for Toland to write to some of the leading members elect.

I have no hesitation in saying that he will be supported by all the leading and personal friends of the President here —

---

[1] Representative from Pennsylvania.   [2] Representative from Pennsylvania.
[3] President of the Bank of Pittsburgh and President of the Pittsburgh Manufacturing Company. Senator from Pennsylvania, 1831–1834. Later Minister to Russia and Secretary of War in Tyler's Cabinet.

such as Major Barry,[1] M[r]. Van Buren, Major Eaton, Major Smith, Major Campbell &c &c. In fact I think if he will consent to let his name be run that he can be elected. Should he determine on this he ought to come on here, at least two weeks before Congress meets. Write me in relation to this scheme.[2]

BIDDLE TO GEORGE HOFFMAN

Washington Nov[r]. 22nd 1829

Dear Sir

. . . The best feelings are entertained toward the bank by those whose opinions are most valuable and most useful. I am very desirous of making & for that purpose, am particularly solicitious to avoid giving, at the present moment, any occasion for the revival of a jealousy which has been recently and deeply felt, in regard to the apparent exclusion or omission from the Local Boards of persons favorable to the present administration. My stay in Baltimore was too short to allow me to consult with you on the subject, but M[r]. Colt mentioned the names of five gentlemen who were to be nominated and all of whom, it appeared, were in opposition to the present administration so that out of the whole 13, there are only two gentlemen who are in political harmony with the administration. You know, my dear Sir, how entirely indifferent I am to what are called politics & how unwilling I am to introduce things of that kind into the affairs

---

[1] Postmaster-General under Jackson.

[2] The whole plan ultimately failed, as the Pennsylvania delegation, with the exception of Mr. Hemphill, determined to support Mr. Clarke. Accordingly Toland's name was not even submitted as a candidate. However, the real importance of this letter lies in the fact that Lewis broached Biddle on the subject. The letter indicates that Lewis was trying to get in touch with Biddle on political affairs and that he fully realized the latter's influence.

of the Bank. At the same time, it is proper in itself, as well as highly expedient, not to give unnecessary offence & not to do anything which might have the appearance of partiality. I am afraid that this great disproportion, tho' entirely accidental, may be the ground of objection & reproach. . . .

ALEXANDER HAMILTON [1] TO BIDDLE

New York Dec. 10th 1829

Dear Sir.

If, after the receipt of your first letter, sufficient time had remained for any valuable interference, on your part, at Washington, and you had not appeared quite so confident in your conclusions, I should have endeavoured to prove, that you were under a delusion. The die is now cast;[2] it therefore, only remains for you, to make the best of an unpromising cause. I have no doubt the executive was perfectly sincere, and of this there is internal evidence sufficient, in the alternative he proposes. I am confident, had the subject been examined by him, without influence, he never would, for a moment, have entertained the project of establishing a National Bank, the dangerous tendencies of which are so entirely at variance with his patriotism.

As I have trespassed thus far, I feel, as if I would rather proceed, than retreat, with an assurance of my best respects.

[1] Son of the great Alexander Hamilton. Born May 16, 1786; died August 2, 1875. With the Duke of Wellington in Portugal in 1811 and served as aide-de-camp to General Morgan Lewis in 1814. In 1823 one of the three United States Florida Land Commissioners. Last years spent in real estate speculations in New York.

[2] Cf. Richardson, J. D. (editor), *Messages and Papers of the Presidents* (Washington, 1896–1899), vol. II, p. 462.

In presenting to your consideration, the reflections that have occurred in my mind, I can forsee no injury, and consequently offer them gratuitously. In the first place, I would suggest the propriety of abstaining from the expression of any opinion intimating a want of fairness and integrity in the President; I am satisfied he feels no personal hostility and consequently no conduct of the bank ought to create such a feeling. I would next observe, have no confidence in Van Beuren;[1] as an aspirant for the Chief Magistracy, he is without principle, and totally destitute of sincerity. In the West, especially in Kentucky, the friends of the Administration are against you, & on the majority in this State, you can make as little calculation; these are sufficient causes to govern this gentleman; he may smile and seem gratious, it will only be to deceive. Under these circumstances, do you not think it would be very unwise policy to make any application to Congress, in relation to the Bank at the present session? You can lose nothing by the delay, and may acquire, independent of the opportunity to explain the character of your operations, the nature of the exchanges and the absolute impossibility, in any well regulated and decently administered Institution, to equalize the currency, the chance of some political changes, either here or in Europe, which may have propitious influence on the measures of our government. To anticipate any congressional patronage, in the existing state of things, in direct opposition to the President's avowed sentiments, the secret but artful hostility of aiming intriguers, with the whole host of Jackson Papers, would be to encourage expectations, certain to be disappointed, and if unsuccessful, ruinous. There

---

[1] This is the accepted view of Van Buren by the followers of the Bank, as is shown by the later correspondence.

can be no doubt as to the difficulties you will have to encounter, and there is as little question that precaution is your only dependence.

The affairs of the Bank must not be brought under discussion, through any *friendly* suggestion; if its opponents should commence the charge, the defence would afford a fair opportunity for explanation, and one a less ungracious to expose the anti republican scheme of a government bank, and the absurd expectation that the currency could be equalized by any, however organized. It would not be more absurd to contend that the government ought or could regulate our exchanges on Europe. These variations are the rights and consequences of free commercial intercourse, and any influence that prevents extravagant changes affects all that is desirable; and I venture to predict, if a perfect equality ever be established, it will be of short duration, a deleterious stagnation; the paper fountains would overflow, until the country was deluged with irresponsible emissions. It is not improbable, Mr Barbour, encouraged by the Executive thrust, may renew his proposition to sell the stock held by the Government, which would afford a favourable opportunity for every necessary explanation; acting on the defensive, you avoid the natural prejudices of the mind, to prejudge and exclude information, and may make friends, instead of creating enemies. The nation can have no interest in the sale of the stock, for whatever may be its present price; without the interference of the bank, it would bring par value; if such be the fact well understood, the proposition would be defeated and the Bank will have gained, without risk, the opportunity for explanations.

To them who have observed the political horizon with

attention, there is no part of our internal history better established, than that the present affords no certain index of the future, lest it be to teach the lesson of prudence.

I wish not to trespass longer; in the cause of the public, I am a volunteer, and while I do not transgress too far, harmless, in which situation I have the honor to be your

BIDDLE TO ALEXANDER HAMILTON

Phil[a]. December 12th, 1829

Dear Sir

I received this morning your favor of the 10th. inst. which I have read with great pleasure. The view it presents are quite sound & correspond exactly with those entertained here. My impression is that these opinions expressed by the President are entirely & exclusively his own, and that they should be treated as the honest tho' erroneous notions of one who intends well. We have never had any idea of applying to Congress for a renewal of the Charter at the present session — and of course should abstain from doing so now. Our whole system of conduct is one of abstinence and self defence

BIDDLE TO GEORGE HOFFMAN

Phil[a]. Dec[r]. 15, 1829

My Dear Sir

I had this morning the pleasure of receiving your favor of the 14th. You may readily imagine my surprize at seeing the remarks in the message after all I had mentioned to you in Baltimore. But it is better to try to repair it than to regret it — and I am not sure whether it may not on the whole do good by satisfying the country of the usefulness of the institution & spreading a very salutary dread of the monster whom it is proposed to substitute for it. The consolations on the present occasion are, that this is a measure emanating exclusively from the President in person, being the remains of old notions of constitutionality,[1] that it is not a Cabinet measure nor a party measure; that the whole foundation of the reproach of the want of a sound currency is so notoriously the very reverse of the fact; and that it has produced in all quarters the most decided disapprobation. . . .

BIDDLE TO NATHANIEL SILSBEE [2]

Phil^a. Decr 17th. 1829

My dear Sir
    . . . But seriously, I do not feel the least anxiety about this sortie of the President, who with, I am sure, the best intentions, has erred from want of information — what I regret & deeply regret, is the loss of individual property which it will occasion and the wound it will inflict on the credit of the country. When I look over the list of Stockholders & see the number of females, of trust estates, & societies charitable & religious, it is melancholy to see their interest thus injured. This is particularly the case with South Carolina which owns, what two weeks ago was worth more than five millions of dollars. In regard to public credit, it is very fortunate that the Chief Magistrate of the Country should make an official declaration of its insolvency, — should pronounce that what it pays to foreigners in dividends & capital & what it receives for revenue is an unsound paper. . . .

---

[1] For Jackson's early views on the Bank, cf. Bassett, *op. cit.*, vol. II, pp. 589–590.

[2] Senator from Massachusetts, 1826–1835.

MEMORANDUM [1]

Between Oct., 1829 and Jan. 1830

Mr Biddle

(Gen'l Jackson) I was very thankful to you for your plan of paying off the debt sent to Major Lewis. (N.B.) I thought it was my duty to submit it to you. (Gen'l Jackson) I would have no difficulty in recommending it to Congress, but I think it right to be perfectly frank with you — I do not think that the power of Congress extends to charter a Bank out of the ten mile square. I do not dislike your Bank any more than all banks. But ever since I read the history of the South Sea bubble I have been afraid of banks. I have read the opinion of John Marshall [2] who I believe was a great & pure mind — and could not agree with him — though if he had said, that as it was necessary for the purpose of the national gov^t there ought to be a national bank I should have been disposed to concur; but I do not think that Congress has a right to create a corporation out of the 10 mile square. I feel very sensibly the services rendered by the Bank at the last payment of the national debt & shall take an opportunity of declarring it publicly in my message to Congress.

[1] This memorandum is in Nicholas Biddle's handwriting of a conversation he had with General Jackson in Washington. This letter Professor Catterall took for a letter of President Jackson (cf. Catterall, *op. cit.*, p. 184), which was later corrected by Professor Bassett in the latter's *Life of Jackson* (vol. II, pp. 599, 600). However, as published in Professor Bassett's *Life of Jackson* the memorandum does not bring out the significance of the extract. In order to do this it is necessary to keep the two parties distinct; and with this in view the editor has designated, in parenthesis, whether it is Biddle or Jackson who is talking. For the correction and final statement on this most important point the editor is indebted to Mr. Edward Biddle.

[2] Marshall on McCulloch *vs.* Maryland. Magruder, Allan B., *John Marshall* (Boston, 1892), pp. 194–197.

That it is my own feeling to the Bank—and Mr Ingham's also. He & you got into a difficulty thro' the foolishness — if I may use the term of Mr. Hill—(N.B. writes) observing he was a little embarrassed I said (")oh that has all passed now.(") He (Jackson) said with the Parent Board & Myself he had every reason to be perfectly satisfied — that he had heard complaints & then mentioned a case at Louisville—of which he promised to give me the particulars.

(N.B.) I said (") well I am very much gratified at this frank explanation. We shall all be proud of any kind mention in the message—for we should feel like soldiers after an action commended by their General.(") (Gen'l Jackson) Sir said he it would be only an act of justice to mention it.

Biddle to Samuel Smith [1]

Phil^a. Jany 2nd. 1830

My dear Sir

. . . The expressions in the message were the President's own—not dictated nor suggested by any body else —& inserted in opposition to the wishes, if not the advice of all his habitual counsellors. It is not therefore a cabinet measure, nor a party measure, but a personal measure. As such it is far less dangerous because if the people know that this is not an opinion which they must necessarily adopt as a portion of their party creed—but an opinion of the President alone—a very honest opinion though a very erroneous one—then the question will be decided on its own merits. . . .

---

[1] Cf. sketch of life in Niles, April 27, 1839.

BIDDLE TO JOHN POTTER ESQ.

Phil^a. Jany 9th. 1830

My dear Sir

In our conversation yesterday, you expressed a wish to know the situation in which the Bank stands with regard to Messrs. Gales & Seaton of Washington. I will explain it to you with pleasure, as I presume the facts will remove an erroneous impression with respect to the Bank as well as those gentlemen themselves.

They were formerly in succession, Directors of the Branch in Washington, & their debt amounted at one time to about Sixty thousand dollars. In January 1828 being myself in Washington, I found it about Fifty thousand Dollars, which I thought much too high. I therefore resisted a recommendation to place one of them in the Board & advised a reduction of the debt which has accordingly been done, so that I believe the whole responsibility of both parties does not now exceed between eleven & twelve thousand dollars, there having been paid by a sale of their property since March last more than $30,000. Even of the present debt, about $5000 was not a loan from the Branch but was transferred from the Bank of Columbia in the settlement of its affairs with the Branch so that of the sum actually lent, the amount now due is, as you perceive, very small.

In Novr. 1828, they applied for a loan of $15,000 from the Parent Bank—and their application was much recommended by their friends on the ground of the usefulness of their paper and the probability of its discontinuance if the loan were not made. But the Board refused to make the loan. They thought that the only true course of the Bank was to lend its money on business principles and with adequate security — that no distinction could be made between its friends and its enemies and that to go out of its way to make a loan to the editors of a newspaper would be to depart from its system of total indifference and entire abstraction, with regard to politics. In the present case too, the Bank might place itself in the very unbecoming attitude of sustaining at the seat of Government a paper opposed to the existing administration.

You will think well of our impartiality when I mention that in running my eye over the Washington Pay List, to see the liabilities of Messrs Gales & Seaton, I remarked that our friend the Editor [1] of the Telegraph has between $11 and $12,000 — an amount about the same as the Editors of the Intelligencer. In truth, you know, my dear Sir, how constantly & strenuously the Bank has resisted every thing like political influence believing as we all do that the moment the Institution is subjected to any party, whether in power or out of power, it becomes a curse to the country.

I have spoken to you freely about the pecuniary affairs of these parties — circumstances, which as a member of the Board I wish you to know & I confide them entirely to your judgment and discretion.

BIDDLE TO JOHN McKIM JR ESQR

Phil^a. Jany 18th. 1830

Dear Sir

I have received your friendly letter of the 16th. inst for which I thank you. You ask my opinion about the fate of the Bank. I will tell you very frankly. I do not think this attack

---

[1] Duff Green of Missouri. *The Telegraph* was established in 1826 as a Jackson organ.

upon it will do any harm, & I think it will rather benefit it. I think so for two reasons — First, that the ground of the attack (its failure to produce a sound & uniform currency) is well known by every man in the country to be unfounded, the currency issued by the Bank being more sound & uniform than that of any country in the world at this moment. Second, the substitute proposed for it is one which no man who values the liberties of the country could agree to establish. These things will be perfectly understood before long, & cannot fail to operate in favor of the Bank. I think therefore that the Stockholders need be under no uneasiness. The Bank is at this moment in a high state of prosperity, having during the last year divided 7 per cent, & made all the proper reservations—and still retaining a surplus profit out of the years work of $223,000. What other Bank has done the same?

WILLIAM B. LEWIS TO BIDDLE

(*Confidential*)   Washington 3 May 1830
My D. Sir,

I rec^d. yours of the 27 ultimo the day previous to Judge Overtons departure, and consulted him with regard to the appointment of suitable persons to fill the places of those directors of your Nashville Board as will have shortly to retire. We found considerable difficulty in making proper selections, but have agreed to recommend the following named gentlemen.

Thomas Crutcher
Alexander Porter
Francis B Fogg, or E. H. Foster
Bernard Vanlier
Joseph Vaulx.

The first named gentleman is one of the earliest settlers in the Country — a man of great moral worth, and is at this time and has been for nearly thirty years, one of the Treasurers of Tennessee. You cannot, I should think, do better than to appoint *him*. Mr. Porter was a member of the Nashville Board when it was first organized — an Irishman by birth, but has been a resident of the State upwords of thirty years and has lived, I should think, 25 years in Nashville — a man of good moral character, of wealth, and *needs none of your money*. I have served with him and know he makes a good and safe director. Fogg and Foster are partners in law, both men of business and of high standing — Foster was a member of your first Board. Mr Vanlier is concerned in some of the iron works of this State — he is a native of Penna. — a man of good moral character, well off, safe and judicious — at least this was his character when I left Nashville, and I have no reason to believ it has undergone any change. Mr. Vaulx must be known to you as he has served two years as a director. He is a safe judicious man — has married into an *influential connection*, and is doing a good business as a merchant. When he was first appointed some objection was made to him on account of his age; but as he has once been a member of the Board, and is several years older than he was, I presume no objection could now be made to him on that account.

I am of opinion that Judge Overton himself would serve if appointed, tho' I am not authorised to say so, never having heard him speak upon the subject. If it would not be inconvenient for him to attend, living 5 or 6 miles from town, it would be good policy to appoint him; he is a brother-in-law of Judge White of the Senate, and a *particular friend* of the

President. If his living in the Country should be an objection, I would advise you to put him in the place of Harding next Year, who also lives in the Country. Two of the Directors who go out this year should be returned to the Board as early as the rule, which governs such cases, will admit of. I mean Campbell and Farqueharsen, both of whom make good directors — particularly the latter. Without wishing to disparage others I verily believe that M^r. Farqueharsen is the very *best* director you have in your Board.

The President is well, and desires me to present his respects to you.

BIDDLE TO WILLIAM B. LEWIS ESQ

(*Private*)   Philada. May 8. 1830
My Dear Sir.

I thank you very much for your favor of the 3d: inst. with the list of names which I must prize, because I know that it is dictated by friendly feelings towards the Bank. As soon as I receive the nomination from Nashville I shall not fail to consult you about it.

Since you left us, I have thought very anxiously about a subject which I mentioned to you, I mean the present disposition of the President towards the Bank. Since his opinions were stated in the Message, he has had an opportunity of examing more attentively the effects & operations of the Institution, of witnessing its utility to the finances of the Government, & of knowing the views of sound & practical men from every part of the Country. He is also, I trust, satisfied that the powers of the Bank have not been abused for political purposes, & that towards him & his administration, the Bank has acted frankly, fairly & cordially. It would be affectation in me not to say that those who conduct the Bank were exceedingly hurt & pained by the opinion expressed by the President, that all their efforts to restore the Currency had failed. Yet, in the midst of their regrets, they knew too well their duties to suffer themselves to give the slightest political bias to the Bank, to be driven or tempted into opposition, or to abate in the slightest degree their zeal for the public service. The President has few more decided personal or political friends than many of those who are concerned in the administration of the Bank. To them, as well as to a large body of citizens, it would be exceedingly gratifying to know the feelings of the President towards the Bank at the present moment, because some of his injudicious friends & many of his opponents seek to make an impression that such is his rooted dislike to the Institution, that he would refuse his sanction to a Continuance of the Bank, were the Charter renewed by both Houses of Congress. The first class say this because they dislike the Bank — the second because they dislike the President; but I hope that neither the President nor the Bank will allow themselves to misunderstand each other, or to be estranged from each other, by the manœuvres or the indiscretions of their respective friends or enemies. Their true attitude is that of mutual Independence & mutual respect, & as far as I am concerned that attitude shall be fairly maintained.

Whenever you have any thing gratifying on that subject which you can with perfect propriety communicate, I shall be obliged by hearing it, & in the mean time, remain as always

CHARLES AUGUST DAVIS [1] TO BIDDLE

N. York 21 My 1830

My Dr Sir

. . . I think it probable I may have mention'd to you that it was believ'd here by many that Mr Van Buren had some agency in it, and the reasons assign'd if not true are at least curious. This — he look'd upon the U.S. B. as a mass of power which might be employ'd to bear on any point or ag^t any point with no inconsiderable force and if a disposition sh'd exist thus in directing its influence politically he as a political man (& having had no agency either in its creation or thro' its changes & trials) naturally concluded it w^d. be less likely to oppose old friends than to adopt new ones or strangers. Hence it was natural that he sh'd not view it with a favorable political eye — it might be perfectly harmless, or it might not — and political men are not always satisfied with uncertainties. Like the old Gun it was safer out of reach & harms way for tho it was said to have neither flint or powder in it still it might go off. At this particular period the *Safety fund system* appear'd — and in theory had no doubt an honest, able aspect — it was so far adopted by Mr Van Beuren then Govr. of the State,[2] as to have been more easily

---

[1] One of the directors of the State Bank of New York. Wilson, *op. cit.*, vol. III, p. 347.

[2] Van Buren's career as Governor of New York was very brief. He was inaugurated January 1, 1829, but resigned March 12, to go into the Cabinet. "His inaugural message is said by Hammond to have been the best executive message ever communicated to the legislature." In this address he outlined the "safety fund" system which had been communicated to him by Joshua Forman. "Under this system all the Banks of the State, whatever their condition, were to contribute to a fund to be administered under state supervision, the fund to be a security for all dishonored bank notes. To this extent all the Banks were to insure or indorse the circulation of each bank, thus saving the scandal and loss arising from the oc-

made his almost exclusively — if successful — than it is now found to shake it from him — that it is suspected of being inapplicable in practice. Had it prov'd successful and met with the general favor it was suppos'd to merit, "Van Buren Safety fund" w^d. have been as clearly identified & recogniz'd as "Clinton & Canal." And if approv'd in one State w^d. most likely have become general — here then was a substitute at hand and "a safe channel for all Gov^t purposes" sh'd the U.S. Bank be dispens'd with — but it is likely to prove otherwise — and turns out among the moves of ill luck which sometimes are made by the most wise and prudent. These are among the leading reasons advanced by the knowing ones here touching Mr Van Buren and his agency in the Message, and if groundless, they are at least curious as I before stated.

I have a very high opinion [1] of Mr V. Buren. I believe him a safe and segacious man, or any way he has the reputation of being "mysterious" — "dark" and "designing"; but unless I am entirely mistaken in my observations of him personally, I should say this impression is created for him more by a negative than a positive course of conduct politically, or rather by a peculiar and unusual system of Caution — few men say less — no man writes less on the passing political

casional failure of Banks to redeem their notes, and making every Bank watchful of its associates. In compelling the Banks to submit to some general scheme the representatives of the people would, indeed, he said, enter into 'conflict with the claims of the great moneyed interests of the country; but what political exhibition so truly gratifying as the return to his constituents of the faithful public servant after having turned away every approach and put far from him every sinister consideration.'" Shephard, Edward M., *Martin Van Buren* (Boston, 1891), pp. 168–170.

[1] Biddle likewise held Van Buren in high regard and often reiterated his belief that the latter was "neither the instigator nor the adviser of the President's remarks."

occurrences — and whilst other great men are wasting their powers & puzzling their wits to explain away or smoothen down the sharp corner of some printed or written opinions & assertions which unfortunately may have outlived the occasion and which may not harmonize with the changes of public sentiment — He is fresh & free from all charges except the important one which friends as well as enemies are ready to lay at his door — the charge of having effected all these changes in public sentiment — no body can say how, when or where. He neither asserts or contradicts — but if he has in reality no hand in thus acquiring political power few men know better how to keep what comes in possession.

It is thro' periods of political excitement that his system is more likely to succeed than in "calm successions," or in other words his capital accumulates faster at such periods, and if I were a politician or party man I'd "back him" for a leader of my party "ag^t. the field": but being neither I only indulge the liberty of sketching occasionally an outline roughly as in this instance of those who direct public affairs, aware at the same time that I can more correctly sketch the range of a market for Iron, Sugar or Coffee. I am in great truth & with high esteem

WILLIAM B. LEWIS TO BIDDLE

(*Confidential*)   Washington 25 May 1830
D. Sir,

 . . . Before closing this letter permit me to say one word in reference to a subject mentioned in your last letter to me — I mean the information you rec^d. of the President's having declared that if Congress should pass a law renewing

the Charter of the U.S. Bank he would put his veto on it.
I told you in Phil^a. when you first mentioned the thing to
me, that there must be some mistake, because the report was
at variance with what *I* had heard him say upon the subject.
In conversing with him a few days ago upon the subject he
still entertained the opinion that a *National* Bank might be
established that would be preferable to the present U.S. Bank;
but that, if Congress thought differently, and it was deemed
necessary to have such a Bank as the present, with certain
modifications he should not object to it. If the President finds
that his scheme is not likely to take, I do not believe he will
be opposed, altogether, to the present Bank. In haste I am

Roswell L. Colt to Biddle

10 June (1830)?

Dear Biddle

Soon after the Presidents first message in which the
subject of the Bank was mentioned Mr Howard had a conversation with Mr Van Beuren [1] in which he told the Secretary
that that part of the message refer y to the Bank—had caused
great surprise. Mr. V. B. answered he knew nothing of it, that
he had not been consulted on the subject, and disapproaved
of that part of the message & that he was not hostile to the
Bank. You recollect I wrote you at the time I was satisfied
Mr V. B. was the author of those obnoxious paragraphs, &
Mr Poinsett says he is sure that V. B. is the man who has
caused us all our trouble. . . .

[1] Van Buren seems to have tried hard to keep aloof from an open attack on
the Bank. The Bank men always claimed he was the cause of their trouble; but
Professor Bassett, in his *Life of Jackson* (cf. chap. 29), shows that Van Buren was
not anxious to be implicated in the various moves against the institution.

HENRY CLAY TO BIDDLE

Ashland 14 th. June 1830

Dear Sir

...Unless I am deceived by information, received from one of the most intelligent Citizens of Virginia, the plan was laid at Richmond during a visit made to that place by the Secy. of State last autumn, to make the destruction of the Bank the basis of the next Presidential Election. The message of the President, and other indications, are the supposed consequences of that plan.[1]

[1] This letter is in Clay's handwriting and is highly significant. It is a well-known fact that Jackson was strongly advised by many of his friends not to introduce the Bank question in his message of 1829. On October 22, 1829, Felix Grundy wrote to Jackson outlining the main features of a National Bank and concluded as follows: "I hope to be in Washington a week or ten days before Congress convenes — and will lose no time before I see you. I intend to set out for Richmond on the 25th instant to see the Virginia Convention in session thence to the city." On November 27, 1829, Ingham wrote to Jackson advising against the Bank attack; on December 17, 1829, Benton sent Jackson a copy of Randolph's idea of a National Bank; while on the same day the Attorney-General likewise opposed introducing the question. (Cf. Jackson MSS. in Library of Congress.) Thus, with the single exception of Benton the Jackson MSS. show that all the friends of the President cautioned Jackson on the expediency of raising the issue. The Van Buren MSS. contain no mention of the Bank message.

Moreover, it is established that Van Buren was opposed to interfering in the struggle. Cf. Bassett, *Life of Jackson*, vol. II, pp. 631, 640, 740.

Yet Professor Ambler, in his *Life of Thomas Ritchie*, p. 131, shows that Van Buren visited Richmond about this period. Therefore the question arises, could the Southern politicians have induced or suggested to Van Buren the idea of an attack on the Bank, holding out to the latter the hope of the next Presidential election, while their main idea was to gain time for their own propaganda? It was in the Virginia Convention of 1829 that the Calhoun doctrine of defending slavery was first enunciated. Therefore the Calhounites, by projecting the Bank and raising a hue and cry, might further their own scheme. However, it was spoiled by Jackson crushing nullification in 1830. Seeing they had failed in this attempt, they immediately came out clearly for the Bank. Thus, in the view of these late historical events Clay's letter suggests many interesting points, for if this suggestion is sound the Bank controversy shifts from Washington to Richmond.

JOSIAH NICHOL TO BIDDLE

Office Bank United States
Nashville 20th. July 1830
(recd Augt. 2, 1830)

Dear Sir

Yours of the 22nd ultimo is duly received, and the request therein contained attended to as far as yet in my power, the President of the United States arrived in Town last Tuesday. I done myself the pleasure of waiting on him, as an old friend, and at the request of a number of our most respectable citizens made him a tender of apartments in my house during his Stay in Town, which he accepted, and left us on Thursday last for the Hermitage; during his Stay at my house I had frequent opportunities, and did not neglect the subject of your letter. I enforced every argument that I could make bear on the subject, or that would be of any service in removing his prejudice. I brought to his view the improvement of our Town and Country since the establishment of this office, and Contrasted the year of 1826 with the present year of 1830. on the Subject of exchange, in the former year We generally paid a premium on Bills drawn on any of the Eastern cities of from 9 to 12 per cent; now 1830, We can obtain Checks, payable at one day after sight at any place where the United States Bank have a Branch at a premium of one half to one per cent — which is little more than pays postage. he appears to be well satisfied with the facilities that the Bank have given to Government and individuals, in transferring their funds from One point to another, and acknowledges that a Bank such as the present only can do so. he appears to be genrally pleased with the Management of the United States and Branches — and particularly so with this office. I have taken considerable pains and gave him all the information I consistently could on Banking Subjects — and belive have convinced him that the Present Bank and Branches could not be dispenced with without Manifest injury to the Country and particularly so to this Western Country, as no other Currency could be Substituted. On the subject of his favourite plan I touched lightly, but let him know that I thought it would be more dangerous to Our liberties than than the U S. Bank. the Only objection he appears to have to the present Bank is that a great part of the Stock is held by Foreigners — consequently the interest is taken from the Country. he is well satisfied that Politicks have no influence in Bank or in the Choice of Directors, and I am well convinced that he will not interfer with Congress on the Subject of renewing the Charter of the Bank. Altho on this subject he keeps his opinion to himself he speaks of You in the most exalted terms and says there is No Gentleman that can be found would manage the Bank better or do the Bank & Country More Justice. I am Sir very respectfully your

BIDDLE TO JOSIAH NICHOL ESQ.

(*confidential*)   Philada. Augt: 3. 1830.
Dear Sir.

Since writing to you this morning it has occurred to me that you may have it in your power to do a great service to the Bank as well as to Genl: Jackson. No man can now fail to perceive that the remarks on the Bank in the President's Message were unfortunate, & have tended to make many sober men uneasy about the stability of our finances & the soundness of our currency. As respects the Bank, it has gained friends by the reports in Congress & by the general discussion of its affairs throughout the Country, so that at present I consider the Bank decidedly popular with the great mass of the Community. As a proof of it we have now before us no less than ten applications for branches — one in New York, one in Ohio, one in Virginia, two in South Carolina, one in Florida, one in Indiana, & I believe that there is a decided majority in both houses of Congress favorable to it.

Under these circumstances the opposition to the President will naturally endeavor to turn the Bank question against him — to represent him & his friends as unfriendly to sound currency.

In this the Bank will give of course no assistance. It means to be as it has been perfectly neutral & unpartial — minding its own business & not medling with other people's & nothing shall force it or seduce it from its strict line of duty. But it is worthy of great consideration for Genl: Jackson & his friends whether it would not be right for them to remove the impression of his & their hostility to the Bank. I do not believe that Genl: Jackson or his particular friends are hostile to the Bank. He expressed his doubts & his belief about it. I am sure he was wrong, but I am equally sure that he was perfectly honest, & if I do not much mistake his character he will if he thinks he has not done justice to the Bank in the first instance, be ready to do it ample justice when on more reflection & examination he becomes satisfied that he can do so. This he will have a fine opportunity of doing & at the same time of disarming his political antagonists of what they may make a powerful weapon at the next meeting of Congress. Genl: Jackson does not perhaps know (for persons in high stations do not always hear the whole truth) that the part of his Message which relates to the Bank has been a source of regret to many of his most attached friends & to most if not all the political associates around him. He has now a fair [1] opportunity of converting that right into pleasure & triumph.

In his next message he will be able to state that since his last message nearly 10 millions of principal of the public Debt were paid off in January & July. In his last message he was kind enough to speak with approbation of the agency of the Bank in making that payment without the least inconvenience to the Country. Now, what I think his friends desire is that he should renew the expression of that approbation — to the Bank it would perhaps be an act of justice — and it would be an act both of justice & policy to himself & his friends by correcting an opinion that has gone abroad that he & they are unfriendly to the Institution. He could say this without looking to the past or the future — without committing himself or his friends — & the friends of the Bank would be gratified by such an evidence that his feelings were kindly towards the institution. This is a very simple & easy thing to do — & yet I believe it would be very useful. Now how shall it be brought about? I have an idea that if any body can do it you can, & if Judge Overton [2] were disposed to aid he could be very useful. I submit the matter to your judgment to do what you may think right. I suggest it to you as a friend of Genl: Jackson & a friend of the Bank — believing that it would be useful to both — but as I have made it a law not to interfere in political matters in case

---

[1] In the manuscript the word "fine" is inserted in pencil.

[2] A land lawyer. Placed on Supreme Court Bench as successor to Andrew Jackson. Woodbridge, J. (editor), *History of Nashville* (Nashville, 1890), p. 516.

you should think the suggestion worth acting upon, you will have the goodness to do it without reference to me.

HENRY CLAY TO BIDDLE

(*confidential*)   Ashland 11th. Sept. 1830
Dear Sir

Major Tilford having mentioned to me that you were considering whether it was proper to apply, at the ensuing Session of Congress, for a renewal of the charter of the B.U.S. and that you entertained some doubts on the subject, I had a conversation with him and Mr. Harper,[1] which I informed them that they were at liberty to communicate to you. I added that, perhaps, I might address a letter to you on the same matter. A leisure hour allows me to fulfill that intention.

It may be assumed, as indisputable, that the renewal of the charter can never take place, as the Constitution now stands, against the opinion and wishes of the President of the U.S. for the time being. A bill, which should be rejected by him for that purpose, could never be subsequently passed by the constitutional majority. There would always be found a sufficient number to defeat such a bill, after its return with the President' objection, among those who are opposed to the Bank on constitutional grounds, those who, without being influenced by constitutional considerations, might be opposed to it upon the score of expediency, and those who would be operated upon by the influence of the Executive.

I think it may even be assumed that a bill to renew the Charter cannot be carried through Congress, at any time, with a *neutral* executive. To ensure its passage, the Presidents

---

[1] Cashier of the Branch at Lexington.

opinions and those of at least a majority of his Cabinet must be *known* to be in favor of the renewal.

President Jackson, if I understand the paragraph of his message at the opening of the last Session of Congress, relating to the Bank, is opposed to it upon Constitutional objections. Other sources of information corroborate that fact. If he should act upon that opinion, and reject a bill, presented for his aprobation, it would be impossible to get it through Congress at the next Session against the Veto.

That a strong party, headed by Mr. V. Buren, some Virginia politicians and the Richmond Enquirer, intend, if practicable to make the Bank question the basis of the next Presidential election, I have, I believe, heretofore informed you. I now entertain no doubt of that purpose. I have seen many evidences of it. The Editors of certain papers have received their orders to that effect, and embrace every occasion to act in conformity with them. This fact cannot have escaped your observation.[1]

If you apply at the next Session of Congress, you will play into the hands of that party. They will most probably, in the event of such application, postpone the question, until another Congress is elected. They will urge the long time that the Charter has yet to run; that therefore there is no necessity to act at the next Session on the measure; and that public sentiment ought to be allowed to develope itself &c. These and other considerations will induce Congress, always disposed to procrastinate, to put off the question. In the mean time, the public press will be put in motion, every prejudice excited and appeals made to every passion. The question will

---

[1] This was quite true, for by this date the *Washington Globe* and the other Jackson prints were beginning their strenuous attacks on the Bank.

incorporate itself with all our elections, and especially with
that as to which there is so great a desire that it should be incorporated. It will be difficult, when Congress comes finally to
decide the question, to obtain a majority against the accumulation of topics of opposition.

But suppose, at the next Session, on the contingency of
your application for a renewal of the Charter, instead of postponing, Congress was to pass a bill for that object, and it
should be presented to the President, what would he do with
it? If, as I suppose, he would reject it, the question would
be immediately, in consequence, referred to the people, and
would inevitably mix itself with all our elections. It would
probably become, after the next Session, and up to the time
of the next Presidential election, the controlling question in
American politics. The friends of the Bank would have to
argue the question before the public against the official act of
the President, and against the weight of his popularity.

You would say what ought the Corporation to do? I stated
to the above gentleman that, in my opinion, unless you had
a satisfactory assurance that your application at the next
Session would be successful, you had better not make it. If,
contrary to my impressions, you could receive such an assurance from both departments of the Government, who would
have to act on the case, *that* would present a different state
of the question, and would justify the presentation of your
petition.

If not made at the next Session, when should it be made?
I think the Session immediately after the next Presidential
election would be the most proper time. Then every thing will
be fresh; the succeeding P. election will be too remote to be
shaping measure in reference to it; and there will be a disposi-

tion to afford the new administration the facilities in our fiscal affairs which the B. of the U.S. perhaps alone can render. But suppose Gen¹ Jackson should be again elected? If that should be the case, he will have probably less disposition than he now has to avail himself of any prejudices against the Bank. He will then have also less influence; for it may be loosely asserted, at least as a general rule, that the President will have less popularity in his second than in his first term. And that I believe would emphatically be the fate of the present President. At all events, you will be in a better condition by abstaining from applying to renew the charter during his first term, than you would be in, if you were to make the application and it should be rejected. Upon the supposition of such a rejection, and that the question should be afterwards blended with the Presidential contest, and Gen¹. Jackson should be elected, his re-election would amount to something like a popular ratification of the previous rejection of the renewal of the charter of the Bank. Indeed, if there be an union of the Presidents negative of the Bank bill with the next P. election, and he should be reelected, would it not be regarded as decisive against any Bank of the U.S. hereafter?

My opinion, upon the whole, then is, that it would be unwise to go to Congress without something like a positive assurance of success at the next Session; and that the Corporation, without displaying any solicitude in regard to the continuation of its charter, had better preserve, in the able and faithful administration of its affairs, which it has of late years manifested, and go to Congress at the first moments of calm which shall succeed the approaching Presidential storm.

I hope I need say nothing, by way of apology, to satisfy you of the friendly feelings which have prompted this letter;

nor to impress you with the propriety of receiving it in the confidence with which it is written. I add assurances of the constant and cordial regard of

—— TO COLONEL HUNTER [1]

Washington 30 h. Octr 1830

My Dear Sir

. . . Your institution is destined however to encounter a Severe Struggle, for the renewal of its Charter. I see in various quarters of the Union evidences of determination to resist it, and it is not the least striking of these, that Mr Clay — who we all know is latitudinarian enough to have no constitutional scruples on this, or on any other Subject — is unwilling to Commit himself upon this measure — the inference is obvious. He doubts the result of the application for the new charter, and is unwilling to hazard his popularity by becoming its advocate. But for the course pursued by South Carolina, Mr Calhoun, & M^r McDuffie might have rendered service. as it is — I Know not how far they will have the power.

BIDDLE TO WILLIAM B. LEWIS ESQ.

Phil^a. Octr. 31st. 1830

My dear Sir

I have been prevented by other occupations from saying to you that on examining the Louisville business, I found I could not consistently adopt your suggestion. It seems that out of 9 there are 4 gentlemen friendly to the administration. This is accidental, but I am glad of it, for the fact shows that there was no principle of exclusion — that the business men

[1] Cashier of the Branch of the Bank of the United States at Nashville. Collector of the Port in 1843. *American Almanac, 1843*, p. 92.

were taken indiscriminately from all parties & the division is sufficient to prevent any political partiality on either side, which, however, I believe neither side feels nor exercises. To introduce new members — members so well qualified as those now there — for the purpose of making any political balance, would be wrong in itself & would expose us to the very imputation we wish to avoid of looking to party considerations. On the whole, therefore, I thought it better to let the business considerations prevail over politics. The only regret I feel is, that I had it not in my power to agree to what might perhaps have gratified you.

BIDDLE TO HENRY CLAY ESQR

Philadᵃ Novʳ 3ʳᵈ 1830

My dear Sir

I have purposely delayed answering your favor of the 11ᵗʰ of Septʳ until I could speak with some degree of confidence as to the course which will be adopted in reference to the subject of it. In the mean time I have read repeatedly and with renewed interest all your remarks, proceeding as I know they do from one who with ample materials of information & great sagacity in employing them gives the result of his reflections with a sincere desire to serve the institution. For this in any event you will accept my grateful thanks.

After keeping the subject long under advisement in order to observe the latest development of facts, I am now satisfied, that it would be inexpedient to apply at present for the renewal of the charter. My belief is from all I have seen & read & heard, that there is at this moment a majority of both Houses of Congress favourable to a renewal, and moreover that the President would not reject the bill. The temptation is therefore great to take advantage of a propitious state of feelings like this. But then the Hazard is not to be disguised. A great mass of those who if they were obliged to vote at all would vote favourably will prefer not voting if it can be avoided, and the dread of responsibility, the love of postponment & the vis-inertia inherent in all legislative bodies would combine to put off the question during the approaching short session. To pass both houses & be rejected by the President, to be rejected in either house, to be postponed in either house, to be brought forward in any shape and not be finally and favorably acted upon are degrees of evil — but the mildest of them a great evil, much to be deplored & to be avoided if possible. My impression then is that nothing but a certainty of success should induce an application now. To this I am the more inclined because time is operating in favor of the Bank, by removing prejudices, and diffusing a general conviction of its utility.

Having made up my mind on the subject, I am gratified that this, which is the first expression I have made of this opinion, should be communicated to one whose views have so largely influenced my own. It will always afford me great pleasure to receive the benefit of your further suggestions on this or any other subject, being with great respect and regard[1]

JOSEPH HEMPHILL TO BIDDLE

Washington Decr — 9 — 1830

Dear Sir

After receiving the Message [2] of the President, M^r. McDuffy & myself are of the opinion, that it is the true inter-

---

[1] On the same day Biddle wrote to Hunter presenting the identical arguments.
[2] Richardson, *op. cit.*, vol. II, pp. 528, 529.

est of the Bank of the United States to apply f
of its charter at the Present Session — the rea
ing now will be fair & such as must be appr
ing had been said in the Message, perhap
would have been to lay quiet at the pre
public mind will be uncertain as to the fate of the
rafices may be made by the time & the currency of the Cou
try effected; it is of importance that this question should be
settled as early as possible; as it has been the second time
introduced by the President, the bringing of it can do no harm
& if it fails it can be renewed before the next Congress. . . .
If I was with you I could explain more fully why the application should be now made.

JOSEPH HEMPHILL TO BIDDLE

Decr. 9– 1830 Washington

Dear Sir

At present I think it had better not be mentioned out of the board that there is any intention to make an application for a re-charter this Session. This is for yourself only.

ROBERT SMITH TO BIDDLE

Confidential   Washington Decr. 13, 1830
Dear Sir

I gathered from a conversation with Major Lewis, of the President's family, that altho' the President is decidedly in favor of a Bank such as he recommended to Congress, yet if a bill were to pass both houses, renewing the charter of the Bank U States with certain modifications, the President would not with hold his approval. What these modifications were, I could not distinctly understand; but I believe that

the principal one was to take from the Bank the right of establishing branches in the states, unless with the consent of
the states, & it was intimated that a provision of the kind
would really be beneficial to the Bank, in as much as our
career if the jealousy with which the States regard the Bank
would be removed, & it was not doubted but that sooner
or later every state would solicit the establishment of a
Branch. It was also intimated that the holding of real estate
by the bank was very objectionable. The right to do so however, is so essential to the safety of the Bank, that it cannot
be perceived how the relinquishment of it can be yielded. . . .

BIDDLE TO JOSEPH HEMPHILL

Philad. Dec. 14. 1830

My dear Sir,

I take the earliest opportunity which my occupations
have permitted to consult you on the subject of attempting
the renewal of the Charter during the present session of
Congress.

Until the arrival of the President's message my impressions
were these. I believed that there was a decided majority of
both houses of Congress who, if they had been obliged to vote
at all, would have voted for the renewal. But not being
obliged to vote, they would avoid voting. Many would say
that the question was premature, that they ought not to forestal the judgment of their successors, that it was a short
session — in short the indifferent & the timid would combine with the opponents of the Bank to postpone the question. Once brought forward & postponed, it would of course
be blended up with the elections, & become one of those political matters judged exclusively by party considerations.

On the other hand if it passed through both Houses, & was negatived by the Pres^t., from that time forward it would become a question between the Bank & him, & if he were reëlected, he would construe it as a decision by the nation against the Bank, & act accordingly. There was also not unmingled with these views the hope that as the President had mentioned the subject to Congress he would have left it to them, & that time & experience would have made him more wise & less pertinacious. Such seemed the state of the case in November.

It is certainly much altered now.

The President has himself again thrust it before Congress, & seems determined to make it an electioneering topic. By inviting the State Gov^{ts}. to strengthen themselves by usurping the whole circulating medium of the country, he will probably excite them to instruct their delegations in Congress to oppose the charter, & it is to be presumed that in no event will he sanction a bill for the re-charter. . . .

I believe it greatly for the interest of the country to settle this question during the present session. My doubt is whether it would be expedient in reference to the ultimate settlement of that question for the Bank to *ask* for a renewal. But the benefit of settling it may possibly be obtained without the risk of prejudicing the Bank in case of failure by another course which is this.

The Committee of Ways & Means [1] have now the President's Message before them. If that Comm^e. were to say that this is a question which must not be left in its present position, that all the great interests of the country are hazarded by this suspense, & altho' they did not intend to stir it, yet

[1] McDuffie was chairman of the Ways and Means Committee.

now that it has been agitated it ought to be put to rest — if they would say this, the way would be open. If the Comm^e. were to say to the Bank whether it would take at once the renewal & on what terms, we should answer by return of mail in a manner no doubt satisfactory, & the Comm^e. might then report a bill of a single section continuing the Charter for twenty years after the expiration of its present charter on the payment of the stipulated bonus. In this way the recharter would present itself, not so much in the light of an application by individuals, but as a financial measure, introduced by the financial organ of the House. If it succeeded — well. If it failed, the Bank might hereafter come forward with its proposal without prejudice of its having been once defeated. . . .

John Norvall [1] to Biddle

Philadelphia, Dec. 16, 1830.

Dear Sir,

. . . My opinion, if it be worth anything to you, is, that the bank ought forthwith to make application for the renewal of its charter. If a bill for the purpose should be passed, General Jackson will be more afraid to put his veto to it than after his re-election. If he should negative such a bill, the fact will go far toward preventing his re-election. Besides, the present congress is probably more favorable than the next will be to the bank. In any event, it appears to me to be the interest of the stockholders and officers to bring the matter at once to issue. . . .

[1] Editor of Anti-Federalist paper in Philadelphia, 1816–1832. Later moved to Michigan and was Senator from that State, 1837–1841. Cf. sketch of life written by his son in *Michigan Pioneer Collections*, vol. III, pp. 140–147; also Bingham, Stephen D., *Early History of Michigan* (Lansing, 1888), pp. 496, 497.

JOHN NORVALL TO BIDDLE

Philadelphia, Dec. 19, 1830

Dear Sir,

I am going on with the examination of the list of members, with a view to ascertain who are for, and who are against, the renewal of your bank charter. Mr Letcher,[1] of Kentucky, tells me that there are 74 opposition members, who, he is satisfied, will vote in solid phalanx for the bank. At least 22 of the 26 members from Pennsylvania will vote for it. They, added to the 74 will make 96. Nearly all the South Carolina, a portion of Virginia and North Carolina members, will vote for it; and scattering Jackson votes in all the other states will be obtained for the bank. Upon the most moderate calculation, 130 votes may be considered as certain. That number will leave, in the house, a minority of 84. In the senate, of 48 votes, 22 opposition members may be set down as certain for the bank. General Barnard[2] of our state, and Mr. Livingston[3] of Louisiana, General Hayne[4] and Judge Smith[5] of South Carolina, and Mr. Tazewall[6] of Virginia, Jackson members, are for it. These make 27, leaving a minority of 21. There is also General Smith of Maryland, making 28, and leaving a minority of 20, with the probability of two or three more Jackson votes. The preceding statement is the most unfavorable in the project congress for the bank. . . .

[1] Representative from Kentucky.   [2] Senator from Pennsylvania.
[3] Senator from Louisiana. Later Secretary of State, 1831–1833.
[4] Representative from South Carolina.
[5] Senator from South Carolina.   [6] Senator from Virginia [Tazewell].

BIDDLE TO MR. ROBINSON ESQ.

(*private*)   Philadᵃ Dec. 20–1830
Dear Sir

     ... In respect to Gen¹ Jackson & Mr Van Buren I
have not the slightest fear of either of them, or both of them.
Our country-men are not naturally disposed to cut their own
throats to please any body, & I have so perfect a reliance
on the spirit & sense of the nation, that I think we can defend the institution from much stronger enemies than they
are. In doing this we must endeavour to reach the understandings of our fellow citizens by the diffusion of correct
views of a subject which is much understood. You will receive
herewith a copy of condensed analysis of Mr Gallatin's
article on Banks, so far as it relates to the B.U.S. ...

ROSWELL L. COLT TO BIDDLE

                                 Bal. 29 Janʸ 1831
Dear Biddle

     ... Tis said that Van Buren & Calhoun have kissed
& made up their dispute — it is a fact that Calhoun has
dined with Mʳ Van Buren — and now the Secretarys party
are crowing under the idea, that Calhoun is courting the
favor & forbearance of Mr V B — at which it is Said that Mʳ
C. is not a little vexed. If Jackson determines to run again
for the Presidency, & Calhoun does the Same, as he says he
will, then Van B. & his party will denounce Calhoun & throw
him off as they have Duff Green. The Clay party are trying
to get Calhoun to separate himself from Jackson — they say
that heretofore he was sound on the leading questions, U.S.
Judiciary, Bank U States, Tariff & internal improvements,

and that all he has to do is find some fit & proper occasion to come out & declare that his views on these important subjects are the same he had formerly entertained — this the Clay party tell him. Clay is our first Choice — You are Second, but that we cannot carry our party for You if You are against the Judiciary, the Currency, the finding employment at home for our surplus Labour, or new avenues through which to distribute the product of that Labour — and it is hoped he will listen. I fear not.

BIDDLE TO WILLIAM B. LAWRENCE, ESQ.

Phil^a. Feby 8. 1831

Dear Sir,

    . . . What I can do & will do is this. It is obvious that a great effort will be made to array the influence of the Executive & all his party against the Bank. It is not less evident that our most effectual resistance is the dissemination of useful knowledge among the people, and accordingly I am endeavoring to convey to all classes real & positive information in regard to the working of the institution & its beneficial influence on the prosperity of the nation. To do this newspapers must be used, not for their influence, but merely as channels of communication with the people. If you think the one in question a useful vehicle of information I will employ it — and in this way.

I have many articles about the Bank — articles of interest to a general reader & which would occupy no more space than would be necessarily given to articles on other topics, nor occasion I presume any extra expence — such for instance as M^r McDuffie's & Smith's reports or the extracts from Mr Gallatin's article. For the insertion of these I will pay either as they appear or in advance. Thus for instance if you will cause the articles I have indicated and others which I may prepare to be inserted in the newspaper in question, I will at once pay to you one thousand dollars. If this may facilitate the arrangement you propose I shall be glad. There is as you perceive nothing in this communication which I should care to conceal, but as it might be misconstrued, I inclose your letter to me & request that you will have the goodness to return what I have written to you. It will give me great pleasure to see you on the 15th, and in the mean time I am with sincere regard & many thanks for your presenting the subject to me.

BIDDLE TO JOSEPH HEMPHILL

Philada: Feb: 10. 1831.

My Dear Sir,

I have had the pleasure of receiving your letter of the 8th: inst. inclosing a letter from Mr. Green,[1] expressing his wish to borrow from the Bank twenty thousand dollars. I will submit it to the Board at their next meeting. In the mean time I can only say that it will receive from them a kind & respectful consideration as a matter of business, without looking to the past or the future. The Bank is glad to have friends from conviction, but seeks to make none from interest. For myself, I love the freedom of the Press too much to complain of its occasional injustice to me, & if the loan be made, it shall be with a perfect understanding, to be put into the Note if necessary, that the borrower is to speak his mind about the Bank, just as freely as he did before — which I take to be "ample room & verge enough."

[1] Duff Green of the *Telegraph*.

BIDDLE TO ENOCH PARSONS [1] ESQ.

Phil^a. Feby 28th. 1831

Dear Sir

... In the general views expressed in your letter I entirely concur. It is deeply to be regretted that the President has taken this course, and we must endeavor as much as possible to counteract its effect. But our weapons are truth and reason — our appeal is from the passions to the understanding, & the dissemination of correct views of the nature & operations of the Bank is the most efficient engine we can employ. Further than this we ought not to go. I should lament deeply that those connected with the Bank should be active or zealous or conspicuous in political contests. This would be wrong in itself: it is a violation of that perfect neutrality which is the first duty of the Bank. It would be injudicious too, even on calculation, since no advantage to be derived from their efforts would overbalance the general evil from their actual or supposed interference. ...

BIDDLE TO JOSEPH GALES ESQR.

Phil^a. March 2. 1831

Dear Sir

... On this whole subject of publication, my theory is very simple. I believe that nine tenths of the errors of men arise from their ignorance — and that the great security of all our institutions is in the power, the irresistible power, of truth. I recollect well when twenty years ago I opposed in the Legislature [2] of my State the measures taken to prostrate

---

[1] Enoch Parsons, a lawyer of Hartford. Cf. Trumbull, J. H. (editor), *Memorial History of Hartford County* (Boston, 1886), vol. I, p. 130.

[2] A good sketch of Biddle's early career is given by Conrad, R. T., *Sketch of Nicholas Biddle*, in *National Portrait Gallery of Distinguished Americans*, vol. III.

the former Bank, how much of the opposition to the Bank was the result of downright ignorance of its meaning and its operations, and I have lived to see the very individuals the most zealous in the work of destruction, candidly confess, as they have grown older and wiser, that they did not properly appreciate the institution. I know what was then wanting — and I am resolved that it shall not now be wanting. I saw the manner in which the small demagogues of that day deceived the community — and I mean to try to prevent the small demagogues of this day from repeating the same delusion. For this, there is but one course, the free circulation of plain honest truths by means of the press. There is one mode in which you can much assist me. It is by the transmission of a list, such as your long practice has enabled you to accumulate, of citizens with their respective addresses in various parts of the United States. Your own subscription list, with the additions which you propose to make for increased diffusion of your paper, would form excellent materials & I would gladly defray the expence, if necessary, of copying that list which, for greater convenience, should be divided into States

BIDDLE TO JAMES HUNTER Esq.

(*private*) Bank U States
May 4. 1831

Dear Sir
 . . . The President has undertaken to say of the Bank that which is wholly without foundation & to denounce the institution. The whole influence of his government, & of the presses subservient to his government, is employed in endeavoring to break down the Bank. In this situation, the

Bank can only find safety in such explanations of its proceedings as will satisfy the country that it has been justly assailed & that its operations are highly beneficial. But how it is to make these explanations, except thro' the press, the only channel of communication with the people? And if it employs that channel, why should it ask of printers to insert its explanations gratuitously? If a grocer wishes to apprize the public that he has a fresh supply of figs, the printer whom he employs for that purpose never thinks of giving his labor for nothing, but charges him for his trouble in inserting the advertisement. If the Bank in a like manner wishes a printer to insert information about its concerns, why should it not pay him for his trouble? The payment for the printing of documents thus disseminated is not only so proper but so just, that one is amused by the affected squemishness of the other printers who do not happen to be employed when they denounce the Bank for circulating documents which Congress itself has ordered to be disseminated by means of extra copies, and what is worse than all, paying the printers for their labor. . . .

BIDDLE TO J. HARPER

(*private*)   Bank U. States
                                                     June 29. 1831

Dear Sir

Your favor of the 16th is duly received & the contents are extremely satisfactory. I was sure that the statement was a calumny, & am glad that we have it in our power to prove it so.

I have heard various accounts of M^r. Blairs'[1] connection

---

[1] Cf. Catterall, *op. cit.*, p. 256, note on this topic.

with the Office, such as his being indebted & settling his account by paying ten per cent of the principal, immediately previous to his leaving Lexington to establish himself at Washington. Have the goodness to let me know the particulars of that transaction.

MEMORANDUM [1] BY BIDDLE

Octr. 19, 1831.

About ten o'clock today M^r. McLane, Sec^y of the Treas^y called to see me at the Bank. He had come to Phil^a principally for the purpose of conversing with me after he had seen the President.

He now stated that he had seen the President, and explained to him the course which he proposed to pursue in regard to the Bank. He had done this in order that there might be no misapprehension on the part of the Pres^t of his views & the consequences which might result from what he proposed to say in his report.

He said to the President that he thought the act of Congress which directed the Secretary of the Treasury to report annually to Congress made it the duty of that officer to present his own views & on his own responsibility and that the Executive stood rather in the light of a mediator between him (the Sec^y) & the Legislature. That such had always been the construction of the powers of the Secretaries. (This was obviously an infusion by Mr Dickins to whom I left a volume with all the passages marked which I thought might encourage this opinion.) He proceeded to explain to the Pres^t what his intentions were. He means to speak of the power of the

---

[1] Catterall, *op. cit.*, pp. 209–211, note. This memorandum is quoted in full in Catterall's book and the subject discussed in full in the above-mentioned pages.

Gov^t to pay off the whole of the debt on the 3^d of March 1833 with the aid of the Bank stock; that this stock if sold out would occasion alarm in the country & the panic would sink its value; whereas he was satisfied that the Bank would take it at a reasonable price, not less certainly than eight millions. This would give him an opportunity of speaking of the Bank in the most favorable manner, recommending the continuance of the charter of the present Bank in preference to a new one, with such modifications as without injuring the institution might be useful to the country & acceptable to the Executive. This he meant to present in the strongest manner he could to Congress. All this he explained particularly to the President who made no objection whatever. For greater precision he had put down the heads of what he meant to say in his report & showed them to the President. Mr Livingston by request of M^r McLane was present at this meeting.

It had been previously understood between Mr Livingston & M^r McLane that the Pres^t should say nothing in the message about the Bank. The President acquiesced tho' reluctantly in this, because he thought he could not well be silent with consistentcy. But in my (N B's) conversations with him M^r McLane I had expressed the opinion that his silence would not be so useful as his mentioning the subject. The matter was therefore renewed with Messrs Livingston & Mc Lane & the Pres^t and it was resolved that he should introduce the subject in this way — that having on former occasions brought the question before the Congress it was now left with the representatives of the people.

M^r McLane with a view to show the Pres^t the full extent to which his report might lead, said that perhaps when his report was presented & referred to the Comm^{ee} of Ways &

Means M^r McDuffie in his present mode of thinking in regard to the Bank might choose to introduce a bill into Congress for continuing the Charter & if so he (M^r McLane) could not with the views which he entertained of the Bank make any opposition to it. The President said he would be sorry if the question were forced upon him in that way.

I said it would be necessary to scan very accurately the Pres^t's speech so that there might not be a shade of opinion expressed against it, or any declaration that having once expressed his views & having no reason to change them he would now leave it to Congress &c. M^r McLane said certainly no such expression could or should be introduced, as it would not be in harmony or consistency with his own (M^r M's) report.

M^r McLane said that he would be willing to charter the Bank without any bonus, but intimated that he thought a large bonus would be required, & said that this should be considered in our proposed purchase of Bank stock.

He said that he thought the greatest danger of the Bank was from those who wished to pull down this Bank in order to build up another, that a Mr West of Salem had been very pressing on that point. I said there were I believed some capitalists in Boston & New York who were anxious about it, but I thought they had little political weight. He said that the argument was that to continue it would be a monopoly.

In regard to the period of applying for a renewal, he does not wish to be considered as the adviser of the Bank because it might be imputed to him that he was acting in concert with the institution, but he renewed the opinion which he expressed at Washington that it was doubtful (indeed he seemed to be more inclined now to think it inexpedient) whether it would be expedient to apply this year. His idea was that if it were put to the President as a test, he would be more disposed to reject it on that very account. The Pres^t is now perfectly confident of his election — the only question is the greater or the less majority, but he is sure of success & wishes to succeed by a greater vote than at the first election. If therefore while he is so confident of reelection this question is put to him as one affecting his reelection, he might on that account be disposed to put his veto on it, if he be as it were dared to do it. For what I see, says M^r McLane of the character of Genl Jackson, I think he would be more disposed to yield when he is strong than when he is in danger.

The footing then on which the matter stands is this:

The President is to say that having previously brought the subject to Congress, he now leaves it with them.

The Secretary is to recommend the renewal.

This latter point pleases me much. When I saw him at Washington he did not think he could go so far as to originate a recomendation of the Bank, & I therefore examined all the reports of all the Secretaries to show that the proposals for the Bank all originated with them & I left the volumes of these reports in Mr Dickin's hands marked, so that he might urge them on the Secretary's attention.

He thinks he can present the Tariff question strongly — he will then press with equal strength the Bank question & if he can arrange the question of the public lands (the surrender to them of the lands within their limits at a certain price so as to make the landholding states pay in stock to the old States the proportion which the latter have a right to) the Bank would be put in such company & on such a footing that even Mr Benton would not attack it.

On his way to Mr Carroll's with the Pres^t. the latter adverted to the inconsistency of those who pulled down the old Bank & built up the new — & particularly of the objection then made that foreigners were stockholders. This he considered an unfounded objection. (He mentioned this to me at Washington.)[1]

Some surprize was felt by the Pres^t of the Bank at perceiving in the report of the Secretary of the Treasury the following phrases:

"It is not perceived that there is any sufficient justifica-"tion in the grounds of the transaction as assumed by the "Bank for an arrangement in any form, by which so large " an amount of the public funds should be retained by the "Bank at the risk of the Gov^t. after it had directed their "application to the payment of the public creditor."

The reason of the surprize was this. On the 14th of Octr. 1832, the Chief Clerk of the Treasury Department addressed a letter to the Pres^t. of the Bank written obviously & avowedly at the request of the Secretary of the Treasury for the purpose of enabling the Pres^t of the Bank to contradict certain statements about the three per cents which appeared in a New York paper of the 12th of October. The letter, tho' not itself written for publication, was written professedly as the basis of a publication by the Pres^t of the Bank, and authorized him to vouch certain things. Having no taste for newspaperisms, the Pres^t of the Bank never answered and indeed never read the New York paper, but if he had answered it, he would have asserted the fact vouched for by the follow-

[1] Biddle evidently added to the *Memorandum* from this point at a later date because the following references are to the Secretary of the Treasurer's report of 1832. Cf. Reports of the Secretary of the Treasury, 1829–1836, vol. III, p. 295.

ing extract of the letter referred to, a letter written by the Chief Clerk of the Treas[y] at the request of the Secretary containing suggestions by the Secretary of what the Pres[t] of the Bank ought to publish. The suggestion was in these words:

"Nor has the Treasury any reason to object to the course "which the Bank has pursued in regard to the European "holders of the 3 per cents. On the contrary that measure "appears wise & prudent, & well adapted to prevent the "embarrassments which the sudden withdrawal of so much "foreign capital from the country would necessarily produce."

This was on the 14th of Oct[r]. 1832.

Another reason of the surprize of the Pres[t] of the Bank was that on the   of November 1832 he was waited upon by the Chief Clerk of the Treasury who announced himself as coming from the Secretary of the Treasury to make enquiry about the Certificates of stock. The Chief Clerk stated not once nor casually, but frequently & emphatically, what he had written on the 14th of October, that the Secretary was perfectly satisfied with the measure itself, but only desired that the Certificates should appear soon in order that the doubts of others might be removed, & he pressed the Pres[t] of the Bank to write a letter to the Secretary explaining the matter. In consequence of this request, the Pres[t] of the Bank wrote a letter to the Secretary on the   . If it had not been clearly & repeatedly stated that the Secretary was entirely satisfied & wanted only the means of satisfying others undoubtedly this letter would never have been written. The Pres[t]. of the Bank did not know — did not wish to know, & certainly would never have asked to know what the opinions of the Secretary were on the subject. The communication therefore to nim that the Treasury deemed the measure wise & prudent, and that the Secretary was satisfied with it was wholly gratuitous and in truth it might as well have been spared, since really it does not seem strictly proper to treat the Bank in this way—to denounce its measures in public at the same time that you praise them in private.

The Pres^t of the Bank was also surprized at that passage in the report of the Secretary he states that various considerations "have suggested an enquiry into the Security of the Bank as the depository of the public funds."

His surprize arose from two circumstances.

The first was that on the 31st of Octr. 1832, the Secretary addressed to him a letter requesting to know what the Bank would give for 3,919,666.66 francs — about $700,000 — being the first instalment of the French indemnity.[1] In that letter he stated that "*it would be sufficient for the Treasury to receive a credit for the amount in the Bank of the U.S. one month after the payment of the bill in Paris say on* the 2^d of March next," adding that "if as I presume an arrangement for the transfer May be best made with the Bank, I will thank you to state the terms."

It seems strange, that the Secretary at the same time that he announces to Congress his fears about the solvency of the Bank, should ask that very Bank to take in its own hands $700,000 additional money of the public, not to be paid for until the 3^d of March next.

The other reason of surprize is that the Secretary on the requested to know of the Bank what it would give for a bill on London for the 3^d instalment of the Danish in-

[1] Cf. MacDonald, William, *Jacksonian Democracy* (New York, 1907), pp. 204–207.

demnity amounting to about $244,000. Here then the Secretary, in the midst of his anxiety for the safety of the public monies in the Bank, actually proposes to place no less than a million of dollars more of that very public money in that very Bank — sure never was insolvency so much flattered before.

JOHN TILFORD TO BIDDLE

Lexington Nov 11. 1831.

Dear Sir

Mr Clay was elected to the Senate of the United States by a majority of nine Votes.

In a conversation with him a short time ago, he mentioned that he had about a year [1] since, thought that the Stockholders of the Bank of the United States, should not for some Two or three years ask for a renewal of their Charter, but that he now thought differently and would advise an immediate aplication to be made by them. I give the information to you, as the opinions of prominent men may be desirable on this subject at this time.

BIDDLE TO NATHANIEL SILSBEE

Philad^a. Novr. 21. 1831

My dear Sir

Without having come to any determination in regard to an application to Congress at the aproaching session for a recharter of the Bank, it is thought better to provide against such a contingency by relieving our friends in both houses from an embarrassment which might grow out of their connexion with the Bank. With this view in the elections of Direc-

---

[1] Cf. letter of Clay, September 11, 1830.

tors for the present year, we have omitted those who are members of Congress. In writing today to Mr Greene I have suggested the same course in respect to yourself. As we have already claimed your services whenever we could obtain them, & I hope we will long continue to enjoy them, it is unnecessary to say a word in regard to this omission, which under existing circumstances, I am sure you will perfectly understand, and I trust appreciate. Hoping soon to see you on your passage southward, I remain with great respect and regard.

EDWARD SHIPPEN TO BIDDLE

(*Confidential*)   Louisville 6 Dec. 1831
Dear Sir
     I have seen a letter from the Private Secretary of the President to a gentleman in this City, in answer to a communication addressed to the President on the Subject of a renewal of the Bank Charter. The substance of that letter is, that the Pres^{dt} does not consider himself pledged against a renewal, and that if Congress passes a Bill with *proper modifications* of the Charter his approval will not be withheld.

     I have taken some pains to ascertain the objections to the present Charter, and the modifications which it is thought will insure the Executive sanction. I give them to you with the only object of putting you in possession of the views held on this interesting subject by those who are deep in the secrets and favor of the President.

     1st Prohibit the establishment of more than two Branches in each State.

     2. The Stock now owned by government to be sold to in-

dividuals, in a manner that will prevent a few persons from monopolizing it. The Sale of the Government Stock will satisfy many in the North, and remove the existing objection of the President to a *partnership* between the Gov^t. and a Corporation.

3rd Limit the power or capacity of the Institution to hold real Estate. Say, the value of that description of property in possession of the Bank shall not at any time exceed 10 or 15 millions of dollars.

4. Take from the Corporation the power to loan money on a pledge of merchandize.

5. Give to the President and Directors of the Bank authority to appoint two individuals to sign *all* the notes issued (for the President & Cashier) and let *all* the paper emanate from the Mother Bank.

6. The existing provisions in relation to Government deposits, and Direction of the Bank, to be preserved.

7. Render the Corporation Suable in the Courts of the Several States by making the service of process on the President or Cashier of the Branch, & where the cause of action arose, a service on the Corporation.

It is believed that the modifications suggested will ensure the renewal of the Bank Charter. They are not calculated to impair the usefulness or efficiency of the Institution, and if *proposed by the Corporation*, they will really be adopted by Congress. By proposing the necessary modifications, the Bank will strengthen herself with the people, prevent an angry discussion in Congress, which might result in making the question of renewing the Charter a party test, and ensure the sanction of the Executive to the modifications solicited by the Bank, and adopted by Congress.

I give you these suggestions and opinions only on account of the source from whence they emanate. They are urged with apparent zeal in favor of the Bank, and altho' I am forbidden to mention names I have no doubt it was expected I would communicate their ideas to you.

My own opinion is that the object is entirely political. The popularity of the President must fall in the West,[1] if his hostility to the Bank is continued. The letter of the Private Secretary urges the necessity of proper modifications, which cannot be suggested by the President, and from the tenor of that letter, and the anxiety manifested by the party here, I think they are desirous to have the Bank question settled by a renewal before the next Presidential canvass, with any modifications to free the Pres^{dt} from the charge of an entire abandonment of his original opposition.

SAMUEL SMITH TO BIDDLE

Wash^{t}. 7th Decr 1831

My dear Sir

I had last night a long conversation with McLane and I am authorized by him to say that it is his deliberate opinion and *advice* that a renewal of the Charter ought not to be pressed during the present session in which I concurr *most sincerely*. The message is as much as you could expect. It shows that the Chief is wavering. If pressed into a *Corner* immediately neither McLane nor myself will answer for the consequences. But we both feel confident of ultimate success if time be given for the P^{t} to convince himself of the Error into which opinion long formed (prejudice if you pleased)

[1] For a careful discussion and analysis of President Jackson's popularity in the West, cf. Dodd, William E., *Expansion and Conflict* (Boston, 1915), pp. 20–39.

had committed him. Every day new Converts are making. Every day the utility of the Bank is becoming better known, and its popularity increasing. The mind of the President is getting better informed. And the increase of its friends cannot fail to have a favourable Effect on him therefore do not push him out of time. Give full play to the members of the Administration. Every one of whom (except Taney) are favourable; his opposition, I think, arises out of the mistaken Idea that the Bank has operated politically. Can you give me the means of Conquering that Idea.

M N. Mangum of N.C. a new Senator is a warm advocate of the Bank; he lodges with your friend

ROBERT GIBBES TO BIDDLE

confidential   Baltimore 11th. Decb. 1831.
My Dr. Sir

I have just heard a conversation which I deem sufficiently interesting to write you about, as it concerns the Bank of the U.S. Of its accuracy you could have no doubt did you know the individuals.

From the Presidents message, and the Report of the Secy of the Treasury we were all lead to believe that the powers that be were in favor of re-chartering that invaluable institution. Now to the facts — Barry,[1] Woodbury, & Taney [2] are hostile. These three are under the influence of Blair, Lewis, Kendall & C.O. who still rule our Chief Magistrate, and who himself is an enemy to the Bank in despite what he is made to say in his message. But on Mr. McLane's Report have we placed our hopes; now the "Globe" denounces his

[1] Major Barry, a close friend of President Jackson.
[2] Later Secretary of Treasury under President Jackson.

sentiments, and the Paragraph formed for that purpose was so objectionable, that on being shewn to M^r M^cL. he declared that was it published, he would send his resignation the next morning — it was accordingly modified as it appeared in that paper. Neither Barry or Woodbury saw the Report until it appeared in print. The President of course had it submitted to him, and was persuaded *at the time* to give it his sanction. But has since read with satisfaction the Richmond Enquirer which says that it will require a majority of *three fourths* of Congress to carry the measure into a Law.

I write you these remarks hastily, as they may be of service to you to know the actual state of affairs at Wash^t. in order to advance the all important subject which you must have so much at heart. I fear you will yet have much trouble with our wise *governors*. You have most heartily my good wishes and I am almost prejudiced enough to say and that of every honest man in the Community.

C. F. MERCER [1] TO BIDDLE

(*private*)   Washington D.C.
                                                  Decr 12th. 1831

Dear Sir

. . . Two years ago I earnestly advised you not to attempt the renewal of the Charter of the Bank of the United States, in the hey day of Genl. J^ns administration. I told you what I dare say you had already discovered that his party, I meant its active leaders, would quarrel among themselves, and knowing his hostility to the Bank, I advised you to await that result.

I now as confidently recommend it to you to press this

[1] Representative from Virginia.

Congress at this session for the renewal of your Charter for reasons too numerous and important to be compressed in the compass of a letter which I really have not time to write. I will however present to you a part of them, and my object being wholly disinterested I shall study brevity in my language rather than effect. Gen'. Jackson's popularity has declined much more among men of intelligence than with the great body of the people. It has especially declined in Congress. But his election is as certain as his life. He hates your Bank and has reason enough to do so. His silly notions respecting it have been exposed with your approbation, and he is mortified or vexed as well as angry.

Altho I hold his election to be certain every body else does not do so. But no one can doubt but that his reelection will increase the effect of his influence over this Congress.

Calhoun is friendly to your bank and he will certainly not be again Vice President.[1] He has little influence, but where it exists it is powerful and it exists among your enemies to the South.

McDuffy has ability and influence & talents and integrity and he is still the the friend of Calhoun, Chairman of the very committee to whom your memorial if presented would be referred.

Van Buren your enemy is in England.[2] If a candidate four years hence for the presidency his influence will be felt to your prejudice.

If you wait till the next session of Congress remember

---

[1] Calhoun's career as Vice-President is discussed by von Holst, H., *John C. Calhoun* (Boston, 1898), pp. 61–103.

[2] A sketch of Van Buren's ministry to England is given in Shephard, Edward M., *Martin Van Buren* (Boston, 1891), pp. 191–203.

it is the short session and will not allow time to mature your bill. Consider also that by that period Jacksons success will have been ascertained and his power enlarged and invigorated.

The Sec^y of the Treasury and Js Cabinet probably are now on your side. They may not continue to be so because the persons who fill these political stations may be changed. . . .

HENRY CLAY [1] TO BIDDLE

Washington 15th December 1831.
read 20th Dec^r & Referred Comm^ee
on the Offices.[2]

My dear Sir

. . . Have you come to any decision about an application to Congress at this Session for the renewal of your Charter? The friends of the Bank here, with whom I have conversed, seem to expect the application to be made. The course of the President, in the event of the passage of a bill, seems to be a matter of doubt and speculation. My own belief is that, if *now* called upon he would not negative the bill, but that if he should be re-elected the event might and probably would be different.

---

[1] On October 4, 1831, Clay wrote to Francis Brooke on the need of re-chartering the Bank as follows: "I think the Charter of the B. of the U.S. ought to be renewed upon equitable conditions. I am perfectly willing to abide by the reasons which I assigned for a change of my opinion (the only change of opinion I ever made on a great pol. question) relative to that institution, and which are to be found in my public speeches." And again on December 25, 1831, writing to Brooke: "The Executive is playing a deep game to avoid, at this session, the responsibility of any decision on the Bank Question. It is not yet ascertained whether the Bank, by forbearing to apply for a renewal of their Charter, will or will not conform to the wishes of the President. I think they will act very unwisely if they do not apply." Cf. Colton, Clay's *Works*, vol. IV, pp. 316, 322.

[2] These words are in red ink in the original manuscript.

SAMUEL SMITH TO BIDDLE

Washington, Decr. 17. 1831

Dear Sir

This morning M^r. Clay, on returning a visit I had paid him, took occasion to broach the subject of the renewal of the Charter of the Bank of the U. States, by enquiring whether I had any precise information as to its purpose to memorialise Congress on the subject. I replied that I had not; that I had myself been inclined to think that, as the subject was national, and had so repeatedly and recently received the notice of the Executive, it might be the best policy to let the Gov^t act upon it without the special interposition of the Bank, as it would in this event be acted upon on large public considerations, free from the prejudices which might arise on viewing its bearings on private interests. He expressed his dissent from this opinion; said the present was the most favorable time to get the charter; that a majority of the two Houses was for it; that he himself should vote for it; that M^r. Buckner, the new Senator from Missouri, had told him he would do so; that the President had unquestionably the last summer declared (stating the name of the individual to whom he made the declaration) that either the Bank or Andrew Jackson must go down; that it was probable that, if two Houses passed a Bill, the President would approve it previous to the next Presidential election, but that if not passed previously he did not doubt his rejecting it; in fact, that now or never, was the time to act with any chance of success.

I stated to him that in conversation with several members of Congress, personal friends of the President, and others of like character, they had expressed great solicitude that the subject should not at this session be pressed by the Bank, declaring at the same time their friendship to the Bank, with the fear, if so pressed, the measure would be considered by the President as an electioneering one, and would scarcely fail to be felt by him as personal, and being so viewed impel him, in the assertion of his independence, to put his veto on the Bill, that it might not be alleged that he was influenced by a regard to a re-election; that the Secretary of the Treasury was adverse to the subject being taken up at this time; and that if the discussion were deferred, as public opinion, particularly in the West, was becoming more favorable, the President, yielding to its influence, would be apt to become himself less adverse to a continuance of the Charter.

He said that his information corraborated mine; but that he did not believe the effect on the President would be such as was represented; that if the Bank memorialised Congress it would be but following in the wake of the President; that if they did not, he doubted whether the subject would be effectively brought forward; that many of the members would avail themselves of the circumstance to wave the discussion of the subject; that, further, it should be considered that if the pressing it by the Bank should be viewed by the friends of the President as an electioneering measure aimed against him, there was another aspect of the subject under which those opposed to the President, and in general friends to the Bank, might consider the delay to memorialise, especially after the actions of the stockholders on the subject, as an electioneering step against them; that already rumors of a coalition to this effect was circulated; and that in regard to the feeling in the West, it was quite doubtful; he believed they (the representatives) might without injury vote for a renewal, but there would be little sensation there let the decision be what it might. . . .

Altho' these views are probably familiar to you, and you may, thro' other channels, be possessed of the facts I have stated, I have supposed there might be a use in communicating them, with the opinion . . . that the views and reasoning of Mr Clay are in the main correct. I may add, that you know him sufficiently well to admit, that, however glittering the prize of ambition may be, he is remarkable for the habitual exercise of dispassionate judgement and clear perception. I would add, however, my aprehension, that, altho' the discussion will shew a majority in favor of the Bank, there will be a sufficient number of members voting with its enemies for an indefinite postponement to defeat the passage of a Bill this session. . . . I am, with unfeigned respect

DANIEL WEBSTER TO BIDDLE

Washington Decr 18. 1831

My Dear Sir

The state of my health & the severity of the weather have prevented me, since my arrival here, from being much abroad. Nevertheless, I have seen a great number of persons, & conversed with them, among other things, respecting the Bank. The result of all these conversations has been a strong confirmation of the opinion which I expressed at Philadelphia that *it is* expedient for the Bank to apply for the renewal of its Charter without delay. I do not meet a Gentleman, hardly, of another opinion; & the little incidents & anecdotes, that occur & circulate among us, all tend to strengthen the impression. Indeed, I am now a good deal inclined to think, that after Genl Jackson's re-election there would be a poor chance for the Bank. I am well informed, that within three days, he has in conversation with several Gentlemen, reiterated his old opinions, somewhat vociferously, & declared them unchangeable.

I have thought, My Dear Sir, the best advice I could give you, is, that you come down here, yourself, & survey the ground. You will have access to men of all parties, & can digest your information, compare opinions, & judge discreetly upon the whole matter. In my judgment, this is your true course, & ought to be immediately followed.

I am, Dear Sir, always faithfully

BIDDLE TO ASBURY DICKINS ESQ.

Phil^a. Decr. 20, 1831.

My dear Sir,

. . . M^r McLanes report is all that his friends could wish — enlarged liberal, wise, & statesmanlike. It is much fitter for a President's message than *the* President's message itself & I wish with all my heart that the writer of it was President. The style of the paragraph in that message about the Bank, with the commentary of the Globe, the Richmond Enquirer, & the Standard, I confess shake my confidence much. It is not in such an ambiguous tone that a President should speak or make his dependants speak.

THOMAS CADWALADER TO BIDDLE

Washington 20. Dec: 1831.
Tuesday Eve:

My dear Sir,

This is merely to report my arrival & that I am quartered at Barnard's Hotel.

I had some talk with my companion, the Senator,[1] who seems disposed to give all the aid he can, tho' he hangs in doubt as to the policy of starting the application *now*, unless it can be ascertained that we have $2/3^{ds}$, in asmuch as he has lately had intimations, from a quarter w^h he considers entitled to full credit, leading him to apprehend a Veto, on a smaller vote: at the same time he acknowledges that the chances of such negative may be greater after the Election. Of his Colleague & Brother in Law (W.) he speaks doubtingly. He will give me however all he can gather about him, as well as about the members below from Penns^a & says he will *help along.* I have sent a note to M^r McLane, asking to fix a time tomorrow morning to talk with me, & you shall hear from me after seeing him.[2]

THOMAS CADWALADER TO BIDDLE

Barnard's [3] — Washington
(*Private*)   21. Dec. 1831.

My dear Sir,

      I yesterday reported my arrival. I have had this morn-

---

[1] This must refer to the Senator from Pennsylvania.

[2] These and the following letters of Cadwalader throw much light upon the political moves in Washington in the fall of 1831. Professor Catterall states that John Sergeant and Daniel Webster were largely instrumental in Biddle's coming to his final decision to memorialize immediately for the re-charter of the Bank. However, these statements are not substantiated by any direct proof. It is quite correct to say that Sergeant had a great influence on Biddle's moves — especially in local politics and in the later re-chartering of the Bank by the State of Pennsylvania. But there is no evidence to show Sergeant's or Webster's power in the present issue. On the other hand, the Cadwalader correspondence shows almost conclusively that Biddle was mainly swayed by what his agent in Washington reported.

[3] Barnard's Hotel was at the northwest corner of Pennsylvania Avenue and Fourteenth Street. Frederick Barnard had succeeded Basil Williamson as proprietor in 1824. Bryan, Wilhelmas B., *A History of the National Capital* (New York, 1916), vol. II, p. 59, note 6.

ing a long & frank conversation with M^r McLane. He says *positively* that the President will reject the Bill, *if the matter is agitated this* Session. He (the Pres^t.) & those about him w^d regard the movement, before the election, as an act of hostility, or as founded on the idea that his opinions w^d bend to personal views, & that his fears w^d induce him to truckle. M^r: M^cL. is *sure* that under such circumstances he w^d apply his veto, even if certain that he w^d thereby lose the Election. The question he says cannot now be started without being regarded as a party one, & the influence of the government w^d be thrown upon *it* so that we should lose a large number of votes which under other circumstances we should gain — the rejection not being considered as a final one — as the question may be renewed at the next session, or a subsequent one, the Veto once given the President w^d never swerve, & that 2/3^{ds} w^d be required on any subsequent trial. Accordingly to the Sec^y's view of it, therefore, we are now to see whether we can rely on 2/3^{ds} under the circumstances averted to, namely the operation of party feeling, & Gov^t influence and to that inquiry I devote myself. M^r. M^cL. seems to have canvassed the Senate thoroughly, & we have gone over the names together. He gives us — Maine, Mass^{tts} Rhode Is^d Connecticut & Vermont — two each & New Hampshire making   II

N. Jersey 2. — but if this session, strike off Dickerson — say then   I

Penns^a Wilkins positively against us *this Session* & Dallas too *as he thinks,* tho both for us at another time — Delaware —   2

tho' if Rodney takes Clayton's place he is *contra.*

Maryland (if *this Session,* we lose *Smith!!!* for *certain*),   I

N.Carolina — Mangum — (our friend) w^d vote with the
> party

if brought on *now* — Brown against us —
S.Car^a *Hayne dead ag^t the Bank* — Miller ag^t;
us *now*. Georgia Forsyth — on one side but
for this Session w^d be adverse. Kentucky (Clay),   I
Tennesee — Grundy w^d work for us strongly *bye & bye*,
> but now w^d be contra. Ohio & Louis^a 4

Indiana — Hendricks favorable, but w^d go with Gov^t
if *now* to vote — Hanna resigned.
Mississippi — Ellis — like Hendricks — Pointdexter *dead con.*
Illinois — *both contra.* Alabama — Moere *con.*
King — in favor, but w^d go with party if *now* to vote.
Missouri — (Buckner) $\underline{\text{I}}$

                                                      21

If M^{c}L.'s views are right (& he tells me they are chiefly
founded on personal communications) this is discouraging
as to the *present* session. As to the H. of R. he considers Maine
all contra; New Hampshire divided; Mass^{tts} all in favor, so
R. Isl^d Conn^t: & Vermont, N.Y. 15 dead against, 4 doubtful — the rest in favor (including Root & White — both of
whom at present session w^d vote contra).
Jersey, all favorable — Penns^a all favorable, but half
> against if *now* agitated — Del^e 1 pro.

Maryland, 2 doubtful — Mitchell dead against, the rest
> in favor — but 2 of them ag^t *now*.

Virg^a 4 only viz: Barber, Mercer, Newton & Doddridge —
> on our side

N.Car^a 3 pro: all the rest *con* — including in the latter yr
> Cavzna Shiphard.[1]

[1] Must be William B. Shepard.

S.Car^a all con — except McDuffie & Drayton.
Georgia — Wilde only for us. Kentucky 5. pro: 7. con:
Ten^ee Arnold & Bell pro — but not if *now tested.*
Ohio—all *pro.* Louis^a all *con.* so—Indiana, Illinois, & Alabama.
Miss^i doubtful, Missouri pro 1. —
These are M^r McLane's impressions. All will be cautiously
sifted by information from other quarters.

I have seen McDuffie, & am to have my *talk* with him
tomorrow morning: Had a note also from Genl Smith—with
whom I am to confer. 9 P.M. I have just left M^r McLane
— with whom I have passed the Eve. We have gone over
the ground again — he re-iterating & enforcing his views &
opinions as before expressed, amounting to this — if you
apply now, you assuredly will fail — if you wait, you will as
certainly succeed. He thinks Genl. J. will *hereafter* sign the
Bill, if it appears that a large portion of *the People* are for the
Bank. He tells me Cass Livingston & *Barry* are decidedly for
the Bank, & Woodbury also favorable to it — the 2 later
w^d work against it if the question is agitated before the Election. Taney fixed against us — he is latterly *radical* on all
points — *par example*, he thinks the Judges ought to hold
their appointments only for 4 or 5 years. I write, as my letter
shews, hastily — no time to read over — People calling —
all the P.M. & it is now being late. I will get together before I
leave this place materials on which the Board may make calculations — giving as I shall do, the authorities on w^h I depend. My object is to correct the votes on w^h we may rely
in case of an application *at this Session.* With that information before us, the decision may readily be made.

I have a great deal of private matter opened to me w^h will
better to talk than to write on.

THOMAS CADWALADER TO BIDDLE

Washington
Barnard's 22. Dec: 1831

My dear Sir,

I yesterday gave you the ideas of M^r McLane & have to day had a conference with M^r McDuffie. He leans strongly to an immediate application — but is much staggered by what I learned from M^cL. He now thinks we must ascertain our strength carefully & not start the business unless sure of a majority under the circumstances adverted to in my last. He was entirely candid & confidential — has no good will to the Administration & is disposed to view their movements with doubt & suspicion. He will not give up the idea that the P. will be more likely to sign the bill now than after the Election, & under any circumstance he thinks we ought to *go on*, if we can poll a certain majority. Let the P. then veto, if he *finds freedom* to do so — in the face of his Message & M^cL's Report — & we may bring on the measure with a fair chance of the 2/3^ds next year. We are now getting exact information as to the vote — in w^h he will help. Tomorrow after ten, I meet Genl Smith & dine with him & McDuffie at M^r McLanes. That triumvirate & my unworthy self are to discuss the subject in conclave at the Sec^y's office on Saturday Eve.

All our Penns^a members of the H. of R. (except Horn, Dewart,[1] & Mann) are said to be for us, even in the teeth of the P — that part I shall better sift, before I rely on *all* — Ford & King, I do not feel sure of. I shall look closely at those of them who voted for Stevenson,[2] fearing their steadiness

[1] This evidently refers to Lewis Dewart, Representative from Pa., 1831–1833.
[2] Andrew Stevenson of Virginia, Speaker of the House in 1831.

in acting counter to Executive influence. M^cD. doubts whether that feeling will operate as powerfully as has been supposed — he calculates on the odium it w^d produce, affecting equally the acting & the acted upon.

Observe that I give you, as I go along, what I hear from others. When I get all the materials to be gathered, & hear all opinions, I shall make up my own. The conference of Saturday Eve: may perhaps open new lights — tho there will be in it more of diplomatic reserve than in my previous tête-à-têtes with the Individuals. I keep my eyes & ears sharply open & hear a great deal more than seems to be worth recollecting

I am interrupted & must close —

Thomas Cadwalader to Biddle

Washington 23. Dec: 1831
Barnards

My dear Sir,

Gen. Smith entirely goes with the administration in his objections to the agitation *of the question* at this Session — it will be made a Jackson & anti-Jackson vote, as he says, it being entirely impossible to persuade the Pres^t that we are acting under any other than a hostile feeling to him. Under that view of the subject, *in a vote of this Session*, Smith says, we lose in the Senate 10 votes which we might count in our favor next year — viz;

Jersey 1. Dickerson
Penns^a 2 (Dallas *told S. so.* Wilkins is *certain* for the party)
Maryland 1 (Smith*! ! ! as he himself tells me.)
N.Car: 1. (Mangum)
Georgia 1. (Forsyth)

Mississippi 1. (Pointdexter — not certain — as he is sound
      with the Pres^t:)
Illinois 2 (Kane & Robinson (both supposed friendly —
      but strong *party men*)
Indiana 1 (Hendricks — doubtful if he w^d vote for us at
  10   all — another man to be in Hanna's place —
      dead contra.

* Smith failing us, you will think the question settled *for this session* — & so it is, unless we can turn the administration men from their objections to a present movement of it. This I shall perhaps know in a few days. The conference with McLane, Smith & McDuffie is put off to Sunday. Genl. S. & also M^{c}L. & M^{c}D. advert often to the general impression that the Bank operates powerfully ag^t the Jackson party — they themselves having no such notion:— I have said to each of them that your Letter Book [1] contains the best evidence to the contrary & would shew, if it c^d be looked into, that we not only endeavour to keep the Bank & city offices out of the political vortex, but dissuade the officers of the Institution from being prominent as party men. I recollect letters to that point extracts from which c^d be used in a quiet way by Smith, as he thinks, with a powerful effect — I advise you sending them if no objection strikes you to your so doing. . . .

I therefore now close — with one remark — that as far as my consultations with our friends have gone, the Jackson portion of them argue against starting the question at this Session — and the Clay portion are equally anxious for its present agitation. . . .

[1] This is quite true. Cf. Biddle to David Sears, January 5, 1824; Biddle to Isaac Lawrence, April 22, 1825; Biddle to Campbell P. White, November 27, 1827.

BIDDLE TO THOMAS CADWALADER

Phil[a]. Dec[r]. 23. 1831

My dear Sir,

Your favor announcing your arrival & your second giving the result of your first interview are received. I have not had yet an opportunity of apprizing our friends S. & C.[1] of the state of things but shall do so this afternoon. The views of M[r] M. are sufficiently discouraging, & I shall wait anxiously for the further lights which you will give.

I inclose a paper of which I have no other copy — which therefore you will have the goodness to send back when you have no further occasion for it, or to bring it if you come soon. It is an extract from the minutes of the old Bank of the U.S. by which you will perceive that as early as the 6th of Jan[y] 1807 — four years before the expiration of the charter, and when it had nearly as long to run as ours has, the stockholders met & prepared a memorial which was not however presented until the following session of Congress — say 1808 (as this is the substance of the extract it is not worth while to send it)*

* Whence may be argued that if they began so early, we involved or provoked as we have been, cannot be reproached with a premature movement. I am particularly anxious to know the opinion of M[r] M[c]Duffie in whose judgment in this matter I have the highest confidence.

BIDDLE TO THOMAS CADWALADER

Phil[a]. Dec[r]. 24. 1831
Saturday night

My dear General,

The mail which should have arrived this morning did not reach us till night, so that I have just received your favor

[1] Sergeant and Clay.

of the 22ᵈ inst which is very interesting. On this whole matter I have heard much & thought more since you left us. I of course abstain from forming any definite opinion, but I will mention to you exactly my present state of mind. It is this. If Mʳ McDuffie could insure a reference to the Committee of Ways & Means, & a favorable report of that Committee, I would not hesitate to try it, if I could rely on a majority of one only in each house. Once fairly launched by the Comᵉᵉ I think we could succeed by a larger vote — but this you know better than I do. I have not said this to anybody except yourself — but all my reflections tend that way. With your letter comes a second from Mʳ Webster renewing with increased conviction his opinion expressed in the most decided manner of the expediency of it.

THOMAS CADWALADER TO BIDDLE

> Washington Sunday
> 25 Dec: 1831

My dear Sir

My last letter to you was of Friday — I have yet recᵈ no communications from you. Yours of the 23ᵈ is just brought in & *contents* noted. This morning was appointed for the conference between the Secʸ: Gˡ Smith Mʳ McDuffie & myself. the Secy: is however ill, in bed — & we must await his convalescence.

I have had much talk with Mʳ Webster (who is now at Annapolis) Mʳ. Silbee present. He (W.) seems decidedly for starting the memorial if we are sure of a bare majority in the 2 Houses — & even indeed if we are sure of a majority in H. of R. where we of course must *begin*. He says the Senate *will not throw out the Bill, if passed below* — & he thinks the

Pres^t. will not reject it—threaten as he may at present. entre nous, it is evident that W's opinions are guided, in some degree, by party feelings—as seems to be the Case with most of the Clay men. I must therefore measure opinions with fair allowances, Mr Adams, with whom I have consulted, & with whom I shall again confer takes cooler views—& is more disposed to look at the question under all its aspects; leans towards postponing unless a strong vote can be ascertained. Having rec^d the N. York *reports* this morning, I believe I may now sum up our supporters in that delegation at 14—three others are marked doubtful. In Maine, from the best information I can get we shall have 1. vote (Evans)— we certainly have all the Mass^{tts} R. I^d Conn^t: & Vermont— in N. York 14—all for Jersey—22 from Penns^a besides Horn (who next year w^d vote for B^k with *certain restrictions* — as Dallas tells me) & Mann (perhaps) Delaware 1. Maryland 7. Virginia (as polled by Mercer & Archer—Archer dead ag^t us on constitutional grounds — but polling his Delegation *on honour* & after conversing with each member— who agree in the result (6. N.Car: as polled by Y^r Kinsman Shephard—(who is *for* the B^k) 6—*certain*—S.Car: 2 (McDuffie & Drayton) Georgia 1 Kentucky 5—Ten^{ee} 1. (certain) besides Bell who will vote with *us if he can.* Ohio 14. certain—Louis^a 3—certain & Missouri 1. certain—giving for the Bank 116—& leaving against it 97. These pollings I have gone over with McDuffie this morn^g: & he confirms them— we look therefore, allowing for absences, to 20. majority—w^h he thinks good ground to go upon—supposing the Bill Safe in Senate—as to that Body—I ran them over in a former Letter —now again, more *knowingly.* Maine Mass^{tts} R.I.^d Connecticut & Verm^t 2 each—N.Ham. 1. *certain* (making) = 11.

N.Jersey (taking off Dickerson if now agitated ag^t: wishes of Pres^t. *certain*) — 1

Penns^a (W. & D. both torn with contending calculations — but I have reasons to believe they will consider State interests as paramount to *be explained when we meet.*

Del = 2 & M^d 1. (Genl. Smith told me he must desert if now pushed — maybe not — but let him pass) (certain) 3 w^d vote for B^k thro' *thick & thin* — N: Car: (Mangum told McDuffie he w^d & believes his colleague
Brown will go with him — but say *certain*) —   1
Georgia Forsyth our friend — but probably not with us *now*
Kentucky 1. Ohio & Louis^a 4 — *certain*   5
Tens^{ee} — Grundy in favor — but cannot *now go it.*
Mississippi — Pointdexter anti Jackson & believed with us 1
McDuffie will ascertain however — Missouri (certain)   <u>1</u>
now believed certain (if Pointdexter is right) —   25

With us another time — Dickerson — Smith — Forsyth & Grundy — perhaps Brown — say 5 = making 29 or 30 on another occasion. — Under these circumstances McDuffie leans in favor of *going it* now — & so do I — but we think it best not to *decide* till after the Conference with McLane & Smith. We have full confidence in M^{c}L's candour — as to his belief that J. will put on his veto — but the old Gent^m *may* shake in his intentions — and, if he return the Bill, he may state objections that perhaps may be yielded to by us. We sh^d in fact have hopes of him on a future occasion, if he takes any other than the broad ground of the *constitution.* We might be blamed for losing this Session (the *long* one — moreover) & tho' we go counter to the administration men — who are interested in postponing, we keep the other party with us — some of whom w^d be lukewarm, Webster w^d *be cold*,[1] or perhaps hostile, if we bend to the Gov^t influence. I do not yet *decide* — but *incline* to *suppose* that after the council at the Treasury, I shall advise the Com^ee to start the memorial. I shall not do so however unless McDuffie's opinion is decidedly that way, for he is our main stay — & if we make a blunder I have told him that I shall throw it on him.

All agree that when started, the H. of R. must lead — & all say it will not be committed to the Com^ee of W. & M. but to a special one — 7. will be the number & of *course* the Speaker will appoint — 4 for & 3 against — so say McDuffie & all — no danger of his breaking a custom so fixed. Everything then depends on having the proper man as chairman. McDuffie promised to move the Commitment of the Memorial — w^h puts him in that position & thus gives us a fair chance.

Thomas Cadwalader to Biddle

Washington 26 Dec: 1831

My dear Sir:

I have your letter of Saturday night — (24th inst.) and am glad to find the leaning of your mind, as to the question of present action or postponement, to be in the direction of my own *notions* . . .

In my estimates of votes I counted Findlay of Ohio as for us — he is decidedly adverse. We have however Genl Duncan of Illinois our firm friend — who was considered against

---

[1] Professor Catterall, in his book on the *Second Bank of the United States* makes the statement, on page 218, that this remark was made in a footnote by Cadwalader. However, the above extract shows that it was in the regular context of the letter.

us — & I have reason to hope that several of those marked
doubtful on my list — will be on our side . . .

I shall not consult Dallas & Wilkins as to the policy of acting now — knowing they w^d incline to postpone — & not
wishing to ask advice, under strong probabilities of going
against it. They are now well inclined to help us to votes —
& Wilkins, tho' always protesting for non-commitment on the
B^k question, is, as I verily think, more warm in our cause
than D — being more linked in the great points of State Interest — to w^h, as he admits the extinction of the B^k w^d
carry a death blow. On tariff & internal improvements he is
Quixotic — Dallas has a cooler *head*, if not *heart*. . . .

My yesterdays Letter gave my ideas as to the modus ope-
randi in the H. of R. if now to go *on*. I am more in doubt
as to the course in the Senate when the Bill goes up. As to
Smith, after his confession to me of adhesion to Palace influence we must understand with him, in a candid & friendly
way, that he must hold back, & that some other Champion
must head our Column — who it ought to be is the question
— as to power of talent, we w^d at once designate Webster
— but the name carries a deadly bearing of party feeling,
w^h it seems to me w^d counterbalance the good we might derive from him in other respects. M^c. Duffie may perhaps
enlighten me in the darkness in w^h I confess myself now to
be enveloped — & I mention the difficulty, now in time, to
you, for the benefit of your views . . .

Expect, *very shortly after that Conference at the Treasury*,
to receive my opinion as to the policy of now presenting the
memorials — or waiting for a less stormy occasion. You may
as well have the papers ready.

THOMAS CADWALADER TO BIDDLE

Washington 26. Dec 1831

My dear Sir

Your last letter is of Saturday night (23ᵈ instᵗ) ansᵈ by me yesterday — Nothing to day from you.

Mʳ Peter R. Livingston [1] (Brother of the Secʸ: of State, in whose House he is living) came to see me last Eve. He is strongly of opinion that we ought to start an application now. He says his Brother McLane & Cass [2] wᵈ prevent the veto tho' they are all desirous of saving the Presᵗ. from the neces-

[1] Peter Livingston was largely instrumental for the election of William H. Seward as Governor of New York in 1834. "Livingston had been a wheel horse in the party of Jefferson. He had served in the Senate with Van Buren; he had taken a leading part in the convention of 1821, and he had held with distinction the speakership of the Assembly and the presidency of the Senate. His creed was love of republicanism and hatred of *Clinton*. At one time he was the faithful follower, the enthusiastic admirer, almost the devotee of Van Buren; and, so long as the Kinderhook statesman opposed Clinton he needed Livingston. But when the time came that Van Buren must conciliate Clinton, Livingston was dropped from the Senate. The consequences were far more serious than Van Buren intended. Livingston was as able as he was eloquent and Van Buren's coalition with Clinton quickly turned Livingston's ability and eloquence to the support of Clay. Then he openly joined the Whigs." Alexander, De Alva S., *A Political History of New York* (New York, 1909), vol. I, pp. 402, 403.

[2] Lewis Cass did not agree with President Jackson in his attack on the Bank. On September 23, 1833, Cass made an appointment with Lewis to discuss the matter of the removal of the deposits. "Cass commenced the conversation," wrote Lewis, "by remarking that his object in desiring to see me before I left was to inform me that he had determined to resign his seat in the cabinet, and wished to converse with me upon the subject before he handed his letter of resignation to the President. He said he differed with the President with regard to the measures which were about to be adopted for the removal of the public deposits from the United States Bank, and as his remaining in the cabinet might embarrass his operations, he owed it, he thought, both to himself and the President to withdraw." Lewis urged him to acquaint Jackson. Cass was finally induced to remain in the Cabinet, but in a later Cabinet meeting, when asked his opinon on the measure, Cass simply and frankly said: "You know, sir, I have always thought that the matter rests entirely with the secretary of the treasury." McLaughlin, A. C., *Lewis Cass* (Boston, 1898), pp. 154, 155.

sity of acting one way or the other, before the Election — they look to Penns^a with great anxiety. M^c. Lane calculated in his talks with me on half that delegation voting postponement, in conformity with the wishes of the administration phalanx. Now I do not think they can shake more than four of them, if *so many* — & the more I see of the Senators D. & W. the more satisfied am I that the opinions lately expressed as to their votes are well founded. They are strongly inclined to aid the wishes of the Palace men in dissuading from moving the question this Session — but whenever moved they must support it.

M^r. Livingston has been, as you know, an active & powerful worker in the politics of N York. He enters zealously into this B^k question — (probably from Party feeling — a Member of the *Clay Convention*) besides the 14 favorable votes of his State on w^h I have before counted, he says he *can*, & *will*, bring over some of those marked on my list as *doubtful* — viz: Angel, Babcock, Cooke, Hogan, Lansing, Lent, Pierson, Reed & Soule. He is now engaged in that good work & is to report the result. When the subject comes up much warmth, say indeed violence, is to be expected — & we may find some shaking, on whose firmness we now count. I am fully in the belief, however, that we shall gain more from those marked "uncertain" & now by me counted as adverse, than will make up any losses from my present list of *yeas*. . . .

BIDDLE TO SAMUEL SMITH

Phil^a. Jany 4, 1832

My dear Sir,

You will hear, I am afraid with regret, tho' not with surprize, that we have determined on applying to the present

Congress for a renewal of the Charter of the Bank & that a memorial for that purpose will be forwarded tomorrow or the next day. To this course I have made up my mind after great reflection & with the clearest convictions of its propriety. The reasons I will briefly explain. 1. The Stockholders have devolved upon the Directors the discretion of choosing the time of making the application. If we should omit a favorable opportunity we would commit an irreparable error, & would be permanently reproached with it by the Stockholders. Now these Stockholders are entirely unanimous in their opinions and in a case of such grave responsibility their wishes are entitled to great consideration. Unless therefore there should be some very strong reason against it, the application should be made. 2. Independent however of this, I believe That this is the proper time. The Charter will expire in March 1836 — Unless the present Congress acts upon it, we must wait 'till the Congress of December 1833, & could not expect from them any decision before after March 1834 which would bring the Bank within two years or 18 months of the expiration of its charter. Now whether the institution is to be continued or destroyed that time is too short. Until the question is settled every thing will be uncertain. No man can look ahead in either public or private affairs as to the state of the currency & there will be constant anxiety about our whole monied system. The Bank too ought to know its fate so as to close its affairs without inflicting deep & dangerous wounds upon the community by sudden shocks & changes. I believe therefore that this is the best time for settling the question. If the Bank is to be continued the country ought to know it soon. If the Bank is to be destroyed the Bank & the country ought both to know it soon.

The only objection I have heard to it, is, as far as I understand, this: that in about a year hence there is to be an election for a President of the U.S. — and if the application is now made, the gentleman who is now President will take it amiss & negative the bill — while if the Bank will refrain from applying until after his election is secured, he will probably be permitted to abstain from negativing it. This seems to embrace the whole case — Let us look at it. In the first place then, neither I nor any of my associates have any thing whatever to do with the President or his election. I know nothing about it & care nothing about it. The Bank has never had any concern in elections — it will not have any now. To abstain from anything which it would otherwise do, on account of an election, is just as bad as doing anything on account of an election. Both are equal violations of its neutrality. There are many politicians who want to bring it on because it would benefit their side. There are many other politicians who want to put it off because that would benefit their side. Hitherto they have been urged to bring it before the last Congress in hopes that it would injure the present incumbent — now they are urged to postpone it because postponement would benefit him. The Bank cares not whether he is benefited or injured. It takes its own time & its own way.

In the next place what appears to me I confess wholly inexplicable is why the friends of the present incumbent who are also friends of the Bank, if they think the Bank question likely to injure the President, do not at once take the question out of the hands of their adversaries. If the President's friends were to come forward & settle the Bank question before the election comes on, they would disarm their antagonists of their most powerful weapon. I am very ignorant of party tactics, & am probably too much biased to be a fit judge in this case, but such a course has always seemed to me so obvious that I have never been able to comprehend why it was not adopted.

But again what is the reason for supposing that the present incumbent will be offended by bringing it forward now? What possible right has he to be offended? What too has he meant by all these annual messages — declaring in 1829 that he could not "too soon present it" to Congress — repeating the same thing in 1830 — and reiterating it in 1831. Was this all a mere pretence? that the moment the Bank accepts his own invitation he is to be offended by being taken at his word.

But moreover he is to negative the bill. That is to say, he will agree to the bill hereafter, but because he thinks it will interfere with his election he will negative it now. Truly this is a compliment which I trust he does not deserve from his friends, for even I who do not feel the slightest interest in him would be sorry to ascribe to a President of the United States a course much fitter for a humble demagogue than the Chief Magistrate of a great country. He will sign a bill, which of course he must think a good one, when his election is over — but he will not sign this bill, which he thinks a good one, — if it is likely to take votes from him at an election. And after all, what security is there that when his election is over, he will not negative the bill? I see none. On the contrary I am satisfied that he would be ten times more disposed to negative it then than now. Now he has at least some check in public opinion — some in the counsels of those around him — then he will have neither. And now, my dear Sir, I have tired myself as I have certainly you with these opinions which you think very erroneous & very disrespectful perhaps to the President. But

I wanted to explain precisely the course of thinking which has brought me to my present conclusion. The only regret which accompanies it is that it has not the concurrence of M^r McLane & yourself to whom the Bank as well as myself personally owe much for the manner in which you have both sustained the institution. I cannot express to you how much I am concerned at not being able to adopt the suggestions of M^r McLane who has behaved so handsomely in this matter. But we must each in our respective spheres of duty follow our own convictions with mutual regret but still with mutual respect.

To you I always looked forward as a friend & advocate of the Bank whenever the question of its renewal was agitated. I shall be very sorry on many accounts that from a difference of opinion in regard to time you will be constrained to with hold your aid — but I assure you it will abate none of the regard for you — & the fullness of these explanations will I hope satisfy you of my anxiety to State to you frankly & distinctly the motives which lead me to a conclusion, differing I believe for the first time — from Your's on the Subject of the Bank.

Louis McLane to Biddle

Washington Jan. 5. 1832

Dear Sir,

General Cadwallader has returned to Philadelphia, and I apprehend with impressions, favorable to an attempt to renew the charter of the Bank of the United States at the present session of Congress. When he consulted me upon the subject soon after his arrival here, I frankly & distinctly discouraged the attempt and on grounds which I believe well entitled to weight. Other Counsels however, and, as I think too sanguine expectations of support from Congress, appear to have had greater influence: and it has occurred to me as proper that I should communicate my opinions directly to you.

I do not profess to be in a situation to become the adviser of the Bank, and I desire to be irresponsible for the future decision of the Directors and the stockholders. The position I occupy in the Government, however, and that in which the late annual report which my sense of public duty constrained me to make has placed me in relation to the Bank and may possibly place me in relation to any immediate attempt to re-new the Charter, make it necessary for me to prevent mis-apprehension from any quarter distinctly to state my own opinions. This will at least leave me uncommitted for the future whatever weight may be given to my views.

I feel constrained therefore to say that I am decidedly op-posed, both on principle and on grounds of expediency, to an attempt to renew the Charter of the Bank during the *present Congress.*

The annual report, for the reasons stated in it, recommends the renewal of the charter "*at the proper time,*" thereby ob-viously excluding any premature renewal which should be inconsistent with the principle and term of the charter and not necessary to the safety of the stockholders, or the inter-ests of the debtors and convenience of the community at large.

The charter of the Bank will not expire until one year after the termination of the next Congress: before that period Congress has no authority, without the consent of the Stock-holders, to alter its provisions; and a law passed in the interim can only take effect after the expiration of the present charter.

Unless it could be shown that all the remaining period of

the charter is necessary to accommodate the business of the Bank to the ultimate decision of the Government this would be no just pretence for requiring that decision at this time, and perhaps no greater motive for doing so than there was during the last session. To me there appears to be no such necessity; and it does not follow that those friendly to the institution could be expected to make their final decision at this time.

In the case of such a Corporation as that of the Bank of the United States the Government is entitled to so much of the term of the Charter for the benefit of full experience and of amply taking the good management of the corporation, as may be consistent with the public interest. Independently of this right a subject on which there is so great a diversity in public opinion, involving so many important interests of all classes of the community, and which has already attracted a large portion of public attention should not be disposed of without again affording an opportunity of a distinct expression of the will of the people. The present Congress has not been chosen with any direct reference to this question, and there are no constitutional means of ascertaining the sense of the people before the elections preparatory to the 23d. Congress. Favorable as I am to the continuance of the Bank, if I could be persuaded that a decided majority of the people of the United States were certainly opposed to re-chartering it as at present organized, I could not consent, with the principle of Government which I hold, to forestall, by any premature action, the force of public sentiment, or to exclude the advantage of other counsels with a fuller knowledge of the subject.

It must be obvious that both the interests of the present Banks and the general expediency of such an institution re-

quire that the consideration of the subject should be separate
from party questions, with which it has properly no concern;
and it is equally clear that in the present state of political
parties, whatever may be the motive of the friends of the
Bank, it must undoubtedly be mixed up with topics altogether unfavorable to a dispassionate judgement.

It is not unreasonable to infer that these considerations will
have their weight with the members of the present Congress;
who will see nothing in a refusal to legislate at present inconsistent with the maintenance of their own views under more
favorable circumstances.

I have no right, nor do I profess in any manner, to speak
for the President; his opinions are before the Country in his
official messages in each of which he has invited the People of
the United States to an investigation of the subject. But independently of the views he has heretofore avowed, and however they might be ultimately affected by a deliberate expression of the will of a decided majority of the People of the
U.S. it would be unreasonable to expect that he could now
consent finally to foreclose the investigation which he himself has invited, before the public sense has been constitu-
tionally declared ascertained.

For myself I must say that holding the principles I do and
have here expressed, as one of the constitutional advisers of
the President I could not consistently interpose an objection
to the exercise of his negative upon a bill rechartering the
Bank during the present Congress, unless presented to him
as one of and in connection with a series of measures for ad-
justing, upon principles of compromise, all the great interests
of the Country.

I deem it unnecessary to repeat my opinion of the expediency or necessity of a National Bank on the grounds and for the purposes I have heretofore publicly stated, but I will not disguise the solicitude I feel lest any premature attempts to re-charter the present Bank by exposing it to the influence of party feeling and prejudice, should hereafter encourage the preference to an entirely new institution.[1]

DANIEL WEBSTER TO BIDDLE

W. Jan. 8. (1832?)

My Dear Sir

I cannot but think you have done exactly right. Whatever may be the result, it seems to me the path of duty is plain. In my opinion, a failure, this session, if there should be one, will not at all diminish the chances of success, next session.

I suppose the memorial will make its appearance, in the Senate, thro the V.P. My notion will be to let the administration Gentlemen take the Disposition of it, for the present, & see what they will do with it.

JOHN CONNELL [2] TO BIDDLE

(*Private*)   Washington 10 Jany 1832

My dear Sir

. . . Mr Adams [3] told me, that if you had not petitioned, as you did, that it had been his intention to have

---

[1] This letter shows that Biddle's view of political theory was that formerly advanced by Alexander Hamilton; while McLane, in the above letter, is advancing the Jeffersonian theory. It was largely owing to the fact that the nation — especially the West — at this time held to the Jacksonian theory of the sovereignty of the people (a natural outgrowth of the Jeffersonian ideas) that Biddle later encountered the hostility of the populace — beyond the natural antipathy of the Westerner to banks and banking in general.

[2] A director of the Bank of the United States in 1838. Cf. Report of Committee of Investigation, 1841, p. 64.

[3] Cf. *John Quincy Adams Memoirs* (Philadelphia, 1876), vol. VIII, p. 457.

offered a Resolution, instructing the Committee of Ways & Means to report a Bill, renewing the charter of the Bank; and this, he probably would have done the present week, for *substantial reasons* which he assigned, founded altogether upon great public considerations. . . .

BIDDLE TO GARDINER GREENE[1] ESQ.

(*private*)   Phil Jan 16ᵗʰ 1832

My Dear Sir

The Bank having after great consideration presented a memorial for the renewal of the charter, the citizens of Philad are forwarding petitions on the subject of a similar measure [which] will be transmitted by the State Banks. It would be greatly desirable to have the same thing done elsewhere. I have written to-day to our friend Col. Perkins & I wish you & our other friends would endeavour to have a strong & general expression of the sense of your community so that Congress may be apprized of the real sentiments of the country.

BIDDLE TO HORACE BINNEY[2]

Phil Jan 25ᵗʰ 1832

My dear sir

In regard to the bonus for a renewal of the Charter my views are these —

As the bonus is in fact only another name for a tax, and like all other taxes disables the Bank to the extent of it from

[1] Alleged to be the wealthiest citizen of Boston. Winsor, Justin (editor), *Memorial History of Boston* (Boston, 1883), vol. IV, pp. 29, 30.

[2] A distinguished lawyer, the son of Dr. Barnabas Binney, a surgeon in the Revolutionary War. Binney first became acquainted with Biddle at the meetings of the Tuesday Club, a literary society organized by Dennie in Philadelphia. Binney and Webster were the legal advisers of the Bank. Cf. Oberholtzer, E. P., *Philadelphia, A History of the City and its People*, vol. I, p. 413.

giving facilities to the community, a Bonus should not be pressed by Gov^t beyond a very moderate limit, particularly as the Gov^t is now very rich instead of being needy as it was at the time of granting the Charter.

But if the Bank must pay, I do not think it ought to pay more than the sum of $1,500,000: nevertheless it would not be proper to decline the charter because more was asked & I should be disposed to go as high as two millions or if necessary three; between this last limit & the original sum of a million & a half lies the debateable ground. I think you might at once agree to any sum not exceeding three millions. If more were required or more were insisted upon during the passage of the Bill through the House it would be a subject of further reference to the Board. To the extent I have mentioned, I am sure there would be no difficulty.

CHARLES JARED INGERSOLL [1] TO BIDDLE

Washington Feby 2. 1832

Dear Sir,

I saw the President for the first time yesterday — introduced by Mr Livingston who kindly volunteered his carriage and personal attendance for the purpose. Thus auspicated my reception was extremely gracious and flattering. There was a great deal of free and general conversation of which the topics were the French treaty, the Mexican treaty, the tariff, Mr Van Buren's rejection and his pending negociation, Mr Clay, and Governor Hamilton of South Carolina. I feel satisfied that from the beginning by gradual and proper advances I may eventually and à propos bring about a tête-

---

[1] At this time a strong advocate of the Bank. Later, however, Ingersoll turned against the institution when Biddle urged open war against Jackson. Cf. Meigs, W. M., *The Life of Charles Jared Ingersoll* (Philadelphia, 1897), pp. 167–185.

à-tête communication on the bank, to which end my future intercourse in that quarter shall be directed. I understand from Dickins with whom I had some confidential chat and shall repeat it frequently that General Jackson's antipathy is not to the Bank of the United States in particular, but to all Banks whatever. He considers all the State Banks unconstitutional and impolitic and thinks that there should be no Currency but coin, that the Constitution [was not] designed to compel paper altogether as any part of our monetary system. This view of his doctrine conforms to a report which you shewed me not long ago made by him — to the Legislature of Tennessee;[1] it coincides with some similar notions that I have long indulged myself, and at any rate to be apprised of the theory of his sentiments will be useful to me as it supplies a platform on which to approach him. If his prejudices are honest they may fairly be dealt with. Louis Williams[2] of North Carolina says that all his opposition to the Bank of the United States was fomented if not created by Van Buren who calculated that he could render his ascendancy in New York subservient to the prejudices of Virginia, and that Pennsylvania would acquiesce, which three States thus united would give him a broad basis for the future Presidency. . . .

BIDDLE TO HORACE BINNEY

Phil^a. Feby 6th. 1832

My dear Sir

It strikes me that the resolutions of our legislature will place M^r. Dallas in an attitude equally new, and imposing;

[1] Jackson was the author of the Tennessee law of 1820 creating a loan office. Cf. Bassett, J. S., *Andrew Jackson*, p. 592; Sumner, W. G., *Andrew Jackson*, pp. 158, 159 (3d edition).
[2] Representative from North Carolina.

offering an opportunity of distinction, which a young statesman could scarcely hope for in his dreams, & which the oldest
statesman might pass a whole life without encountering. It
seems to me, his position is precisely this — He wishes to
be the Pennsylvania candidate for the Vice Presidency and
then

> "Glamis — and thane of Cawdor
> "the greatest is believed."

The Pennsylvanians are disposed to assist him and to exclude
M^r. V Buren. To promote this M^r. Dallas should identify
himself with all the Pennsylvania interests, more especially
those interests to which M^r. Van Buren is supposed to be
hostile. He should therefore go immediately to the President
with these resolutions of Penn.[1] in his hand — he should
warn him against irritating our State, especially as the offence to her is wholly gratuitous. He should say to him you
are not opposed to this bank essentially; you mean to agree
to it with certain modifications. Now let me mediate between
you and the Bank; let us agree on the modifications; the Bank
will consent to them, and I will report them, the rechartering
of the Bank will thus become a measure of yours — you will
gratify Penn^a. — you will take from your adversaries their
most formidable weapon, and secure the ascendancy of your
friends. If the President will do this his success is certain, if
M^r. Dallas will do this, besides sustaining his father's work,
& conferring a great blessing on the Country, he will assure
to himself distinguished consideration through the nation.

---

[1] These resolutions carried under the able leadership of Ingersoll, who declared "that the constitution of the United States authorizes and near half a century's experience sanctions, a Bank of the United States as necessary and proper
to regulate the value of money and prevent paper currency of unequal and depreciated value."

I do not know how he is disposed for such an enterprize, but he ought to give ten years of his life for this chance of attaining it. Tell him so, and if in half an hour afterwards he is not on his way to the Presidents, — why then — the stars have conjoined for him in vain.

BIDDLE TO CHARLES JARED INGERSOLL

Philad^a. Feb^r. 6. 1832

My dear Sir

It occurs to me that the present is a crisis for Genl. Jackson, & for the Bank. The Penn^a delegation, and eminently Mr Dallas, now have an opportunity of doing great good; and of acquiring great distinction. Let them go forward, and mediate between the President and the Bank, — make him name his modifications; make the Bank agree to them, make the re-charter an administration measure. You see at a glance all this. Do put them up to it; make M^r. Livingston and M^r. McLane stir in it. It is a real coup d'état. Try if you cannot bring it about, without loss of time.

CHARLES JARED INGERSOLL TO BIDDLE

Washington. Thursday evening
9 February 1832

Dear Sir,

An article signed *Tulpe Hocken* destined to appear in the Sentinel, and another signed *incognito* sent to the Enquirer of Philadelphia, each adapted to the various tastes of the readers of those different papers, the first designed to corroborate the spirit of Pennsylvania, the second to inculcate a beleif that the President has no constitutional objections to the Bank, but that the Vice President and his adherents are opposed to it, will serve to shew you that I have been paving the way for just such a coup d'état as your letter of the 6ᵗʰ received to day suggests and after [having] well digested my project I went to the Department of State yesterday to break ground: But Mʳ Livingston was with the President and I was obliged to defer the overture till to day, which I am not sorry for, as your letter come to hand in the mean time has confirmed my views and shaped them with precision. I now proceed with much satisfaction to report to you substantially what took place. When I saw Mʳ Livingston, as I did this morning soon after the receipt of your letter, I told him that I wished to speak freely with him respecting an important measure which he had often mentioned with great apparent freedom to me, assuring him that he might rely implicitly on my confidence and my disposition to render a service to General Jackson's administration consistent with what I deemed the welfare of the country: I then explained to him the state of parties in Pennsylvania, that the confidence of the people in General Jackson is undiminished as is well known to the adherents of Governor Wolf, but that they have the whole party organization of the State in their hands, and while they dare not openly oppose General Jackson's re-election, yet that many if not most of them are inclined to be in opposition to him. I repeated all the circumstances of the publication by the Philadelphia members of the Legislature last spring in answer to the charge of bribery [1] which was

---

[1] C. J. Ingersoll early in 1831 introduced certain resolutions, with the knowledge and consent of Biddle, in favor of the Bank. These resolutions were passed by a decisive majority, having at one stage met with serious repulse, and after having had a clause added in favor of distribution of the surplus revenue among the States, which Ingersoll voted against. Soon after the *New Hampshire Patriot*

intended to strike at the President, and would have done so much more forcibly than it did, but for the mitigation of some of whom I was one, and I added that the resent attempt to get up a Van Buren party in Pennsylvania had been a complete failure. I then mentioned the recent almost unanimous resolutions of the present Legislature sustaining those of the last in favor of the bank of the U S and said that he might depend upon it, therefore, that collision between the State and the President would be a dangerous & unfortunate occurrence for the latter for which surely said I there is not the least occasion, for why should he risk any portion of his popularity against an object entirely disconnected with politics, and so purely fiscal that if the Secretary of the Treasury were to tell the President that he found a frying pan the most convenient means of managing the finances, I should suppose the President would agree to it, especially as I understood he has no constitutional scruples. After more of these preliminaries than I can altogether repeat, I asked Mʳ Livingston if under these circumstances it would not be the simplest resolution of all the supposed difficulties to take the Bank out of the hands of Mʳ MᶜDuffie and the opposition, modifying its charter so as to suit it to the President's opinion and passing it as a measure of the Administration, Mʳ MᶜLane taking the place which Mʳ Dallas occupied and General Jackson the example of Mʳ Madison in [']15–16 when the Bank was created. I further more offered to see Mʳ Dallas, expressing my confidence that he would cordially cooperate in such a movement. Finally, I

charged and the *Washington Globe* reprinted the charge of bribery. To this Ingersoll and other members of the legislature from Philadelphia and its vicinity hastened to publish an indignant denial. This was dated May 18, 1831, and first appeared in the *American Sentinel* of Philadelphia and was widely copied. Meigs, *Ingersoll*, pp. 167–185.

told Mr Livingston all that General Smith had told me as to the wish of the President's immediate advisors, that the Bank question should be put by this Session. Mr Livingston rec^d. my communication with the utmost apparent cordiality, acknowledged the force of the argument and said the proposed mode of proceeding was exactly that one which he thought ought to be pursued. I then inquired if the President would oppose the Bank on the ground of its unconstitutionality; he answered that he would not, but that he had certain notions of his own as to the frame of the charter which ought to be complied with. Let his friends frame it as they will, said I, provided their alterations are not destructive of the Institution. What are they? First that it should hold no real estate but what is indespensably necessary. Granted, there is no harm in that. Secondly, that the State should not be prevented taxing it. Thirdly, some addition to the Capital so as to let in new subscribers, and Lastly there is another provision, which he could not call to mind; very well, said I, I have no authority to remould the charter. I interpose only as the friend of Mr Biddle of the Bank, and the Administration, but I have no doubt that any reasonable modifications will be acquiesced in, only take the subject out of the hands of the President's opponents and let it be brought before Congress in such a shape that his friends may support it, and I offered to call upon Mr Dallas forthwith. Mr Livingston desired me to defer doing so for a few days promising in the mean while to have a full understanding with the President — he said he knew there were some who wanted him to veto it, and that he does not know what are the present sentiments of the Secretary of the Treasury whose official situation puts it out of his power to be passive or neutral as General Smith had said he designed to be. For himself Mr Livingston acknowledged that the President's various messages invited the immediate action of Congress upon the subject. I told him that as I had no object in view but the public good which I considered identified with the re-charter, I had no objection whatever to wait on the Secretary of the Treasury, or the President and speak to them in the same tone of candour and earnestness that I had used in communicating with him. Mr Livingston replied that the President would hear me with perfect attention & thankfulness and we agreed that at a proper time I should call upon him. In the mean while Mr Livingston will take the earliest opportunity of a full explanation with him, which he probably could not accomplish today because there is a large diplomatic dinner at the President's but he will try tomorrow. . . .

BIDDLE TO GEORGE McDUFFIE

Philad^a. Feby. 10. 1832

My dear Sir

. . . I cannot doubt, whatever may be the result, that we have done well in applying at the present session. When we were first warned against it lest it should affect the interests of one of the candidates for the Presidency, such a course seemed so entirely foreign to the duties of the Bank that we could not acquiesce in it for a moment. At a later period when we were counselled to abandon it, lest the influence of that candidate should crush the institution; that course seemed equally inadmissable, and we determined, that having begun, we would go through at all hazards; and that it was better even to be defeated in a fair field than to retreat. Into that field you have now probably led us; and on you much of the fate of the institution will depend. I have often heard the contemporaries of Mr Calhoun, in the Congress of 1816, speak with admiration of the talent, and tact, the gentleness and the firmness with which he carried the present Charter through the H of Reps. and we rely that the union of the same qualities will enable you to be equally successful now. . . .

BIDDLE TO CHARLES JARED INGERSOLL

Phil^a. Feby. 11. 1832

My dear Sir,

. . . Here am I, who have taken a fancy to this Bank & having built it up with infinite care am striving to keep it from being destroyed to the infinite wrong as I most sincerely & conscientiously believe of the whole country. To me all other considerations are insignificant — I mean to stand by it & defend it with all the small faculties which Providence has assigned to me. I care for no party in politics or religion — have no sympathy with Mr Jackson or Mr Clay or Mr Wirt [1] or Mr Calhoun or Mr Ellmaker [2] or Mr Van Buren. I am for the Bank & the Bank alone. Well then, here comes Mr Jackson who takes it into his head to declare that the Bank had failed & that it ought to be superceded by some ricketty machinery of his own contrivance. Mr Jackson being the President of the U.S. whose situation might make his ignorance mischeivous, we set to work to disenchant the country of their foolery & we have so well succeeded that I will venture to say that there is no man, no woman, & no child in the

---

[1] William Wirt of Maryland, Attorney-General under Monroe and presidential candidate on the Anti-Masonic ticket of 1832.

[2] Amos Ellmaker, Vice-Presidential candidate on the Anti-Masonic ticket of 1832.

U.S. who does not understand that the worthy President was in a great error. . . .[1]

It remains to see how its evil consequences may be averted. It seems to me there is no one course by which his friends may extricate him not merely safely but triumphantly. He has made the Bank a Power. He has made the Bank a deciding question as to his own selection. Now let him turn this power to his own advantage. As yet the Bank is entirely uncommitted — the Bank is neither for him nor against him. In this state let his friends come forward boldly, & taking the Bank out of the hands of their enemies, conciliate back the honest friends whom their rashness has alienated, and who think that the only difficulty which he has yet to overcome is the dread of their internal convulsion to which the prostration of the Bank will lead. The most extraordinary part of the whole matter is that the President & the Bank do not disagree in the least about the modifications he desires. He wishes some changes — The Bank agrees to them — and yet from some punctilio which is positively purile his rash friends wish him to postpone it. Do they not perceive that his enemies are most anxious to place him in opposition to the Bank? And should not every motive of prudence induce him to disappoint their calculations? The true & obvious theory seems to me to disarm the antagonists of their strongest weapon — to assume credit for settling this question for the administration. If the present measure fails, it carries bitterness into the ranks of the best part of the opposition. If it succeeds without the administration it displays their weakness. If the bill passes & the President negatives it, I will not say that it

[1] This paragraph is crossed out in the original. It might be noted that this part of the letter is stronger in its tone than the remainder.

will destroy him — but I certainly think it will & moreover I think it ought to. I can imagine no question which seems more exclusively for the representatives of the people than the manner in which they choose to keep & to manage the money of the people.

... I suppose the President has been made to believe that the Bank is busy in hostility to him — you know how wholly unfounded this is. For myself I do not care a straw for him or his rivals — I covet neither his man servant — nor even his maid servant, his ox nor any of his asses. Long may he live to enjoy all possible blessings, but if he means to wage war upon the Bank — if he pursues us till we turn & stand at bay, why then — he may perhaps awaken a spirit which has hitherto been checked & reined in — and which it is wisest not to force into offensive defence.

Ponder over these things — and believe me

BIDDLE TO CHARLES JARED INGERSOLL, ESQR.

Phil^a. Feby. 13. 1832.

My dear Sir

... Here is the Bank which most assuredly has been in its proper sphere, perfectly true, and faithful, to the administration; and which has never suffered itself, even while it believed itself very unkindly treated, to be betrayed into the slightest departure from its duty to the Gov^t. All the members of the Gov^t. can bear witness to this. The President himself has no hostile feeling towards the Bank, he is disposed to agree to its renewal with certain modifications, and the Bank is disposed to accept these modifications. And yet with no real difference between them, they are now playing into the hands of his enemies, who desire nothing better than to see us at variance. This certainly cannot be right. Is it not wiser for the Presidents friends to disarm at once his antagonists, of their strongest weapon, to settle the question at once; and thus unite all the Presi friends before the next election? This seems so clear, and obvious, that I am astonished that his friends do not immediately take the matter into their own hands, and settle it their own way.

Now what should prevent this reconciliation? If the President is restrained from making any advances, I have no such feeling, & I will make them myself. You know that I care nothing about the election. I care only for the interests confided to my care, and so far from having the least ill will toward the President, so far from wishing to embarrass his administration, I will do every thing consistent with my duty, to relieve it from trouble, and will go nine tenths of the way to meet him in conciliation. This is very easy. The whole can be settled in five minutes.

For instance, the President wishes some modifications in the charter. Well, let him take the charter and make any changes he likes, let him write the whole charter with his own hands, I am sure that we would agree to his modifications; and then let him and his friends pass it. It will then be his work. He will then disarm his adversaries, he will gratify his friends, and remove one of the most uncomfortable and vexatious public questions that can be stirred.

Now why could not this be? The moment is propitious and if done soon it will be done triumphantly. Do think of all these things, & if as a friend of the President, as well as of the Bank, you can accomplish this work of peaceful mediation, you will relieve both parties from an apparent misunder-

standing, you will confer a real benefit upon the country &
especially gratify,

Yours with great regard

CHARLES JARED INGERSOLL TO BIDDLE

Washington 21 Feb 32

Dear Sir

Thus stands the cabinet — The Secretary of State
with us with all his heart & all his head, anxious to be the
author of the President's conversion, who, he says, ought to
be fixed if any thing can fix him by Tibbit's Scheme. M^r. L.
is confident of succeeding, but has done nothing since my
last, not having had an opportunity of bringing the subject
before all the members of the cabinet together, not, in the
first instance, in form, nor till after he has secured a majority of them — he says he is constantly and hard at work for
us; but the bad weather and other interruptions have put
him back, but he promises every thing The Secretary of the
Treasury [1] with us, but so variable in his moods, so much
cooler at times than at others that M^r. L. says he is at a loss
what to think of him, after said M^r. L. — all the pains I have
taken with him.

The Secretary of War [2] with us entirely

The Secretary of the Navy [3] with us

The Atty Genl [4] against us — but M^r. L. hopes to con-
vert him — I found him just now closetted with Kendall, of
whom and Lewis I do not despair. My good understanding
with the Editor of the Globe is well settled. The Bank has
not a warmer or more active friend than Judge Wilkins.

[1] Louis McLane of Delaware.   [2] Lewis Cass of Ohio.
[3] Levi Woodbury of New Hampshire.   [4] Roger B. Taney of Maryland.

M^r. Livingston agrees with me as to the mollesse of his colleague. I expect to see you this week. In haste

The scheme of some of them, said M^r. L. is a bank of the US in each State, but that I consider impossible.

The more schemes and places the better.

CHARLES JARED INGERSOLL TO BIDDLE

Washington 23 Febr^y 1832

Dear Sir

... It is my fortune to have other subjects of confidential liaison with M^r. L. which operate favorably as inducement to similar understanding respecting the bank. After arranging those subjects yesterday at his house where I saw him, when I was about leaving his study without mentioning the bank — for he had told me the day before that it would require some days, and I am very cautious not to torment him with it — he himself introduced it by saying, I suppose you'll see Biddle at Philadelphia and let him know how matters are as to the bank. No doubt, said I. Well then, continued he, I wish you would ascertain from him whether the bank will agree to the President's views of the terms for a new charter, and he proceeded to recapitulate them. As my memory might fail me in some particulars, said I, suppose I make a written note of them. Very well, he rejoined — and accordingly I sat down at his desk, made the enclosed minute, with his assistance, read it to him when done — and we parted on the footing of his unreserved declaration of his desire that I would submit them for your approbation or otherwise, as may be. Tho' I send the original protocol — as it may be called, which I have dated and signed that you may keep it in Rei Vei testimonium — yet I proceed to rewrite the items, as the memorandum made yesterday is not perfectly plain from the hurry of writing it.

1. Government to have no interest in the bank.

2. President of the US empowered to appoint a Director at each branch so that government may be represented at each.

3. States authorized to tax the property both real & personal of the bank within the said States in like manner as the States may tax other property within them.

4. The bank to hold no real Estate but such as it may be constrained to take in payment or security of its debts, and to be compelled by law to sell that within stated time.

The foregoing I understand from M^r. L. are the President's terms.

5. A certain proportion of the stock or capital to be thrown open to new subscriptions, which may be done by prorata reduction of the present capital, or by addition to it.

This — 5 — is not the President's requirement: but M^r. M^r. L. seems to be very tenacious of it, always urging that it will facilitate very much the recharter.

6. The Directors to nominate annually two or three persons of whom the President to appoint any one as President of the bank.

This — 6 — neither the President nor M^r. L. like. It is the suggestion of others — he said. . . .

BIDDLE TO CHARLES JARED INGERSOLL

Phil^a. Feby. 25th 1832.

My dear Sir

You are the Coryphaeus of Ambassadors. Talk not to me of Talleyrand or Luchhesini,[1] or even the great

[1] A distinguished diplomat of Frederick the Great. "His commanding

magician of New York. Your letter of the 23ᵈ. inst has given me great pleasure & I have answered it in a tone which I think will smooth all difficulties. If it pleases, the next thing is to obtain some overt act, some decisive committal — for the extreme mobility of the principal person in our drama, makes me anxious to see him fixed — irretrievably committed. What is specially to be desired is, that he should with his friends, announce decidedly a suspension of hostilities, & then a firm & durable peace. This will give an impulse to their friends in Congress who may thus unite in promoting the object. Here again I rely on your judgment & skill so conspicuously displayed hitherto.

While I am writing your son has called & shown me your letter to him, of which due notice has been taken. . . .

BIDDLE TO CHARLES JARED INGERSOLL, ESQ.

Philadᵃ. 26ᵗʰ Feby. 1832.

My dear Sir

I yesterday wrote a hasty letter explaining my views in regard to the modifications suggested of the Charter of the Bank. In addition to what was then said of the disposition of the Bank, to acquiesce in any modification which may protect the rights of the States from any encroachment by the Bank I will now add that if the President wishes to stipulate that no new Branch shall be established without

demeanour and vivacity of speech, added to great powers of work, and acuteness in detecting the foibles of others, made him a formidable opponent. Further, his marriage with the sister of Bischoffswerder, until lately the King's favourite adviser, added to his influence, which, as was natural with a foreigner, inclined toward the attractive and gainful course. Long afterwards the saviour of Prussia, Baron von Stein, classed him among the narrow, selfish, insincere men who had been the ruin of nations." Cf. Rose, J. H., *William Pitt and the Great War* (London, 1912), p. 203; also cf. Seeley, *Stein*, vol. I, p. 65.

the assent of the State in which it is proposed to locate it, I think there would be no objection to it on the part of the Bank

In truth I believe there is no change desired by the President which would not be immediately assented to by the Bank. And this it is which gives me so much regret, to find the President & the Bank apparently estranged while there is really no difference between them, and to see the Presidents friends lose the present opportunity of settling the question so well, & so advantageously for him.

CHARLES JARED INGERSOLL TO BIDDLE

Washington 1 Mch 32

Dear Sir

   ... In handling your letter to Mr Livingston yesterday I made good use of the crisis which the annoying resolution occasions. He assures me, and you may rely, that the President has nothing to do with it, nor with Root's resolutions.[1] Not at all, said M^r. L. He wishes to end the business this Session. If such a bill goes to him as he can sign he will sign it without hesitation. If not, he will be equally prompt to reject it. Thus we have the mind of the President without doubt, if M^r. L's word is to be taken, of which I have not a particle of misgiving and I feel confident that his is the predominating influence. When I told him so, he said certainly the President knows that he seeks nothing, not even to be where he is, and can have no motive but the honor of the admin— ...

[1] Introduced in the House of Representatives as an amendment to Clayton's resolution. Rejected in the House March 8, 1832, by a vote of 88 ayes to 92 nays. *Cong. Debates*, vol. VIII, pt. II, pp. 1888, 2087.

CHARLES JARED INGERSOLL TO BIDDLE

Washington 6 Mch 32

Dear Sir

. . . I think I have gathered a motive for M^r. McDuffie's [1] almost unaccountable capitulation: if so there was more method than madness in it. The Speaker informs me that M^cD told him that he did not mean nor wish to let the bank be discussed before the Tariff. Hence his yielding to an inquiry which will just occupy in his reckoning the few weeks to elapse before the Tariff becomes the topic. This being so, or at any rate, I have another plan to counteract him: that is, soon after the bank has invited investigation, as I expect it to do tomorrow, and a committee is appointed accordingly, to get the subject taken up in Senate and a bill sent to the h of R if possible before the Tariff is before them. I had an interesting conversation yesterday with M^r. Livingston on this subject. What do you think of a plan, said I, by which Pennsylvania shall yield something of the tariff to the well disposed and moderate of Virginia and the Carolinas in equivalent for their uniting with her in support of such a modified bank as the President approves and thus firmly securing tariff bank and union altogether? I like it very much said he. But can you accomplish it since McDuffie has given way to the enquiry? I do not consider that, said I, indispensible. There is a very strong spirit in Pennsylvania for the bank, I mean in the delegation, and they do not intend to let M^r. McDuffie surrender their desire for his views. I am sensible, said he,

[1] Refers to McDuffie allowing the Clayton Resolution of investigation to pass. Ingersoll and the other Biddle constituents were thoroughly aroused by McDuffie's capitulation. Adams declared he was "either a coward or a traitor"; while Ingersoll "thought it was want of nerve and coolness."

that your delegation is very much bent on the bank. . . .
What do you think, said I, of my prevailing on M^r. Madison to
appear before the public recommending such a compromise?
I believe I c^d get him to do it. Very well, said he: or, I continued, shall it begin at some primary assembly in Pennsylvania? The difficulty now, after all I have understood from
you, is not with the Executive, but with Congress. Yes, said
he, this unlucky resolution of inquiry; but for that I think
there would be no difficulty. The President would sign such
a bill as you and I have arranged. I have never heard him
say so. But I have good reason to rely on it. (I think those
were his very words.)

Thus, you perceive, that McDuffie and Clayton agreeing
in opposition to the Tariff, and that the Tariff is the first
consideration, have, no doubt without concert, contrived
between the resolution of the one and the concession of the
other to postpone the bank lest it should by its combinations
of votes interfere with their primary object and this sus-
pends all the inclining of the President to give way to what
he is I am persuaded more alarmingly satisfied is the settled determination of that State without whose hearty good
will his stan dets.[1] Such is the state of things we have to
deal with. If a Pennsylvanian capable of taking the lead
would now do so on the footing of accommodating the President and the South by some modification (which can be well
afforded) of the Tariff in return for most of them (for I do not
expect all) yielding their objections to a modified bank, it
would be that Pennsylvanians certain road to honor, influence and office. I mean to sound Wilkins about it this very
day. I shall probably meet him at the Atty Genl's dinner or

---

[1] Illegible in the original.

at Serverius ball, and I will make it a point to set the inducement before him. If, as I presume, Dallas was yesterday
nominated at Harrisburg, it leaves W. no better if other
chance of promotion. He has already intimated in the Senate
his desire to compromise the Tariff and I know from M[r].
Livingstons frequent urgency to me that such a movement
would win Jackson's heart. . . .

BIDDLE TO JOHN G. WATMOUGH [1]

Phil[a]. May 11. 1832
10. o'clock

My dear Sir

. . . On the subject of printing & printers I have no
difficulty & no reserve as you may have seen in the course
of the enquiry. The press is the channel of communication
between the Bank & the Country, and I have no more difficulty about remunerating privately for the work done on
account of the Bank, than I would for paying the passage of
the clerks of the Bank, in a steam boat or a stage when they
were travelling on the business of the Bank. Why should we?
If the grocer at the corner wishes to apprize the Community
that he has some fresh figs, he is obliged to pay the Editor
of the Newspaper by the inch, it would not be fair therefore to let the Editor do work in every respect similar for the
Bank, without any remuneration, while he has to pay for
paper & types & printing. I will thank you therefore to ask
M[r] Gales to print six thousand extra copies of his paper containing M[r] Adams' & your report together, and send them
to proper persons in proper places. . . .

---

[1] Representative from Philadelphia County. Cf. results of the investigating
committee and its report in Catterall, *op. cit.*, p. 230.

BIDDLE TO THOMAS CADWALADER

May 30. 1832.

Dear Sir,

On my arrival I [1] began with a full and frank conversation with Mr. McLane on the subject of the Bank and at his suggestion saw Mr. Livingston — after which they conferred — and I saw Mr. Livingston.

The general purport of my communication was this. The investigation has given a new aspect to our affairs — it disarms, or ought to disarm some of the hostility hitherto entertained toward it, and furnishes a new motive for pressing a decision. Under these circumstances it would be very agreeable if the Executive would concur in promoting the object — which we would gladly attain by accepting such modifications as would be agreeable to the administration. I stated moreover the extreme awkwardness of having such a measure before Congress while the Department to which it belonged had no cognizance of it and my anxiety to cooperate with the Executive in modifying and perfecting the measure. I need not detail peculiarity of their situation which makes them passive and all that I could learn from Mr. Livingston was that the awkwardness was irretrievable — and that it only remained to make the bill as unexceptionable as possible.

We have then parted good friends.

BIDDLE TO THOMAS CADWALADER

Washⁿ. June 5, 1832
Tuesday 5 o'clock

My dear General,

For the last week I have been expecting daily to re-

---

[1] Biddle went to Washington May 20, with the idea of conducting his own campaign. This letter is printed in Catterall, *op. cit.*, pp. 232, 233, note 3.

turn home, & was willing therefore to spare you & myself the trouble of corresponding, when we could so much more readily converse about the matter. It has been a week of hard work anxiety & alternating hopes & fears, but I think that we may now rely with confidence in a favorable result. You know how many difficulties are to be overcome — how many hostilities are to be encountered; how many friendly indiscretions and weaknesses are to be repaired, in a work like this. I think moreover that it has reached a point where we may promise ourselves some rest. The Senate are now occupied with what I consider the most decisive point of the whole question — and being obliged to leave the capitol to prepare for some company to dine with me, I write these views as preliminary to the news which the Senators who are to be my guests may bring with them. They have come. This day like yesterday has been consumed in rejecting a very distracting & dangerous proposal to exchange a bonus for the obligation to discount at five per cent. I have been at work all day to get rid of it — and we have succeeded by a vote of 26 to 18 in excluding it. Tomorrow we shall have something decisive.

BIDDLE TO THOMAS CADWALADER

Washⁿ July 3. 1832.
Tuesday evening

My dear Genl,

. . . The Senate immediately agreed to the amendment so that the *Bill has finally passed.* [1] I congratulate our friends most cordially upon their most satisfactory result. Now for the President. My belief is that the President will

---

[1] Bill passed the Senate 28 to 20. *Cong. Debates*, vol. VIII, pt. I, p. 1073.

Nicholas Biddle
From a miniature by Henry Inman

veto the bill though that is not generally known or believed. This however we shall soon see.

DANIEL WEBSTER TO THOMAS CADWALADER

Washington July 5. 1832

My Dear Sir,

Mr Biddle left on yesterday. I feel it to be a duty to express to those particularly interested in the Bank, my sense of the great benefit which has been derived from his presence and attention here. We should have done but badly without him. His address & ability, in satisfying the doubts of friends, softening the opposition of enemies, & explaining whatever needed explanation, have been important cause in producing the result, which has, so far, attended the Bill. I can assure you, that this is not only my opinion, but that of others, also, the most competent observers & judges. At dinner, yesterday, where gentlemen were speaking of the subject, a very distinguished person observed, "that it was only once in a century that a man was to be found so eminently fitted to be the head of such an Institution as Mr B." ... I am, Dear Sir, with very true regard.

W. CREIGHTON TO BIDDLE

Washington July 10th 1832

Dear Sir,

Mr. Van Buren arrived at the Presidents on Sunday night, and to day the President sent to the senate his veto on the Bank bill.[1]

---

[1] Richardson, *op. cit.*, vol. II, pp. 576 *et seq.*

WILLIAM G. BUCKNOR [1] TO BIDDLE

July 12th. 1832

My dear Sir

You will perceive by the Papers to day what effect the Veto has had upon your Stock, and the Stockholders have now the satisfaction of being acquainted with the objections which have influenced General Jackson in refusing a renewal of the Charter. The period has arrived in which those interested in the Bank have no hope but from your exertions and the only means are to endeavour to defeat his election which as far as I can learn may be accomplished by opposing to him one or more of those Papers in this State whose influence & circulation is great and that this can be arranged I am confident. I am only anxious an immediate attack should be made upon him, for to be effective it must be made at once. I have had a conversation with Webb [2] who I am sure is ready, very little is required to turn this state and I think it can be done. I take the liberty of offering you one Suggestion, which is, that at the present moment of excitement it would be a matter of serious accommodation to the Stockholders many of them, if directions were given to the Branch here to lend on the Stock either temporarily or on the 1st. of October without grace when they can have time to make other arrangements. I pray you to believe that this is disinterested as regards myself.

BIDDLE TO WILLIAM G. BUCKNOR

Phil[a]. July 13. 1832

My dear Sir

I had this morning the pleasure of receiving your

[1] Bucknor and Biddle, brokers of New York.
[2] James Watson Webb, editor of the *New York Courier and Enquirer*. Cf. sketch of life in Bennett, James G., *Memoirs* (New York, 1885), p. 105.

favor of the 12th inst. & thank you for the suggestions it contains, which are I am sure dictated by the most friendly disposition to the Bank. The subject, as you may readily suppose, has occupied much of my thoughts, so that I am able to speak of it at once but after very deliberate reflection.

I am very sensible of the value to the Bank of the result contemplated & fully aware of the importance of what you mention in accomplishing that result. But the agency of the Bank in contributing to it is a matter of very grave consideration. When the Bank was denounced by the President, & all the influences of his patronage arrayed against it, it was an obvious duty not to suffer the institution to be crushed by the weight of power — but to appeal directly to the country — and as the whole channel through which the understandings of the community could be reached was the press, we strove to disseminate widely correct information in regard to the Bank. That object is accomplished. The Bank is fairly before the country and large majorities of both houses of Congress have decided in its favor. One individual has however opposed his will to the deliberate reflections of the representatives of the people — and the question now is whether the Bank ought to exert itself to defeat the reelection of that person who is now the only obstacle to its success. On that question I have made up my mind that to interfere in the election would be a departure from the duty which the Bank owes to the country. The first law of its existence is entire and unqualified abstinence from all political connexions & exertions. This it has hitherto practised, and whatever may be the consequences, must continue to practise. The temptations to a contrary course are I feel very great, but

I believe it to be the duty of the Bank to resist them. If I could permit myself to do otherwise, it would have an additional satisfaction in the prospect of serving one who has I think been very hardly and unjustly treated by his political associates.

You will easily believe that I think our differences of opinion on this subject arise merely from our looking at the object from different points of view, for I think in my situation You would probably entertain the same sentiments. I shall always be glad to hear from you whenever you have leisure, & remain.

BIDDLE TO HENRY CLAY [1]

(*private*)   Phil\a. August 1\st 1832
My dear Sir
          You ask what is the effect of the Veto. My impression is that it is working as well as the friends of the Bank and of the country could desire. I have always deplored making the Bank a party question, but since the President will have it so, he must pay the penalty of his own rashness. As to the Veto message I am delighted with it. It has all the fury of a chained panther biting the bars of his cage. It is really a manifesto of anarchy — such as Marat or Robespierre might have issued to the mob of the faubourg St Antoine: and my hope is that it will contribute to relieve the country from the dominion of these miserable people. You are destined to be the instrument of that deliverance, and at no period of your life has the country ever had a deeper stake in you. I wish you success most cordially, because I believe the institutions of the Union are involved in it.

[1] This letter is published in Colton, *op. cit.*, vol. IV, p. 34.

THE BANK OF THE U.S. *to* JOHN S. BIDDLE,   *Dr.*

For 20ᵐ copies Mʳ MᶜDuffie's report from the minority of the Comᵉᵉ appointed to examine BUS.
a 21 $.   420

12ᴹ copies Mr Adams' separate report from same
Coᵐᵉᵉ at 22 $.   264

25ᴹ copies Mʳ Websters speech on the President's
veto message on the Bill rechartering BU.S. 25 $ 500

50ᴹ copies (German & English edition) "review" of
the President's veto Message on the bill rechar-
tering B U S. a $20   1000

10ᴹ copies Mr Smith's report to the Senate on be-
half of the Comᵉᵉ of finance on B U.S. a $12.   120

20ᴹ copies report of Comᵉ Ways & Means to the H
of R. on B U.S. Mr McDuffie Chairman a $10.   200

10ᴹ copies report of the Secʸ of Treasʸ. on BUS. $9   90
Expenses incurred for transportation & circula-
tion of the following documents 748.71
                                                        ———————
                                                        $3,242.71

Philᵃ. Sepʳ. 20, 1832
                          Received payment
                                  JOHN S. BIDDLE

                    BIDDLE TO JOHN TILFORD

                                  Philᵃ. Septʳ 26ᵗʰ 1832

Dear Sir

        I send by this mail Mʳ. Websters speech on the Veto
Message, and also another article reviewing that message. It
is desirable that these should be circulated so as to counteract the injurious impressions which the message was destined
to make against the Institution. You will therefore cause the
papers, as well as Mʳ. Clay's & Mʳ. Ewing's speeches on the
same subject or any other well written articles in regard to
the Bank to be printed and dispersed. If you think any of
these I have mentioned too long or elaborate for general

reading, you can substitute any other matter which may
have the same object. All that I wish to caution you against
is, that abstaining as the Bank does from all connexion with
what are called party politics, you will confine your efforts
exclusively to the distribution of what may be explanatory
of the operations and conduct of the Bank. Confined to that
object exclusively, you may cause to be printed and circulated any amount of such papers as you may consider necessary for the vindication of the Bank and give me an account
of the expense, which you will of course endeavor to make as
reasonable as may consist with the object in view.

BIDDLE TO JOHN RATHBONE JR.[1]

Phil*. Nov*. 21** 1832

My dear Sir

. . . The Bank does not mean to commence any systematic reduction of its loans with a view to winding up its
affairs. It does not mean to begin to close its concerns. It
means to go on in its general business just as if no such event
as the President's negative had ever happened. The only
alteration it proposes is rather in the form than in the amount
of its loans — an alteration which under any circumstances,
it would be disposed to recommend — and it is this — to give
gently and gradually the loans of the Bank the direction of
domestic bills, converting where it can be done the line of
notes discounted, into domestic bills of exchange, which being payable at maturity, will give the Institution a greater
command over its funds. . . .

[1] A powerful financier from New York. One of the directors of the New York
and Erie Railroad. Wilson, *op. cit.*, vol. III, p. 416, note.

COLT (?) TO BIDDLE

Paterson 8 Decr 1832.

My dear Sir

. . . If the Secretary of the Treasury comes out against
the Bank, & which I am now disposed to doubt, since I find
who are interested in depressing Stock, I think You ought at
once, to call a Meeting of the Whole Board and consult with
them, whether a meeting of the Stockholders should not be
called — that the affairs of the Bank may be examined into,
with a view of putting down the calumnies heaped upon its
present administration — the reason given to the Public for
the call might be, to ask directions or instructions from the
Stockholders on the subject of curtailing the discounts &
withdrawing the Southern & western Branches — this would
frighten the men at Washington not a little — it is astonish-
ing what a change the Message [1] has produced — no one
doubts for a moment had this message come out 6 weeks ago
that Jackson would have lost his Election & Yet in 6 weeks
more, it will be the flinging up of Caps & hurrah for Jackson
— he is all right — the Bank must be put down — the Tariff
must be put down — so must the Supreme Court — & the
Lands given to the Western States & internal improvements is
worse than bad. I really think You ought to curtail Your
Discount in Tenessee, Mobile, Charleston, Savanna, & Virginia. I would let these people feel a pressure — but not of
course so as to cause failures — give orders at Same time
that in all instances at the Southern & Southwestern Offices
Where more is offered than they can do, to discount first
the Drafts on the Northern & Eastern Cities & refuse the

---

[1] Richardson, *op. cit.*, vol. II, pp. 599, 600.

domestic Notes unless the discounts are made of better paper to enable the offerer to take up a Note held by the Bank. Your true plan is now to encrease even Your Loans to a man, if You can thereby make a doubtful debt secure, so the great object is now to see how much You can repay the Stockholders, upon the Supposition the Bank is to be wound up in 5 Years. . . .

CHARLES JARED INGERSOLL TO BIDDLE

Washington Jan[y] 18/33

Dear Sir

During the few days of my stay here I have made it a point to ascertain from good authority what the probability is as to the bank of the U S; the result is an assurance that some time during one of the Sessions of the next Congress, the Executive will invite their attention to the subject,[1] and submit a plan, which, with modifications, such as the Legislative and Executive may eventually agree upon, will become the institution. What the plan is I did not inquire. Not withstanding all that has passed it is impossible to travel ever so short a distance as from philadelphia to Washington without perceiving universal preference and undiminished confidence in the papers of the bank of the U S. . . .

JOHN SERGEANT TO BIDDLE

Washington Mar: 2. 1833.

My dear Sir,

. . . Looking forward, tho' the present excitement will

---

[1] On January 4, 1830, James A. Hamilton had furnished President Jackson with a scheme for the creation of five "offices of deposit." Bassett, *Jackson*, vol. II, p. 603.

cease, and the composition of Congress be different and less favorable, there are still to be discerned the elements of hope. The new state of parties will be founded upon a combination of the South, and the leaders of it (the Southern party) are friends of the Bank upon principle, and will be more so from opposition to Jackson. If they succeed in their first object, of uniting the South, they will carry the whole of it in favor of the Bank, either actively or passively, those who cannot act in that direction, becoming neutralised and Quiescent. In the middle and Northern States, and in the West too, their view as to the Bank question will be an argument to gain friends for their party. Against a combination which threatens to be so powerful, Van Buren will have to look for alliances in the North, I think, and in so doing will be obliged to give up his hostility to the Bank. It is quite possible, indeed, that he may come into conjunction with some of its most decided friends. In the mean time, Jackson's influence will be diminishing, and his personal feelings will by no means have the same weight as heretofore. And, besides, I think he will be pressed by so powerful an opposition, that even he will be obliged to behave himself with some decency.

What I have thus hinted at, is no doubt the subject of calculation with those who are looking to the future, and I shall be surprized if even at the next session there be not an altered tone towards the Bank in Congress, less ferocity among its opponents, and more confidence on the part of its friends, who, by the way, can never be too much commended for the zeal and courage they have manifested under the most unpromising circumstances. . . .

John G. Watmough to Biddle

Washington Saturday
March 23. 1833

My dear Sir
 . . . The rumor here now is, that both Van Buren [1]
& McLane are opposed to the removal of the Deposits. I have
no news for you & it only remains for me to repeat the warm
assurance of esteem & regard, with which I shall ever remain,
my dear sir

Biddle to Daniel Webster

Phila. April 8. 1833

My dear Sir,
 I have received your favor of the 7th inst. I have no
information of the intended removal of the deposits, though
my opinion is that they will not *dare* to remove them. Nevertheless it is very desirable that whatever is done in the way
of pacification should be done soon — for if the deposits are
withdrawn, it will be a declaration of war which cannot be
recalled. . . .

Henry Clay to Biddle

Ashland 10th April 1833

My Dear Sir
 I have received your favor of the 25h. ult: and perused
its interesting contents with much satisfaction. Your friendly
solicitude to prevent any estrangement between Mr. W.[2]

[1] For Van Buren's attitude on the removal of deposits, cf. Bassett, *Jackson*,
vol. II, pp. 631, 640, 740.
[2] This letter refers to a former communication of Biddle to Clay on the question of the Compromise Tariff. On March 25 Biddle wrote Clay that he had en-

and myself adds another to the many previous obligations under which you had placed me. I concur entirely with you in thinking that, on every account, such a change in the amicable relations between that gentleman and myself would be very unfortunate.

After the introduction of the Compromise bill, it was manifest at Washington that a few of the Eastern friends of Mr. W., supposing that I had taken a step that would destroy me in the public estimation, indulged hopes that a new party would be formed, of which he might be the sole head. I thought that Mr. W. himself made an unprovoked and unnecessary allusion to me when, in describing the struggles of Mr. Calhoun in a Bog, he stated that no friend could come to his relief without sharing in his embarrassment. Even the female part of the audience understood to whom the allusion was directed. I need not say to you that I felt myself under no sort of obligation to Mr. Calhoun himself or to the State from which he came; that I had experienced nothing but unkindness from both; and that I have come under no engagement whatever with him in regard to the future. If S° Carolina had stood alone, or if she could have been kept separated from the riot of the South in the contest which I apprehended to be impending, I should not have presented the measure which I did.

On a subsequent occasion Mr. W. imputed to me, in a manner I thought unfriendly, an abandonment of the Protective policy. To that suggestion an immediate reply was made. And

deavored to change Webster's opinion on the subject; and that while Webster was visiting in Philadelphia he had prevented the Senator's friends from giving a public dinner for fear it might "furnish an occasion for his less discreet friends to do and say things inexcusable at a moment of excitement." Webster left the city "in a frame of mind entirely satisfactory."

to his chief attack upon the bill itself a prompt answer was given, which you had seen in the public prints. Whatever momentary feelings were excited, during the progress of the measure, I assure you after it was carried that they entirely ceased; and all my sentiments of attachment to Mr. W. returned in their undiminished strength. I took several occasions to evince to him this state of my heart; and I was happy to believe that it was fully reciprocated by him. I assure you that on my part these feelings shall be constantly cherished.

You will have heard from him or others that the Compromise [1] was not offered until after the fullest and freest conferences with him and others. Two distinct meetings at my quarters of 11 or 12 Senators (at the first of which he attended, and to the last he was summoned) took place, in which it was fully discussed and considered. At the last I interrogated each Senator individually, and I understood every one to agree substantially to the bill (for I had prepared a bill) except one, who finally voted for it. Several of those who had, as I supposed, assented to it voted against it.

I do not now think that the course of Mr. W. and other gentlemen from the East and North who voted with him, is to be regretted — certainly not, if the difference of opinion should produce, and it ought to produce, no alienation between friends. Many of them I know so voted, from considerations of policy, rather than from any positive objections to the bill. And the course which they pursued will probably tend to reconcile the South more strongly to a measure, in which it has got a nominal triumph, whilst all the substantial advantages have been secured to the Tariff States. . . .

---

[1] Compromise Bill passed the House, February 26, 1833, 119 to 85; Senate on March 1, 29 to 16.

BIDDLE TO DANIEL WEBSTER

Phil^a. April 10, 1833

Dear Sir,

I wrote to you to day that Mr L. would be in New York. I write to you again to say that I think it would be well to see him. The whole question of peace or war lies in the matter of the deposits. If they are withdrawn, it is a declaration of war. It is wiser therefore to begin the work of peace before any irrevocable step is taken.

ROBERT W. GIBBES TO BIDDLE

Private   Baltimore 13th. April 1833.

My D^r. Sir,

The contents of this letter you will comprehend, when you connect with it a late conversation held by yourself with a mutual acquaintance of ours, and to whom an unexpected opportunity has been offer'd of gaining the following information, on which you may *rely* as of the *highest*, & most *direct authority*.

You need not be informed of the hostility of the Administration to the Institution over which you preside, but the following items must prove interesting. At this moment the opinion of the different members as to the immediate withdrawal of the Government Deposites is asked, and their individual opinion stands thus. In the first place the President considers that he has conquered all of his difficulties but that of the Bank, & this he is determined to accomplish "coute qui coute." Were it left to Kendall & himself they would withdraw the Deposites immediately, but believing as they do, that the Bank has 40 or 50 millions discount in the Western Country, which it will be compelled to curtail, whether or no, they prefer the odium to rest on its Head, instead of that of the Government. M^r McLane considers that the Government would be prostrated by their taking this step, and therefore is adverse to the withdrawal at present. The Post Master Genl. objects to the step at this moment also, but considers the convenience of making his Deposits in State Banks so important, that he contemplates asking permission (which he thinks will not be refused him) of making his separate deposits in them, — more especially as you will not permit him to overdraw, without a *confidential letter* from him to that effect. Taney is for immediate withdrawal. And the influence of such men as Com^e Stewart, Whitney, &c, is exerted to effect this object, which will produce the natural consequence of lowering the market value of the Stock. The present disposition of the influential party is to withdraw the deposits in October next. But the wily *Magician* is for throwing the responsibility on Congress, believing that they will have a sufficient majority to Carry their measure. His hostility to the Bank is implacable; and the various offers made to them by different State Banks tally's much better with their ulterior views than the security offered by the present mode of Deposit. In a few words, — if it be not determined on to withdraw the Deposits in October, the firm belief is, that the President, instead of *recommending* this measure in his next annual Message, will simply state in it some *definite period* when *he* is determined they shall be withdrawn.

I give you the above information at the request of M^r. Oliver, and should any thing further be communicated which we may deem important, you shall be made acquainted with it.

I need not point out the source of this information — but will merely add, that you may rely on the its correctness.

That it may prove of service to you is the sincere wish of

BIDDLE TO J. S. BARBOUR

(*private*)   Phil^a. April 16th. 1833.

My dear Sir

. . . The fact is that the real sin of the Bank in the eyes of the Executive is, that it is refractory & unmanageable. When these people first came into power on a current of overwhelming popularity, to which they thought every thing should yield, they considered the Bank a part of the spoil, and one of their first efforts was to possess themselves of the institution for the benefit of their partizans. We saw all that would follow from the slightest concession — and determined, since there must be War, to begin it in the frontiers by letting them know that they were to have nothing to do with the Bank. From that time they resolved, that as they could not bend it they would break it. This is the whole secret of the opposition to the institution. I know this so well that I feel myself a much more profound Jurist than all the lawyers and all the statesmen of Virginia put together, for in half an hour, I can remove all the constitutional scruples in the District of Columbia. Half a dozen Presidencies — a dozen Cashierships — fifty Clerkships — a hundred Directorships — to worthy friends who have no character and no money. Why, there is more matter for deep reflection in such a sentence than in any twenty of Tacitus or Montesquieu. It would outweigh the best argument of your Madisons & Randolphs & Watkins Leigh's. But that sentence, short and easy as it seems, shall never be written or said: and so we must go on to the end of the chapter, and the charter. . . .

THOMAS COOPER [1] TO BIDDLE

College, Columbia South Carolina
April 27. 1833

Dear Sir

I am in principle opposed to all Banks, and of course to that over which you preside. I wrote the review of that question in the Southern review. I have just written the article on Banks in the Southern Times of this place, which I send by this post. I have not varied in my good opinion of your personal Character, to which I have not omitted to bear willing testimony.

If I could oppose the banking system with success, I would do so; but I cannot. Under these circumstances, I very greatly prefer the renewal of your institution, to the Schemes of Gen¹. Jackson and Van Beuren; & I have determined to open upon them the battery of the Press here. Have you any facts or suggestions that you would be willing to communicate to me confidentially in aid of my design? If so, I will use them as I here propose. If not, all is well; I shall go on, with

[1] A distinguished scientist, writer, and politician of South Carolina. Cooper was born in London, October 22, 1759. After studying at Oxford, Cooper visited France where he became involved in the political struggles of that nation. In 1795 he came to America with Dr. Joseph Priestley; but, once more taking up the cudgel against government, he was tried under the Alien and Sedition laws for attacking the administration of John Adams. From 1811 to 1814 he held the chair of chemistry in Dickinson College; in 1816, the same chair at the University of Pennsylvania; and from 1820 to 1834, the presidency of the University of South Carolina. Dr. Cooper soon became interested in Southern politics and was a strong advocate of nullification. The character of the man can easily be discerned from this and the following letters to Biddle. Cf. sketch of life in Niles, June 22, 1839.

such observations as occur to me. You know me, and I presume will take for granted that I write in good faith, as a Gentleman ought. I am Dear Sir

I have communicated to no one, my intention of applying to you for information, nor shall I. I send you also a pamphlet.

BIDDLE TO THOMAS COOPER ESQ.

Phil\ª. May 6\ᵗʰ. 1833.

Dear Sir

. . . I have observed with great interest what you have written on the subject of the Bank. The truth is, that the question is no longer between this Bank & no Bank. It is a mere contest between Mr. Van Buren's Government Bank and the present institution — between Chestnut St and Wall St — between a Faro Bank and a National Bank. You do not perhaps know that soon after these people came into power, there was a deliberation in Caucus of the most active of the Jackson Party as to the means of sustaining themselves in place — and the possession of the Bank was ranked as a primary object. For this purpose they began in 1829 with an effort to remove an obnoxious President of one of the Branches — which was to be followed by a systematic substitution of their creatures throughout the whole institution. This experiment failed, owing to the firmness of the Directors who determined that they would not permit the interference of the Executive Officers. . . . From that moment they despared of turning the Bank to their political purposes, and have been intent on breaking it down to substitute some machinery more flexible. To that spirit, a new impulse has been given by a coterie of gamblers who having ascertained the views of the Executive before the last session of Congress and believing that they must be fatal to the Bank, made large contracts on time. These executive denunciations not having sufficiently lowered the stock to render the speculations safe or profitable, the parties are now endeavoring to force the Executive into the withdrawal of the public deposits, as a measure that would cover their retreat. This combination of political gamblers and gambling politicians is the key to the whole history of the relations between the Bank & the executive. Against that coalition, all honest men should exert themselves. I am extremely gratified therefore at the opening of that battery of yours, and shall be very glad to supply you with all the ammunition in my power. . . .

BIDDLE TO J. S. BARBOUR [1]

Phil^a. July 11th 1833

My dear Sir

I have had the pleasure of receiving your favor of the 7th inst. and am rejoiced to hear that your avowed purpose of acting next winter in the legislature has brought out an expression of corresponding sentiments in other quarters.

What should be deeply impressed on the minds of the Southern gentleman is, I think, this — that the administration people mean to unite in an outcry against any Bank, & having thus secured the cooperation of the constitutionalists in the destruction of the present Bank, they will then build up one of their own, leaving the Constitutionalists to be laughed at, after having been duped. The question is no longer open. It is a question between Chestnut St and Wall St. — a question whether the Central Gov^t. is to have the

[1] Representative from Virginia.

command of the revenues — a question between a Treasury Bank or an independent Bank.

Mr Gouge [1] was an assistant Editor of a party newspaper devoted to the cause of Mr Jackson & opposed to the Bank. He has retired from the paper and this book is among the fruits of his leisure. The work has attracted so little notice that I had never seen it, tho' I had observed the advertisement of it; nor have I ever heard it mentioned. In consequence of your letter, I have sent for a copy of it, and have run my eyes over it. Mr Gouge has no knowledge or experience of his own on the subject of which he treats, nor do I observe any thing either strong or original in the book, which consists of an accumulation of common place extracts such as any body could get together who wished to support a system of any sort. I ought not to speak so disparagingly, since I observe that he is very civil and complimentary to me personally, but really there does not appear to be much merit of his compilation. It is a book made with the scissors, & what is worse, a dull pair

THOMAS COOPER TO BIDDLE

Columbia S. Carolina
July 12. 1833

Dr Sir

I observe the Jackson administration, to conciliate Pennsylvania, have appointed W. J. Duane to the treasury, a

---

[1] William M. Gouge was the editor of the *Philadelphia Gazette* and for thirty years contributed articles on banking to various periodicals. He was connected for some time with the Treasury Department in Washington. His best-known works are: *The History of the American Banking System* (1835); *The Expediency of Dispensing with Bank Paper* (1837); and *Fiscal History of Texas* (1852). Gouge was a strong advocate of the Sub-Treasury and had great influence in trying to establish this system.

man of plain practical good sense, and I believe of good meaning; but he must of necessity in a short time adopt administration morals, which is a code identical under every administration of every form of government. He has written to the
editor of the *Times*, to send him the series of Essays signed
C. I shall send him the number of July 6 & that of to day
in my own name: I have not kept any but one copy of
the former numbers. I observe Ritchie [1] of Richmond is very
angry: of course: many people here think I abandon my principles; but I do not write for popularity, but for what I consider as just and true under the circumstances. To Gen¹.
Jackson, his proclamation & his force bill,[2] & to those who
support these measures, I have nothing to say but bellum
inter necinum. Degraded as we are, to a government whose
polar star is the omnipotence of parliament, I care but little
about modern politics here, except to oppose them.

BIDDLE TO ROBERT LENOX

Phil^a. July 30 1833

My dear sir
  . . . The gamblers are doing every thing in their power
to bend M^r. Duane to their purposes. But he knows them and
will not yield an inch. I feel entirely confident that he will do
his duty, and will leave his place rather than prostitute it.

I wish to wait a little while until the smoke blows off, before doing any thing very decisive. In the mean time I wish
you would keep within your income — and bring the State

---

[1] Thomas Ritchie, editor of the *Richmond Enquirer*. For Ritchie's actions
during these years see the admirable *Life* by Professor Ambler.

[2] Cf. Houston, David F., *Critical Studies of Nullification in South Carolina*
(Harvard Historical Studies, vol. III, 1896), pp. 128–130, 149; Phillips, Ulrich B.,
Georgia and State Rights (American Historical Association, Annual Report, 1901,
vol. II).

Banks in debt to you: and for the present it is better that you should do it — than that I should say it: for when once we begin, we shall have many things to do, which will crush the Kitchen Cabinet at once

BIDDLE TO SAMUEL SWARTWOUT [1]

(*confidential*)   Philad^a. July 30 1833

Dear Sir

A friend of mine and Mr Duane's asked me two days ago if there was any body in New York to whom I could recommend M^r. Duane, so that he might not be deceived and see things with his own eyes. I said that you were the very man. I have had no opportunity of seeing my friend since, to ascertain whether he had mentioned your name to M^r. Duane. Whether he did or did not however, you have the means of doing much good by frank communications with M^r. D. He I believe knows and feels that the toils of these gamblers are spread for him, and he ought to be helped in his honest efforts to disentangle himself. If these practices could once be brought home to a gang so as to satisfy the President and Secretary of their schemes, the country might be much benefitted

BIDDLE TO THOMAS COOPER

Phil^a. July 31st. 1833.

Dear Sir

. . . There is at this moment a strange scene before our eyes here. M^r. Duane, after much solicitation and with an unaffected hesitation accepted the place of Secretary — but he took it entirely untrammelled & unpledged. He had been a

[1] For Swartwout's activities during these years, cf. Fish, Carl R., *The Civil Service and the Patronage* (Harvard Historial Studies, vol. XI, 1905), pp. 114, 121, 139.

little time in Office when he was required to concurr in the schemes of Jackson and the Kitchen Cabinet against the Bank by withdrawing the deposits. This he refused. A mission has accordingly been set on foot to make arrangements with the State Banks to do the duties now performed by the Bank of the U.S. so as to deprive Mr. Duane of the objection that the change would incommode the public business. Of this mission Amos Kendall is the plenipotentiary, and he is expected here to-day. If he succeeds the attack will be resumed on M^r. Duane. But that gentleman will I am satisfied refuse, as he has already done. He will take a decided, firm, manly stand, and will leave his place rather than prostitute it. This will introduce a new state of things. The Kitchen Cabinet is already against M^r. Duane & will endeavor to expel him — but if he is only firm as I rely on his being, he may do much to break up this nest of gamblers. The result will be soon known. In the mean time I think we may be sure that M^r. Duane will be in flagrant opposition to the Kitchen Cabinet, that he has already refused, and will continue to refuse to yield to them. . . .

BIDDLE TO DANIEL WEBSTER

Phil^a. Aug 13. 1833.

My dear Sir

Altho' we do not feel anxious as to the result of the movements at Washington touching the Bank, still it is thought prudent to prepare for any adverse event and accordingly we have this day given instructions to the Branches to keep their discounts at their present amount — and to shorten the time for which they buy bills of exchange. This will make the institution strong & if any sudden movement is attempted by the Cabinet, proper or improper, we shall be ready. This will, I trust be temporary, as the squall may blow over.

BIDDLE TO THOMAS COOPER

Phil^a August 16th 1833.

My dear Sir

... This I know is their design. This very day, a gentleman in whom I have the utmost confidence, repeated to me a conversation which a friend of his had with M^r. Woodbury. In the course of it, the latter said, "We are not against a bank, but against the Bank" — "We went (this was his precise expression) to *scrabble* for the Stock and to have the Offices." "But," said the other, "what will you do with the constitutional question?" "Poh," said Woodbury, "that we can use to "suit ourselves." And this is what they all intend. I do not believe that a single member of the Cabinet has any constitutional doubts about the matter except M^r. Duane — and he, I incline to think, is almost, if not quite as firm, in his dislike to State Banks. He is entirely and cordially against the movement of Kendall & I cannot doubt he will resist the gamblers. ...

BIDDLE TO ROBERT LENOX

Phil^a Oct 1st. 1833.

My dear Sir

I have received this morning your letter of the 30th ulto. and have since had a long interview with Mr Rathbone to whom I explained our whole situation and views — and to whom I must refer you for more particulars than I have leisure to give.

After a great deal of reflection, we are all satisfied that the best thing to be done is to do as little as possible.[1] The exchange operations are placed by the resolutions passed to-day on a proper footing. We do not give any instructions as to reducing the local discounts, but we shall reduce ours at the Bank, and if you can gradually diminish yours without exciting uneasiness among our customers it would be very good policy. Our wish is not to give an order to that effect lest it might create alarm, but to do it quietly and imperceptibly.

The subject which has given us more anxiety than any other is the treatment of the Branch notes. We are now satisfied that our best plan is to continue to receive them as heretofore — and that your Office should do the same. The idea we have is this. The balances now in Bank will probably be absorbed by the disbursements of the Government and in the mean time the accruing revenue will be left with the new receiving Banks. There it may accumulate, and masses of it may be held sufficient to incommode some of the smaller Branches, to whom it may be suddenly sent. It is better for us therefore to absorb it — if we can — until the measures in operation at the Branches will reduce their issues so much as to make them not trouble us.

The closing of the mail so soon obliges me to stop.

DANIEL WEBSTER TO BIDDLE

Private   Boston Oct. 29. 1833
Dear Sir,
  I write this letter, as a private one, & for the purpose of inquiring whether the course for the adoption of the Bank is yet settled. The removal of the Deposites is a question of

---

[1] This letter follows Secretary Taney's order for the removal of the deposits.

great interest to the Government, & as such will doubtless attract the attention of Congress. It is, also, a matter of moment to the Bank, *as one part of their Charter*. In this point of view, it becomes a question whether the Bank should not lay the transaction of removing the Deposites, before Congress.

This, I have no doubt, you have already considered.

SAMUEL SWARTWOUT TO BIDDLE

N York 23 Nov. 1833

My dear Sir,

I have this moment read your kind letter of yesterday, and am bound to acknoledge that I do not deserve your support in the way proposed, for, from the immensely increasing commerce of this place, the Collector's duties have so much increased, that it is quite impossible for him to attend to the duties of a Director. Hence, it would be improper for me to accept it. I am nevertheless greatly obliged by your kind offer & tender you very grateful thanks for it.

Permit me in this letter to say a word on the subject of the present money pressure. It is dreadful here and no hope of relief excepting thro your Institution. You must be *liberal* and that to a great extent or you will destroy your friends, those who have hitherto sustained your cause and defended your course. Let me interest you to take this course, it is due to your numerous friends and the public at large would give your Institution credit for it. Now that the effect of the late measure has been made manifest, you can relieve the whole community and rely upon it you would recive due credit & consideration for it. I speak to you, my dear Sir, with the freedom of a friend. Would to God the Bank would take a noble, liberal course and thus justify itself to the world.

Nothing but extensive discounts, by your Institution can save your friends & the public in general. All the blame that has hitherto been cast upon you would be turned to commendation. The old friends and dependents of the Bank are perishing for want of aid. Surely the Institution cannot mean this? Rely upon it, my dear Sir, that [if] the Bank and its Branches were now to open the door to the Commercial Community, it would make more friends than it ever had. Its power has been shown, now let its mercy be manifested. The community is precisely in the situation to be most affected & most favourably too, by such a course. . .

DANIEL WEBSTER TO BIDDLE

Washington Decr. 21. 1833

Sir

Since I have arrived here, I have had an application to be concerned, professionally, against the Bank, which I have declined, of course, although I believe my retainer has not been renewed, or *refreshed* as usual. If it be wished that my relation to the Bank should be continued, it may be well to send me the usual retainers.

HENRY CLAY TO BIDDLE

(*Confidential*)   Washington 21st. Dec. 1833.

My dear Sir

. . . If the state of public opinion at Phila^d. should be such as to favor the operation, it would be well to have a general meeting of the people to memorialize Congress in favor of a restoration of the deposites. Such an example might be followed elsewhere; and it would be more influential as it might be more general.

If the local Banks could be induced to concur in such a movement so much the better.

I think it would be expedient to obtain, at the general meeting of the Stockholders in Jan. an expression of their approbation of the conduct of the Board, and particularly of the expenditure which has been made in defending the Bank ag^t. unfounded attacks.

We have before the Senate a nomination of the Gov^t Directors.

BIDDLE TO WILLIAM APPLETON [1]

(*private*)

B. U S
Jany 27th 1834

Dear Sir

... My own view of the whole matter is simply this. The projectives of this last assault on the Bank regret, and are alarmed at it — but the ties of party allegiance can only be broken by the actual conviction of existing distress in the community. Nothing but the evidence of suffering abroad will produce any effect in Congress. If the Bank remains strong & quiet, the course of events will save the Bank & save all the institutions of the country which are now in great peril. But if, from too great a sensitiveness — from the fear of offending or the desire of conciliating, the Bank permits itself to be frightened or coaxed into any relaxation of its present measures, the relief will itself be cited as evidence that the measures of the Gov^t. are not injurious or oppressive, and the Bank will inevitably be prostrated. Our only safety is in pursuing a steady course of firm restriction — and I have no doubt that such a course will ultimately lead to

[1] President of the Branch at Boston.

restoration of the currency and the recharter of the Bank. How soon this will take place, it is of course difficult to conjecture — but I have little apprehension as to the ultimate result.

HENRY CLAY TO BIDDLE

(*Confidential*)   Washington 2ᵈ. Feb. 1834
My dear Sir

. . . My opinion is that no movement should yet be made towards a renewal of the Charter, or the establishment of a New Bank. The Bank ought to be kept in the rear; the usurpation in the front. If we take up the Bank, we play into the adversary's hands. We realize his assertions that the only question is a renewal of the Charter. It is the usurpation which has convulsed the Country. If we put it by and take up the Bank, we may & probably would divide about the terms of the charter, and finally do nothing leaving things as they are. In the other course, the recharter will follow. The Country will take care of that.

HORACE BINNEY [1] TO BIDDLE

Washington 4 Feb. 1834
dear Sir,

I write rather at the instance of Mʳ Webster than at my own motion. He seems to think that the Bank ought to reduce as slowly & moderately as they can — & occasionally to ease off — where it is requisite to prevent extreme suffering. I told him that I supposed that the Bank meant to wind up, as a matter of necessity, arising from the hostility of the Treasury to them — and that if any thing was said by a friend of the currency, in regard to the BK reductions, it ought to

[1] Binney had been sent to Washington to carry on the struggle for recharter.

be said, with the remark that this was the necessary course of the Bank. His apprehension seemed to be, that the Admin was setting into action a strong sentiment of opposition to the Bank, on account of the reductions, & that it was desirable to meet it, either by declarations from the Bank of interested moderation, or something to that effect. My only remark to yourself is that I suppose the Board & yourself are the best judges. . . .

BIDDLE TO JOHN G. WATMOUGH

Phil^a Feby 8. 1834

My dear Sir

. . . You know better than I do what is to happen in Washington. What will happen in the Country unless Congress interposes, is but too manifest — the whole future is full of gloom and confusion. My own course is decided — all the other Banks and all the merchants may break, but the Bank of the United States shall not break. I have asked Com^e. Biddle what is the least sail under which a man of war can lie to in a gale of wind, and he says a close reefed main top sail. So our squadron will all be put under close reefed main top sails and ride out the gale for the next two years. As to those who have no sea room & breakers under their lee, they must rely on Providence or Amos Kendall.

BIDDLE TO JOSEPH HOPKINSON [1]

Phil^a. Feby 21st 1834

My dear sir

I have to thank you for four letters, all very interest-

[1] Distinguished lawyer of Philadelphia. Judge of the United States Court, Eastern District of Pennsylvania, 1828–1842.

ing & very welcome. The last only requires any answer & that
I will give very explicitly. You may rely upon it that the
Bank has taken its final course and that it will be neither
frightened nor cajoled from its duty by any small drivelling
about relief to the country. All that you have heard on that
subject from New York is wholly without foundation. The
relief, to be useful or permanent, must come from Congress &
from Congress alone. If that body will do its duty, relief will
come — if not, the Bank feels no vocation to redress the
wrongs inflicted by these miserable people. Rely upon that.
This worthy President thinks that because he has scalped
Indians and imprisoned Judges, he is to have his way with
the Bank.[1] He is mistaken — and he may as well send at
once and engage lodgings in Arabia . . .

John Sergeant to Biddle

(*Private*)   Washington, Feb. 27. 1834

My dear Sir,

The first thing of real importance I have heard since
I came here was communicated this morning by M^r. Calhoun. He asked me whether I had heard any thing from
M^r. Southard. I told him no. Well, he said, there is a letter
from M^r. S. in which he states as follows — That on his way
to Baltimore (on Tuesday) a New York Jackson man said
to him, "As you are going from Washington, I will tell you
what I would not have told you there. We (meaning himself
and some of his friends from New York) have been talking
with the President about the great and increasing distress,

---

[1] Biddle was urged by numerous friends not to give in to the administration. Many of his New York correspondents assured him that the Regency had
been destroyed and that Jacksonism was dead in their state.

and endeavouring to convince him that this state of things cannot continue — that some thing must be done. He (President) admitted he had heard some thing, but by no means to the extent we stated, of which he seemed to have no idea. The result was that the President drew up some questions for his cabinet, who were to deliberate upon what was to be done." As M^r. Southard has been in Philad^a. you will probably have heard all this, and heard it more accurately. The further fact, stated by M. Calhoun, is material, that there are daily meetings of the cabinet. He told me this yesterday, and then thought they were about changes in the administration. To day, he thinks they are upon the subject of the New Yorker's conversation, and considering the question "What is to be done." If they have come to that point, we shall soon see some movement. Strange as it may seem, I should not be at all surprized if M^r. Taney were to give up the Treasury, and some one else (perhaps Forsyth) take his place. In such an event we shall see a very queer game played. Genl. Jackson will look at the matter, as he does at every thing, singly with reference to himself, and will make any sacrifice that may be necessary to save his own reputation. It is in such emergencies that his greatest skill is exhibited, and it is quite unrestrained by any feeling for others.

M^r. Calhoun thinks they are upon a question of a new Bank. If any project should be brought forward, it will open the way for M^r. C. to bring forward his plan as a substitute. He is fully aware of the advantage would give him — He is at this time the most confident man in either house. He always speaks of the Administration as broken down and gone. . . .

BIDDLE TO SAMUEL BRECK [1]

Phil[a] March 1st 1834

My dear Sir

I have received today your favor of the 26th inst. with the copy of the Governor's Message.[2] I regret on many accounts that paper. It will prolong the distress now existing without effecting any good object, and it is melancholy to see a Governor of Pennsylvania thus aiding in the destruction of Pennsylvania interests. What makes it more shocking is, that up to the very moment of sending the message, those who visited him left him under the strongest conviction that he was decidedly friendly to the Bank. In truth he ought to have been, for so far from frustrating his loan, the Bank actually furnished to Mess[s]. Allen the means of paying the last instalment, as the Governor well knew. Of the effect of his message on the Bank and upon the financial concerns of Penns[a]. you will form some idea when I mention to you the following fact which is a little singular.

A Committee from New York has been visiting the Bank for the purpose of procuring some relief for that city which would of course have reacted on our own State. Yesterday the Board was to have decided it, & I have no doubt that the Bank would have made an effort to give relief — but when we saw the Governors message — saw how totally useless the efforts of the Bank had been to sustain the credit of the State in

[1] A merchant, born in Boston, 1771, and died in Philadelphia, 1862. He was a member of the Pennsylvania Legislature many years, elected as a Federalist to the 18th Congress serving from December 1, 1823, to March 3, 1825; wrote an historical sketch on Continental paper money in 1843. Cf. Fisher, J. F., *Memoirs of Samuel Breck* (Philadelphia, 1863).

[2] Governor Wolf denounced the Bank in his message. Cf. Niles, vol. 46, pp. 26, 27.

appeasing the spirit of the party — and how little reliance could be placed on the men in power, we determined that it was in vain to make an effort — and accordingly, instead of sending the relief expected, we wrote to the New York Committee that the conduct of the Governor of Pennsylvania obliged the Bank to look to its own safety, and that therefore we declined doing any thing at present.

So much for the first effect of the Governors patriotism

BIDDLE TO CHARLES HAMMOND [1]

Phil[a]. March 11. 1834

Dear Sir

... Your remarks in regard to the proposed reduction of the loans at Cincinnati have been read with great attention and interest. Situated as the Bank has been for some time past, its first object was necessarily its own protection, for in its safety the whole ultimate security of the currency must be found. This we have striven to accomplish with the least possible pressure on the community — and thus far the reductions compared with the deposits are so small, that our friends rather reproach us with not having done enough, than to have curtailed excessively. The deposit Banks being now in full possession of the public revenue may employ it in discounts and leave the Bank of the United States the opportunity of gently diminishing its business. That with so wide a circulation as 18 or 19 millions which the receipts of the public revenue may place in the hands of officers who know that no service more acceptable

---

[1] Distinguished lawyer and journalist of Cincinnati. He became associated with the editorial staff of the *Cincinnati Gazette* in 1823 and in 1825 was made editor in chief. Cf. sketch of life in Greve, Charles T., *Centennial History of Cincinnati* (Chicago, 1914), vol. I, pp. 805, 806.

can be rendered than to employ the funds in injuring the Bank, and so many vulnerable points to protect, we shall deem it expedient to reduce the present amount of our loans, cannot be doubted. The Executive, by removing the public revenues has relieved the Bank from all responsibility for the currency, and imposed upon it a necessity to look primarily to the interest of the Stockholders committed to our charge. Our friends must therefore bear with us, if in the midst of the present troubles, we should endeavor to strengthen the Bank so as to make it able here after to interpose effectively for the relief of the Country. . . .

BIDDLE TO SAMUEL JAUDON

Phila March 11. 1834

My dear sir

　　I received this morning your letter of the 9th & read with great interest all its details. You and our friend Mr Chauncey [1] now understand so well the whole ground that I shall join you in any opinion which you may ultimately adopt. Let us go for the practical. If we can get a permanent charter, let us do so — if not, let us take the temporary & make it permanent hereafter. Above all, let us do something soon. The country now wants something to rally to — it requires some point on which to concentrate its thoughts. In the present fusion of opinions, a stamp may be impressed, which will hereafter be more difficult as men's minds cool.

　　I go tomorrow to New York to see into the real state of things.

---

[1] Owner of Fenno's old paper, the *United States Gazette*. Cf. Oberholtzer, *op. cit.*, vol. II, pp. 112, 113.

James Watson Webb to Biddle

Washington D.C
March 18th. 1834.

Dear Sir

I enclose you a letter this day from my assistant Editor in relation to the Money Market. It is the universal opinion of our friends here, that the recharter of the Bank will depend to a great extent, upon the result of the approaching election in New York; & I assure you *that* result, depends upon the course of the Bank. If you extend, or if you do not curtail, and largely too, you must & will lose the election; & I must say in the spirit of frankness, that your friends in New York & in Congress loudly complain that you are continually putting them in the wrong by granting relief and thereby rendering their prediction perfectly futile. M^r. Martin — late of our State — said this morning that many of his associates in the House feel very sore on this Lead, and begged that when I saw you I would say that to retain the friends it has, the Bank must persevere in its curtailments.[1] . . .

Biddle to S. H. Smith [2]

(*private & confidential*)   B U. S.
April 2nd. 1834

Dear sir

I have had the pleasure of receiving your favor of the 30th inst. which I deemed so important, that before answering it, I consulted the Board at their meeting yesterday in the same confidential manner in regard to the subject of it. It is,

[1] Biddle received many solicitations from his friends in the same tenor as this letter.

[2] President of the Branch at Washington, D.C.

as you are aware, a very delicate subject, one of which it is very difficult, and yet very necessary, to decide in advance, on the best course to be pursued. The opinion of the Board, which has my own entire concurrence, is this.

The Bank of the United States has been compelled in self defence to diminish its business and call upon its debtors, and refuse to make loans to a very considerable amount. It is still doing so — and shall do so for some time. If it had the means of lending, it would lend to its own customers. The State Banks have all had the same warning — and should prepare themselves in the same way — nor is it just that these Banks should call upon the Bank of the U S. for the funds which it has been husbanding for itself. If it is not just, neither is it safe. If there be trouble among the Banks, the only security is the Bank of the U. S. It holds its power as a trust for the ultimate protection of our banking system, the fate of which seems involved in that of the Bank of the U.S. and if we begin by venturing prematurely to the support of institutions which may be embarrassed, we may ourselves become too much weakened to make decisive efforts at a later stage of the disasters which are coming.

Under these impressions, the Board have declined invariably for some time past numerous applications for loans from Banks. They think it decidedly best to abstain from making such loans. They think also that it is expedient to abstain from all pledges or promises of support to the Banks. We know not how far such engagements may lead us — and until the Bank is strong enough to make some general movement for the benefit of the country: were [such] palliatives would rather endanger us than do permanent benefit to them. We have been very anxious to make you strong —

and are very desirous that you should continue so — for which reason, we wish the Office to avoid every engagement that would commit its funds. . . . In fact, the examination of the subject to which your letter has given rise, has brought to my notice the circumstance that I have inadvertently omitted to apprize you of the wish of the Bank on the 22nd of January last that you should bring your loans down fifty thousand dollars below the amount at which they were fixed in October — and I mention it now to show you that we have looked to a reduction rather than an expansion of your business. On the whole we should much prefer that you avoid all engagements either for general or particular support of the Banks.

In respect to the balances too, we are anxious that they should not be suffered to accumulate — particularly as the want of confidence among the State Banks may make the Office the depository of their notes. Neither the notes nor the balances should remain long. The explosion of the Bank of Maryland found this Bank (at Phila) in possession of $21,000 of its notes — and we shall in consequence pursue a course of more frequent settlements with the State Banks.

I wish it were in my power to say that we might relieve the wants of the Banks near you. But I much fear that we could not do much ultimate good — and at the present moment we must avoid diminishing our means, so as to keep them unbroken when they may hereafter be most needed.

BIDDLE TO S. H. SMITH

(*confidential*)   Phila April 11. 1834
My dear sir
        The failure of the Bank of Washington confirms the opinion, entertained by you in regard to the District Banks

— and I think renders more and more expedient the course recommended in my last. The Bank has been obliged to day to decline the same kind of assistance to a Bank in Baltimore. It becomes us to be specially careful of the Institution at the present moment, and that care I am sure you will always bestow.

THOMAS COOPER TO BIDDLE

Columbia S. Carolina
May 1. 1834.

Dear Sir

The talking will go on in Congress till nothing is done and the members and the public become weary. In that case, Jackson will hold firm grasp of the public monies, and set the opposition at defiance. I have written to suggest a resolution, that no Appropriation bill be passed till Congress shall have provided by law for some safe deposit of the public monies, out of the controul of the President.

I now venture to suggest, whether in New York and Philadelphia, a resolution might not be gotten up, to stop the custom house collections, in case Congress breaks up, and leaves them in Jackson's power. Is there any other possible plan that will be efficient? I think the mercantile Interests may be brought to do it. If Jackson obtains controul of the revenue we are defeated, and nothing but extensive bloodshed will preserve us from a permanent disposition. Assuredly, our present war of resolutions and proclamations will do us but little good. . . .

I observe, all our delegation, Pinckney, Clowney, speak of your Bank in terms of highest respect, and w^d. willingly vote for an alteration of the Constitution in its favour:

but unless the north under Webster coalesce with Calhoun
nothing will be done this session, if at all. If Jackson seize
the revenue in spite of the Senate, and in defiance of a rejection of the appropriation bill, the game is up, for he has
the means and the inclination of buying up not merely political but military adherents; and half measures will only plunge
us deeper into the whirlpool destined to absorb what little
of freedom remains. Adieu.

BIDDLE TO JOHN S. SMITH

Phil^a May 9, 1834

Dear sir

I have had the pleasure of receiving your favor of the
5th inst. and shall answer it cheerfully. And yet it is difficult
to answer with certainty. The question you propose is "will
"relief be afforded to the country by a restoration of the de-
"posits to the B.U.S. and of harmony between it and the
"Treasury, and this unconnected with the question of the
"recharter." Now the mere deposit of accruing revenue in the
Bank would not of itself justify any immediate expansion of
the loans, unless taken as an evidence of a change of opinions
or of feelings toward the Bank on the part of those who govern at Washington. If there was a cordiality there — if there
was merely a concession of the deliberate efforts to destroy
the Bank which has been made for several years past, the
Bank might be disposed to venture much to produce relief.
At the same time the question of real and permanent stability to the currency is in fact the question of the recharter of
the Bank — and I am satisfied that any thing short of this

[1] Calhoun's and Webster's plans are given in full in Cong. Doc., vol. x, pt. i,
pp. 1004, 1005, 1067, 1068.

can produce only partial and temporary effects. I wish that something were done soon, for before long the evils will grow entirely beyond our control. For five or six months past the Bank has been exerting itself to save Individuals and the State Banks, and but for its interposition the evils would have fallen upon the country with ten fold severity. These efforts however have a natural end — and then, when the several hundred State Banks are left to themselves, the confusion will before long [be] irretrievable. This Bank is now very strong — and shall be kept so — it must be beyond the reach of any possible risk, so as to interpose hereafter when the confusion is no longer sufferable. Till then it must retain a position of calm and quiet strength — and look on anxiously but immovably. It will before long have in its vaults nearly one dollar in specie for every dollar of its notes in circulation.

My impressions then are these:

If the Bank Charter were renewed or prolonged — I believe the pecuniary difficulties of the country would be immediately healed.

If the deposits were restored and the Bank had a reasonable prospect of not being obliged to draw in its loans soon after it had made them, I think the Bank would make an effort to relieve the country, and with the Executive friendly or not hostile, would I think succeed in the attempt.

If the deposits were merely restored and the Executive continues its efforts to destroy the Bank — the institution could not either safely or wisely change its present system, which is that of a gentle reduction preparatory to closing its concerns.

You will see in the frankness of these expressions the evidence of my confidence in your discretion and my expectation that you will consider them as for yourself alone

BIDDLE TO R. M. BLATCHFORD [1]

Phil^a June 4th 1834

Dear Sir

. . . In respect to the other subject of your letter, you will I think readily understand the position of the Bank. Believing as we do that the whole support of the currency must devolve on the B.U.S. and seeing as we think we do, that the disorders and troubles are but beginning, our great effort is to make the Bank not merely strong, but entirely beyond the reach of those who, under the name of the Gov^t. are seeking its destruction In this operation the State Banks fall in debt. Now we must either settle with these Banks or let the debt increase 'till it may grow entirely beyond our control and beyond their means of payment. This is wrong in two respects — first, — because it is not just to the Stockholders of the B.U.S. to give to others the gratuitous use of so large a portion of their capital — and second — because these large balances may become unsafe. For example, the Banks of the City of New York owe to the Branch Bank $700,000. Why should they be allowed to owe that sum? — and what will become of the debt if it be permitted to increase as it probably will to twice that sum? I believe that the State Banks themselves will be benefitted by the restraint of being obliged to settle and so accommodate their

[1] Distinguished lawyer in New York, father of the late Justice Samuel Blatchford, counsel for the Bank of the United States in New York, and great friend of Nicholas Biddle. Cf. sketch of life in Wilson, *op. cit.*, vol. III, p. 490; vol. IV, p. 613.

business to their means. The Bank, as I am sure you are aware, is desirous of protecting the community from the mischief which threaten it, and has been constantly engaged in relieving the Banks and individuals whose solvency has been endangered by the measures of the Treasury. At the same time the Bank would injure itself & not benefit the country, if, after all the warnings which the State Banks as well as individuals have had to diminish their business & provide against the storm, it should venture on the Quixotism of preventing all inconvenience to the public from the measures intended to destroy the Institution. The course which circumstances seem to force upon the Bank is that of gradual & gentle diminition of its business, so as to be prepared to expand or to close its affairs as the country may desire hereafter. I pray you to believe that I shall always be happy to hear from you — and that I am

BIDDLE TO SOLOMON ETTING [1]

Phil^a June 12. 1834

Dear Sir

I have had the pleasure of receiving your favor of the 10th inst. which I assure you requires no apology, as I am always not merely willing, but anxious to learn the opinion of judicious friends of the Bank.

Since the Bank has ceased to be the depository of the public revenue, the indulgence formerly given to the State Banks could scarcely be expected — as it would be unreasonable and unjust to the Stockholders of the Bank of the U.S. to let the State Banks have the use of a large part of

[1] A merchant of Baltimore and one of the directors of the Baltimore and Ohio Railroad. Cf. Scharf, J. Thomas, *The Chronicles of Baltimore* (Baltimore, 1874).

its capital without interest, while they were making interest on it. The Board have therefore made a recent order for the periodical settlement of those balances from the State Banks. The general object was to keep down this accumulation of debt from those institutions — at the same time, nothing was more remote from the desire of the Bank than to oppress the State Institutions. On the contrary we should be disposed to give every reasonable facility in the settlement of the balances. It was probably some misapprehension of the design of the Bank which occasioned the excitement to which you allude & which I trust will cease when the nature of these periodical regulations of the balances is better known from practice.

BIDDLE TO ALEXANDER PORTER [1]

Phil^a. June 14. 1834

Dear Sir

The last mail brought me your favor of the 11th inst which shall not fail to receive immediate attention as soon as we hear from the Branch at New Orleans on the subject. As yet we have had no communication whatever in regard to it.

I regret very much the decision of the House on Mr Clay's resolutions: for its effect will I fear be to render the state of the country much more embarrassing during the summer. The House have it now in their power, by passing those resolutions, to give immediate and general relief to the country. If the House by however small a majority, were to order the restoration of the Deposits, no matter whether it were vetoed or signed by the Pres^t., it would not only relieve the Senate from the reproach of siding against the Pres^t. and the

---

[1] Senator from Louisiana.

people — but it would establish such a relation between the Congress and the Bank, as would induce the latter to make great efforts to restore confidence and prosperity. With such a vote of Congress, twenty-four hours would be sufficient to establish peace, and to insure the return of better times for the country. On that subject my convictions are strong — and were it not for the misinterpretation to which it would be liable, I should go down & talk with you all about it.

Do you think it practicable to carry the resolutions? The majority was 20 which requires a change of only 11 votes. Now I have no doubt that many members like Mr King of Georgia, who are well disposed even to recharter the Bank, but despairing of the recharter, think the restoration of the deposites without being followed by a certainty of a recharter, would benefit neither the country. In this they are mistaken. I think for instance I could venture to say that if such a vote were secured, the Bank would feel no reluctance in giving one, or if necessary, two millions of loans to Louisiana as requested for her relief. This could be done because such a vote is peace and harmony & confidence between the Bank & the Congress. In truth I know of no way in which all the interest on the Western waters could be more immediately & substantially advanced than by such a vote, which it would be in the power of Eleven men, who are sent to Congress to promote these interests, to give in a few days. Could not that resolution be brought up? I should think there were men enough in the House to do that good service to their section of the country, even if it did cost them a frown at the Palace. If you suppose it is at all feasible & that I can promote it, have the goodness to let me know — and in the mean time believe me

BIDDLE TO WILLIAM APPLETON

Phil^a. July 4th 1834

Dear Sir

Your favor of the 27th ult° was duly received and the letter inclosed in it will not fail to receive the respectful attention due to the signers of it.

The Board have deemed it inexpedient to change the course of the Bank during the session of Congress, but when it was ascertained that nothing could be done, upon the adjournment, a Committee was appointed, to consider what measures would be necessary in consequence of that event. This Committee will report in a few days, and in their deliberations, the views contained in the communication you have forwarded will have their due weight. In the mean time, I think it right to say that the paper is written under an entire misapprehension of the course and situation of the Bank. These gentlemen say "it is well understood that the Bank is pursuing a regular system of curtailment apparently at the rate of about a million of dollars per month." Now the fact is that the Bank is not curtailing its business a single dollar; no curtailment of any description has been ordered since January last, and all that was then directed has with a few exceptions been executed, so that the Bank has not I believe a wish to reduce its present amount of loans and certainly has adopted no regular system of curtailment. In respect to your own Office, you know perfectly, that you have been under no restriction of any kind as to the amount of your loans, and that since the removal of the deposits, Boston is the only point in the whole establishment except Savannah (where the business voluntarily fell off after the run upon it) where no reduction was directed, and it is moreover the only place where the discounts have increased, they being at this moment more than half a million of dollars beyond the amount in October.

What has probably induced the belief of this curtailment is the diminition of the apparent aggregate of Loans in the published statements, but these intelligent men of business must perceive that this is the natural result of this season of the year of the maturity of the bills from the South, which cannot be replaced by other bills from the South, as the season of purchasing them goes by, so that these reductions are not compulsory but voluntary and inevitable. Of the nature of these presumed curtailments I can offer no better illustration than what is furnished by the accounts up to the 1st. of July now lying before me showing the following comparison of the discounts during the last month.

	Local Discounts	Dom. Bills	Totals	Foreign Bills of Ecc.	Aggregate
June 1, 1834	34,739,871.21	17,462,041.67	52,201,912.88	1,995,291.80	54,197,204.68
July 1, 1834	34,423,921.72	16,601,051.00	51,021,972.72	3,827,413.03	54,852,385.75
	315,949.49	860,990.67	1,176,940.16	1,832,121.23	655,181.07

Now there is an actual increase of discounts (for the purchase of a foreign Bill is as much a loan as the purchase of an inland Bill) amounting to $655,181.07, altho' of those two classes of Loans, the local discounts and Domestic Bills there is a diminition, but this diminition is voluntary, and so far as concerns the present subject is worth remarking.

The whole diminition in local Discounts is........................315,949.49
of this the diminition at Boston is................................201,137.13

Now you are perfectly aware that the diminition was not directed, nor advised, nor suggested by the Bank — that as far as the Bank is concerned, it is voluntary and forms no part "of a regular system of curtailment." Again; the diminition of the domestic bills is $860,990.67. This is composed mainly of the diminished purchases at New Orleans, Mobile & Charleston to the amount of 851,024.05, of diminished purchases at other Western and South Western Offices amounting to 374,540.27. While at Boston your Domestic Bills of Exchange have increased $385,091.28. Your aggregate business in local Discounts & Domestic Bills has increased $127,-932.14 during the month of June — moreover the loans of the Office are larger, much larger than they generally are at this season of the year, thus,

	Local Discounts	Bills	Totals
June 24, 1830	563,349.59	517,191.01	1,080,533.60
30, 1831	259,428.86	612,585.11	872,013.97
28, 1832	961,732.22	1,044,698.69	2,006,430.91
27, 1833	770,071	3,422,938.08	4,212,955.09
26, 1834	1,248,964.32	1,587,631.16	2,839,595.98

From all this, I think our friends will perceive — 1st. That the Bank is not pursuing any course of curtailment at all. 2nd. That the last months operations have been in fact a considerable expansion of Loans — and 3rd. that of all the Cities of the United States, that which has the least reason to complain is Boston — I say emphatically Boston, because Boston is the only Branch where no curtailments were ordered, the only Branch which has actually and largely increased its Loans — the only Branch which from the removal of the Deposits to the present day, has had no restriction put upon the amount of its Loans. If the Board have found in the situation of the Branch enough to justify the exemption from these restraints, it was not certainly to be presumed the party most favored should most complain.

Having said this much, I could wish to go no farther and yet I ought to add a few words more in regard to the suggestion that "it may even create a necessity for the whigs self defence to separate themselves entirely from that Institution." I regret extremely the use of such phrases since they resolve themselves at last into this, that if the Bank does not do what the Gentlemen wish, the political party to which they belong will denounce the Bank. Now it is true that the Gentlemen who administer the Bank concur in their individual characters with the party just named, and will always be disposed to cooperate with them for general benefit, but nothing could be more immediately & decidedly fatal to that cooperation than the appearance of any disposition to coerce the Bank by political denunciations. If therefore any political party or association desires to separate itself from the Bank — be it so. The parting will be a source of deep regret, but there would be deeper regret at doing wrong to avoid it. The Bank looks only to what it views the interest of the Stockholders and of the country and it will never yield any part of those interests to create or relieve political friends. Already the very suggestion is calculated to be injurious. I did not even venture to read that letter to the Board, because I knew that the tone of it would excite unpleasant feelings and that that portion of the Board connected with the Government might turn to the very great injury of the political party, in whose name these Gentlemen speak, the declarations contained in it. For the same reason I make this a private letter to you, with liberty to communicate these explanations to them. They will I hope perceive in the temper which dictates them a very strong desire that they should be satisfied in regard to the general position of the Bank and especially of its disposition towards them and the community around them. If we are so unfortunate as to fail in this, and

are destined to have the ranks of the enemy swelled by alienated friends, much as we regret the accession of so much re-
spectibility to the adverse party, we certainly will be less inclined to capitulate to their hostility, than to yield to their
friendly suggestions. In a few days I have to apprize you of
the determination of the Board and mean while remain, with
great regard

R. FISHER [1] TO BIDDLE

New York July 7th 1834.

My Dear Sir

. . . Without further preface then I assure you, there
is much dissatisfaction in this City and State among a very
large portion of the friends of the Bank, and those of influence
in the Whig party — and sure am I that it is increasing every
day.

Our Merchants and traders generally have been in hopes
for some time past that circumstances might occur to produce a change of Policy on the part of the Government towards the Bank — that some happy influence might have
sprung up at Washington, and that light might have broken
in upon the chaos, in which the dominant party are undoubtedly involved.

The adjournment of Congress has dissipated this forlorn
hope, and they now begin to look to the present and the
future — to the former suffering under a painful evil, and to
the latter with increased anxiety and alarm.

---

[1] Son of Miers Fisher, a distinguished lawyer. About 1830 Fisher moved to
New York and established the daily paper the *New York American Advocate and
Journal* which was afterwards named the *New York Journal and Advertiser*. He was
a warm friend of Clay; was twice elected municipal judge, appointed Assistant Post-
master of New York by President Tyler; and under President Taylor Appraiser
of the Customs of Philadelphia. Simpson, *Eminent Philadelphians*, pp. 362–364.

The language is general among them, "We have now no chance for relief, but from the Bank of the United States, which institution is called upon, we think by every consideration to extend its loans. As regards the Institution itself, the best informed Financiers in the City (among whom I name Mr Gallatin) declare that this can be done with perfect regard to the Safety of the Institution — and undoubtedly with the best possible policy. The Safety fund Banks of the State, under the influence of the Albany Regency,[1] have considerably curtailed their issues — and refuse to extend them — throwing all the odium of the present extreme scarcity of money throughout this State upon your Bank. Gentlemen from many counties of the State have assured me, that the farmers — men of much influence, believe that their suffering is owing to that assigned cause. The Regency presses are daily filled with articles calculated to induce this opinion, and it is fast gaining ground — Nay, my informants go much further, and declare, that the Regency are delighted with the present state of things, and rely exultantly for their success upon its continuance, believing that they, through the State loan, can turn the relief to their great account. These are the opinions of men entirely friendly to the Bank — and they communicate their information with great reluctance. In this City, I pray of you to be assured, such is the coincidence among our merchants in this opinion, and the excitement thence resulting, that I have *no doubt* measures will shortly be taken (should things remain as they are) that cannot fail to have the most unhappy effect upon the Bank, and the great cause of Constitutional freedom. Indeed I have

---

[1] For the Albany Regency, cf. Alexander, De Alva S., *A Political History of New York* (New York, 1909), vol. I, pp. 293, 294, 324.

heard it talked of, among men of *great influence*, that a meeting of merchants will be publicly called to take into considertion what belongs to them to do for the relief of the Trading Community. There is much talk of taking up Jesse Buel for the Whig Candidate as Governor and some of our Politicians confidently say, if the Bank should continue its present course, it would best comport with his success to go — for A National Bank, and if not denounce the present one, at least to disavow publicly all connection with it. . . .

BIDDLE TO JAMES W. WEBB

Phil^a. July 9th. 1834

Dear Sir

I have this morning had the pleasure of receiving your favor of the 8th inst. We have waited for the adjournment of Congress before taking any final course in regard to the Bank, because 'till then the movement of the Government was uncertain. The subject is now under examination by a Committee of the Board who will probably report in a day or two. My own individual opinion is, that having reached the point of entire safety & being in some sort divorced from the Executive, the Bank is now at liberty to consult exclusively the interest of the Stockholders and the Community. In such a state of things it seems inexpedient to impose or to continue curtailments merely for the sake of any effect they might be presumed to produce abroad, and I shall not be surprised if further reductions of the loans should be suspended. No determination, however, is yet made, and therefore nothing should be said about it in your journal I should think at present.

ALEXANDER HAMILTON TO JOHN WOODWORTH [1]

New York Sep[r]. 14. 1834.

Dear Sir

The success of your exertions at the ensuing election will mainly depend on the course to be pursued by the Bank; the Colera and the drought have done some service, but you alone can prevent an active fall trade in our agricultural products. The regency have resolved, through the Safety Fund Banks, to grant every facility to raise, if possible, the price of grain about the commencement of October, in order to satisfy the farming interest that our embarrassments have passed away and that their policy had placed the future prosperity of the country on a permanent footing — this impression is now gaining ground and unless counteracted will give us an uphill labour — ...

... It has been found expedient to abandon the Bank in our political pilgramage. The people are now familiarly acquainted with the immense power of a national bank and apprehend all kinds of terrible consequences from its exercise, without ever reflecting that in every human institution, possessing the ability to do much good, their must necessarily exist the power to do essential mischief, and that all legislation is more or less subject to the same charge. ...

BIDDLE TO SILAS M. STILWELL

Phil[a]. Oct 30. 1834.

Dear Sir

I received yesterday your favor of the 27th inst which was forthwith disposed of as requested.

[1] Distinguished lawyer of New York.

On the subject of aid from this quarter the fact is, I understand, that the contributions fall on a very narrow circle of
not wealthy people — and that on the late occasion they have
been completely exhausted and a little dispirited that their
exertions have proved so little productive in proportion to
their expectations. I should not think it at all probable that
any thing further could be obtained from them. As to the
Bank itself, I have always made it a point of duty never to
permit its interference in any manner with our political concerns. It was a refusal to become partizans to the present set in
power which has made them its enemies, and it will persevere
in the same neutrality to the end — altho' all the temptations
to depart from that course are obvious & strong, & however
much the consequences may be deplored of the present mis-
rule. We shall not look with less anxiety however on your
great struggle, on which the fate of the country now in a
great degree depends. With the hope that you and the
good cause you support may triumph in that struggle,[1] I
remain

ROSWELL L. COLT TO BIDDLE [2]

Bal. 13 Nov 1834

My dear Sir

. . . The more I have thought about the Bank, the
better I like your idea of applying to your State for a Charter
for 35 Millions — for a Bank to be called the Bank of the U S.
Penn^a to subscribe 7 Millions pay^t in a Stock bearing 4 1/2

[1] The followers of the Bank were defeated in the fall election by an overwhelming vote.

[2] This letter is the first intimation we have in the Biddle correspondence that
the President of the Bank was contemplating an attempt to have the Bank chartered by the State of Pennsylvania.

percts Interest or even 4 — having the Same time to run, they grant the Charter, pledging the faith of the State for Said Debt, & the accruing Dividends toward part of Interest, — this would give your State at least 200,000 a Year as a Bonus, the present private Stockholders of the B U S to have the right to subscribe for the Same number of Shares in the New Bank they now hold in the Old — the unsubscribed Stock to belong to the Corporation with right to Sell as they think proper — the Bank to have the right to establish Branches in all States permitting, & agencies every where on such terms as may be agreed upon. I feel persuaded all the States but N York would grant such privilege & if the[y] refused, place an Agency there — we would grant You the Charter here at once.

BIDDLE TO —— [1]

Phil[a]. Jany 7. 1835

Gentlemen,

I had this morning the pleasure of receiving your letter of the 5th inst in which you apprize me that you had been informed that the Stockholders of the U.S. Bank would accept a charter from this State and you request to know from me on what terms this can be effected — especially mentioning the number of years of the charter with which the Bank would be satisfied — the amount of capital — as well as the premium & other encouragements that would be given to the State in consideration of it.

Having long had reflected much on this subject,[2] I will answer promptly & without reserve.

[1] This letter was evidently a draft of one sent to the committee on banks in Harrisburg.

[2] It was Matthew St. Clair Clarke who first suggested to Biddle the advisability

For a variety of reasons, which I forbear to state because your duties have made you familiar with them, I believe it to be of the greatest importance to our State to appropriate to its own benefit the Capital of the Bank of the U.S. which is about to be distributed & can never be recalled if it once leaves the State.

I believe that considering the general growth of the whole Union — and the extraordinary resources of Penn^a which require only capital to develope them — the sum of ten millions which formed the capital of the first Bank in 1791 — and the sum of 35 millions which formed the capital of the present Bank in 1816 was not more than the equivalent of 100 millions at this time — and that the present institution might with great safety & with great advantage be gradually increased to fifty millions to an amount not disproportionate

of securing a charter from the State of Pennsylvania. Clarke was a co-worker of Peter Force and aided the latter in collecting and publishing the former's great work *American Archives, a Documentary History of the English Colonies of North America.* On October 30, 1832, Clarke wrote to Biddle as follows: "I need only give the outline of what I consider a splendid operation. Only remember *I have given it.* Let our State of Pennsylvania charter the U.S. Bank, less the Gov^t Stock — and in place of Branches, out of the State — create Agencies — or whatever you please to call them. . . . Let the State lay out the Bonus in Internal Improvements and make yourself 'a name & praise among the nations of the Earth.'"

This suggestion evidently impressed Biddle as the above letter and the following actions of the Bank disclose. Moreover, the economic and political aspect of the State favored the Bank men at this particular time. Pennsylvania was already engulfed in the vast internal improvement speculation which characterized these years and was just beginning to feel the effects of her folly. With her commerce sinking beneath the pecuniary agitation of the thirties, her treasury bankrupt, and her citizens overburdened with taxes, the Pennsylvania Legislature was willing to listen to Nicholas Biddle. Furthermore, the Anti-Masonic Party had elected their man, Joseph Ritner, as governor upon an implied promise not to increase the debt nor the taxes, and as the Whigs and Anti-Masons had been voting together on all measures since 1832 under the able leadership of Thaddeus Stevens, Biddle might well deem the time propitious. Cf. *Harrisburgh Chronicle,* May, 1836; McCarthy, Charles, *The Antimasonic Party,* in American Historical Association, Annual Report, vol. 1 (Washington, 1902), pp. 461, 488.

when it is considered how large a sum could be used for the general purposes of trade, manufactures & agriculture — how much might be advanced to the State for the completion of its great Plans of improvement — how large a portion might be given to private associations for rail roads & canals & other objects of general benefit & how much might be judiciously advanced to individuals in the interior for improvements which tho' private in their nature are public in their results. I believe that to give permanancy & solidity to the fiscal arrangements of the State it would be greatly for its interest to extend the charter to thirty years.

I have accordingly endeavored to estimate the value of such a charter — & I have made up my mind to this conclusion which I mention to you at once — because I have not the least ambition to make any arrangement not mutually advantageous & because after all the benefit of this measure to the Commonwealth in its schemes of improvement is far greater than the mere price which may be paid for the charter. The question you will perceive is, what inducement [1] can be offered to the Stockholders in other parts of the U.S. or in Europe to leave his funds in Penn^a. rather than take them home to be employed in other States — and then what reason can be given for accepting a charter from Penn^a rather from any other of the 24 States having an equal with Penn^a to give the charter. As a Pennsylvanian devotedly attached to her interests & her fame I would give more to Penn^a. than to any other State for a Charter — and my effort would be to induce all the other Stockholders to prefer that arrange-

---

[1] New York and later Maryland made generous offers to Biddle when the bill to re-charter the Bank was finally presented to the Pennsylvania Legislature. Both states were most desirous of securing the institution.

ment to either a division of the funds or the acceptance of a charter from any other State. To do which it would be necessary to render the terms beneficial to the State yet not too burdensome to the Stockholder.*

For a charter from Penn^a. for the amount of Stock held by individuals with a power of gradual increase to fifty millions of dollars, and for thirty years, I would recommend to the Stockholders the following terms.

To give to the State $2,000,000 either in cash on the day when the charter was accepted, or in instalments one fourth cash & the rest in equal payments at six — twelve & 18 months, the sum of 2,000,000. To lend to the State whenever wanted six millions of dollars taking their Stock, which need not be repaid before the expiration of the charter, at five per cent, which interest payable semi annually & giving a premium of ten per cent — or if more agreeable to take a four per cent stock at par.

To subscribe the sum of one million to the stock of any rail roads or canal companies which the State might elect as worthy of particular patronage and

To advance at all times to the State a temporary loan of Five hundred thousand at five per cent

Allow me in conclusion to suggest one very important consideration. It is this. The charter of the Bank expires on the 4th of March. The Stockholders are already summoned to meet on the 17th of February to make preparations for the dissolution of the Bank & some final decision will probably be then made for either the division of the funds or an application for a charter from some other authority. It would therefore be highly desirable that the final action of the legislature should be known at that period, so that an immediate acceptance of the charter may be made — or ulterior measures be adopted.

I need not say that in this frank exposition I speak only my own sentiments — I believe such an arrangement would be beneficial to the State and as such it might be offered & would be accepted.

* As far as I understand the financial position of the State it is that a large amount of funds is invested in improvements which do not yet defray their own expenses, but will do so when the whole scheme of improvements is finished. It is desirable therefore to make arrangements for the completion of the improvements and until they become more productive to supply the deficiency of income over expenditure. Both these objects would I think be attained by the following arrangement.

DANIEL WEBSTER (?) TO BIDDLE

Private   Boston May 9. 1835
My Dear Sir

It appears to me that our political affairs are taking a very decided turn, & that if nothing be done to check the current, Mr V.B. will be elected President, by a vast majority. It is entirely obvious, I think, that the movement of the Southern Whigs [1] (as they call themselves) in Mr White's favor has disgusted, deeply, the whole body of our friends in the North. Such papers as the Richmond Whig & Telegraph have endeavored to persuade the People that the question is narrowed down to a choice between Judge White & Mr. V. Buren, & if this be the only issue presented, there is already abundant indication that the whole north, east, & middle too,

---

[1] On the Southern Whigs as a political force, cf. Cole, Arthur C., *The Whig Party in the South* (Washington, 1913).

as I believe, will go for V.B. I do not know whether any thing can be done to change the course of things; but I am fully persuaded, that if any thing *can* be done, it is be done in Penn^a. Your people are awake to political subjects, in consequence of the pendency of an election for Govr. If those who are likely to unite in support of Mr Ritner could unite also in making some demonstration, on National Subjects, & do it immediately, it might possibly have some effect. Whether this be practicable is more than I know.

I have thought it right, My Dear Sir, to express to you my opinion, thus freely, on the present State, & apparent tendency, of things. Our friends here receive letters, every day, & from P^a. as well as from other quarters, calling on them to do more, & say more. But they hardly see what more *they* can do, or say. The sentiment of Massachusetts is known; & it would seem to be for the consideration of others, whether it should be seconded.

You will of course, *burn this*,[1] & let no eye but your own see it. You can judge whether any thing can be usefully done. For my part, I confess, it looks to me as if the whole Whig Strength in the Country was either to be frittered away, or melt into the support of Mr V. Buren.

DANIEL WEBSTER (?) TO BIDDLE

Private   Boston May 12. '35
Dr Sir

One word more on political subjects. It seems truly lamentable that the Nat. Intelligencer should be so unwilling to give, or take, tone, on questions most interesting to us, as a party. Cannot this reluctance be overcome? — If Messrs

---

[1] This is a characteristic entry for a Webster letter.

G. & S. are not disposed to support, at present, any named candidate, they might, at least, preach the necessity of supporting *a* Whig Candidate — *some* Whig Candidate. We are in danger of breaking up, & dividing. Our natural field marshall — he that should rally & encourage us, is the leading paper on our side. But this natural leader seems at present to be without any "objects, and, aim."

I mention this matter to you, because you can judge, as well as any one, whether the subject deems any attention; & if it do, can, better than any one, give an availing hints, in the right quarter. *burn.*

BIDDLE TO D. SPRIGG

Phil^a May 13. 1835

Dear Sir

I have received your favor of the 8th inst. and shall reply to it without the least reserve.

In closing the concerns of the Bank, my great anxiety is to take care of its faithful Officers, and any thing which I can do to serve them, I will do most promptly and willingly. In your own particular case, I am not the less desirous of serving you because you have been comparatively a short time with us, for you have connected your fortunes with the Institution, and that is itself a claim upon me. My impression then is, that the Branch in Buffalo will be soon closed, and that in the contingency of a renewed charter under a state, the agencies of the Bank would be confined to the most mercantile points, as the general superintendence of the currency will no longer devolve on the Bank: so that the Bank would not require your services at Buffalo. I wish therefore that you may succeed in your application for the Cashiership of the Bank in Baltimore — and I will do all in my power to promote your views by communicating with M^r. Anderson. You will receive from M^r. Jaudon by to-days mail a suggestion with respect to another Bank, where he thinks you might be well placed. In short I beg you to believe that it will afford me very great pleasure to promote your views, being, with sincere regard [1]

EDWARD EVERETT TO BIDDLE

Charlestown Mass^ts
3 June 1835.

My dear Sir,

The Ohio Legislature is soon to convene. The Whigs there are now in a majority. I see in a Pittsburg paper a very important Suggestion, which has been repeated or made simultaneously in some others, that if the Whigs at Columbus, at this approaching session, would nominate Mr W. and Genl. Harrison as Vice P. it would have a very decisive effect. If you should be of this opinion, cannot you drop a line to some considerate & influential persons, — members of the legislature or others, — at Columbus?

There is really strength enough in the Country, to elect Mr W., if it could be concentrated & cordially united, in his support.

BIDDLE TO JOHN HUSKE

Phil^a. Aug^st. 6th. 1835

Dear Sir

... In regard to the offer from the State Bank of the Presidency of the Branch at Fayetteville, I think you should not hesitate to accept it. My great anxiety now is, that the

---

[1] This letter is characteristic of the generosity and thoughtfulness of Biddle in his dealings with his friends and especially with all those connected with the institution.

Officers of the Bank should be able to separate from it with the least possible inconvenience to themselves — and I am anxious particularly that they should lose no opportunity of obtaining proper employment elsewhere. If therefore the situation offered be in other respects satisfactory, there is nothing in your relations with the Bank that should induce you to decline it.

This brings me to another matter connected with it on which I proposed to write to you. We are now making arrangements with several of the new Banks to purchase the whole establishment of the Office near them — banking house, debts & all. This plan is very advantageous to the new Bank which thus succeeds to the standing, capital, deposits & custom of the Office, & to the Bank of the U.S. it possesses the attraction of enabling them to close the Office at once. As an example of such a settlement, I will mention what has just taken place at Lexington, Kentucky. The President & Cashier of the Office have been appointed President & Cashier of the Northern Bank of Kentucky — and that Institution has agreed to take the Banking House at the valuation hitherto put up upon it in our schedules — & also to take the whole of the current debt — not including of course the domestic bills — at its nominal amount, giving the notes of the Bank of Kentucky payable in 1, 2, 3, & 4 years with interest at five per cent. The suspended debt the Bank of Kentucky agrees to manage and collect without charge.

Now, if you could make a similar arrangement with the Bank of the State or any other institution, it would be satisfactory to us.

Let me hear from you soon on this subject & believe me meanwhile

BIDDLE TO HERMAN COPE

Phil[a]. Aug[st] 11. 1835

My dear Sir

. . . My theory in regard to the present condition of the country is in a few words this.[1] For the last few years the Executive power of the Gov[t]. has been weilded by a mere gang of banditte. I know these people perfectly — keep the police on them constantly — and in my deliberate judgment, there is not on the face of the earth a more profligate crew than those who now govern the President. The question is how to expel them. I believe that a very large majority not merely of the intelligence and the property, but of the numbers of our countrymen, are disposed to expel them. It remains to see how that majority can be concentrated so as to be effectual. As yet the opinions of the opposition are unformed. No man as yet can combine them: they are not fixed on any one man. But they are fixed on several men who are acceptable to various sections. Then the obvious course is, to make these several men in the first instance embody under them the force of these various sections — and when the common enemy approaches to rally under a leader of their own choice. It is manifestly advantageous to let M[r] Webster lead the New England forces, M[r] White the Southwest, or South — and wherever in any one State there is a strong opposition man — to vote for him as such — and settle the pretensions of the chiefs afterwards. I have said again and again to my friends, I have said it this very morning, "This disease is to be treated as a local disorder — apply local remedies — if Gen[l]. Harrison will run better than any body

---

[1] Cf. Letter of Everett to Biddle, June 3, 1835.

else in Penns^a., by all means unite upon him." That as far as I understand the case, is the feeling very generally of the opposition & Genl Harrison must not suppose that there is in this quarter any unwillingness to give him fair play. On the contrary, he is very much respected, and if our friends are satisfied that he can get more votes in Penns^a than any other candidate of the opposition they will take him up cheerfully & support him cordially.

I have but one remark more to make. If Genl. Harrison is taken up as a candidate, it will be on account of the past, not the future. Let him then rely entirely on the past. Let him say not one single word about his principles, or his creed — let him say nothing — promise nothing.[1] Let no Committee, no convention — no town meeting ever extract from him a single word, about what he thinks now, or what he will do hereafter. Let the use of pen and ink be wholly forbidden as if he were a mad poet in Bedlam. Genl. Harrison can speak well & write well — but on this occasion he should neither speak nor write — but be silent — absolutely and inflexibly silent. . . .

JOHN NORRIS TO BIDDLE

Mifflin County
Browns Mills 16th November 1835

dear Sir,

. . . I have not a doubt but the Legislature of New York would offer at once a most favorable charter for the whole twenty eight million: for they have intelligent men enough to take advantage of everything that would have a

---

[1] This advice shows that Biddle's idea of a campaign was similar to that of Mark Hanna when the latter was managing the candidacy of McKinley.

tendency to increase their wealth & influence in the Union
— whether by commerce, manufactures, or internal improvement.[1] . . .

JASPER HARDING TO BIDDLE

Philad. Dec. 4. 1835

Dear Sir

I have just returned from Harrisburg — every thing
looks as favourable as could be expected, through the kindness of the Speaker, Mr Middlesworth [2] I obtained last
evening a copy of the committees of the House in confidence,
not to show it in Harrisburg to injure him, before it was announced from the chair, I send you a proof slip — Pen-
nepacker the chairman on Banks is a very clever country
member I should think not disposed to throw difficulties in
the way. Mr Lawrence requested me to give you his best
respects.

CHARLES AUGUST DAVIS TO BIDDLE

Private　　　　　　　　　　　　　　New York 6 Dec. 1835
My Dʳ. Sir

. . . The opinion rapidly obtains here that Penᵃ. will
grant you a Charter if Congress declines acting in the matter — and I dont believe one man in a thousand here identified with Trade but wᵈ. rejoice in it — and every time I am
ask'd about it — my answer is — that such will no doubt

[1] The movement for re-charter began in November of 1835. In the early part
of the month Nicholas Biddle began to receive letters from friends both within
the state and in New York advising him to petition the next session of the Pennsylvania Legislature, composed, as it was, of "flexible material." Since New York
seemed specially anxious for a charter, as the above letter indicates, the President
used it to good advantage on the home Assembly.

[2] An old Anti-Masonic leader.

occur provided the State could secure your services and name
to preside over the Bank — but I doubted if you w^d. assent
— that from all I can gather, you intended to wind up the
present institution — and then devote yourself to higher
pursuits than the Story of Banking. It does me good to worry
the dogs on this point — a few evenings since dining at the
Mayors (where were present the delegation to the Legislature
& "other leaders of the party") I took occasion to reply thus
to the Enquiry — and as it was a "winder up" it seem'd to
me the *"Chateau"* tasted better to me afterwards.

WILLIAM B. REED [1] TO BIDDLE

Harrisburg. Decr. 12. 1835.

Dear Sir,

   I have intended from day to day to write to you, but
the very caution and reserve which *we* are obliged to maintain in relation to the Bank measure operate to prevent any
development of feeling and opinion, worth communicating.
I now esteem it especially fortunate that a friend of the Bank
was placed at the head of the Improvement Committee.
That is the only engine on which we can rely and if it fails we
have no chance. Every one at all acquainted with matters
and things here, particularly of late years since the Canal
policy has been pursued, knows that the temptation of a turn-
pike, or a few miles of canal and rail road as a beginning on a
favorite route is nearly irresistible, and I am strongly inclined
to think that now a few of the many members who have toiled
year after year for branches, and who look to this session as

---

[1] Chairman of the Inland Navigation Committee; later Minister to China.
Cf. sketch of life in Scharf and Westcott, *History of Philadelphia*, vol. I, pp. 656,
721–725, 731, 732; vol. II, p. 1167.

their last chance could vote against legislation that would give them their extensions and entrench upon nothing but party prejudices and antipathies. If this feeling cannot be operated on, none other can. An this applies to those who are here not as friends of the state administration and who perhaps not being unwilling to see it embarassed could not be operated upon by the measure, if its effect was to be merely a general relief from taxation. A reference to the map and the Senatorial Districts will illustrate this. The Southern line of Rail Road to connect through York and Gettysburg with the Baltimore and Ohio Rail Road and thence down the Younghegany to Pittsburg would of itself affect the votes of at least three if not four Senators. So with the Erie extension the North Branch, the West Branch survey (all that that District wants). With respect to all these new lines it must be borne in mind that the commencement of the work is all that will be wanted. To be able to go home and boast of having made a beginning is all that is needed. . . . There is another interest too which must not be overlooked in the Turnpikes — relief to them no matter how small a pittance, will be most gratefully received. By the bye, I understand the Canal Commissioners, in their Report take up the tune of the Message and assuming the abundance of funds recommend all the extensions as a matter of course.

With all these views you will easily understand why I consider the Improvement Committee, aided as it may be by the Committee of Ways and Means, a powerful engine to effect our purpose. I shall be glad to have your views in strict confidence as to the course which true policy dictates as respects new banks and increased capital. Petitions are rushing in upon us from all quarters. The Chairman of the Committee on Banks, Mr Pennypacker, is one of the soundest men we have. His idea is to delay action even in Committee upon all these new banks, and having ascertained the precise amount of proposed capital to use it as an argument for the U.S. Bank. This may do very well so far as our city is concerned but I am inclined to doubt the policy in its general application. For example a very strong and respectable application has been made for a new bank at Pittsburg where it seems to be conceded since the closing of the branch that more banking capital is needed. From what I learn from third persons I find that all the Pittsburg members and their friends in the lobby attribute the dilatory action of the Committee who have refused thus far to report a bill, to a secret design on the part of the friends of the U.S.B. to promote its views. They are consequently utterly opposed to the charter. All this I hear indirectly but still I can depend on it. Would it not be better in such a case only, for the friends of the U.S.B. to gain the Pittsburg influence by aiding their project?

I shall be very glad to have your views on this subject particularly as well as on all others connected with the great object we have in view. Whatever you may write I shall consider *strictly confidential* and for my own guidance. It is however essential that I should be fully apprised of all your views. . . .

You are at liberty to show this letter to Mr Sergeant & to any of our common friends.[1]

---

[1] Biddle had already presented some of the members of the committee with an account of a proposed charter according to which the new corporation, with a capital of fifty millions, chartered for thirty years, would give two millions in cash to the state on the day it was incorporated, and furthermore would make liberal concessions to various internal improvement proposals. This outline was "sus-

BIDDLE TO WILLIAM B. REED

Phil^a. Jany 15th. 1836

Dear sir

I have just seen a letter from Harrisburg stating that in a bill for chartering the Bank of the U.S. which is understood to be now before a Committee of which you are Chairman, it is contemplated to introduce a provision [1] that if the Bank "interferes with politics, its charter may be repealed" — and another "prohibiting the Bank from publishing documents." I lose no time in stating to you, that if such provisions, or any thing in the remotest degree resembling them shall be put into the charter, it will be instantly rejected by the Stockholders. They have not asked for this charter — and certainly could not accept it on terms which might be construed into a reproach on their past administration of its affairs

BIDDLE TO JOSEPH McILVAINE

Phil^a. Jany 15. 1836

Dear Sir

I refer you to Mr Wallace for the views entertained of

ceptible of further compression," wrote Biddle to McIlvaine, Biddle's *chargé* at Harrisburg, but the latter was urged to call the attention of the friends of the measure to the sound reasons why the Bank ought to be re-chartered by Pennsylvania. These were: (1) that Pennsylvania would thus become wealthy and surpass New York; (2) no fear of foreign capital, since Europeans had already aided Pennsylvania in internal improvements; (3) Philadelphia had always been the seat of the Bank and would become the center of finances if she re-chartered the institution; (4) that New York's attacks were only designed to break down the Bank in Pennsylvania in order to obtain one in New York; (5) a dissolution would mean the loss of thirty-five million, since foreign stockholders would not support a bank in which they had no confidence. Moreover, the bill was first discussed only by friends of the Bank in the committee without the others being fully informed on the topic.

[1] These provisions were suggested by Governor Ritner and Thaddeus Stevens.

the changes in the bill as stated in your letter of the 13th inst. These are entirely unexpected and I consider them fatal to the whole plan. If the Congress of the U.S. passed the bill in 1832 by large majorities in both houses without annexing such conditions, there is no reason why the legislature of Penns^a. should propose them — and still less reason for our submitting to them. As restrictions, they are unavailing — as indications of opinion, they are offensive; and a single word on that subject causes the immediate rejection of the Act by the Stockholders. I have so written to Mr Reed. Unless therefore these ideas be totally abandoned, I wish the question of the Bank withdrawn, as it seems useless to prolong a negociation which must be abortive.

JOHN B. WALLACE TO BIDDLE

Harrisburg January 18 1836

Dear Sir

Upon conferring with Mr Stevens to-day he agreed without difficulty to waive the section respecting political interferences etc. The Internal Improvement committee are now sitting upon the bill — it will go through that committee to-night & be reported to the House tomorrow — as little delay as possible will take place in urging it through the house. It may be detained longer in the Senate, but its friends will push it as fast as possible. It is expedient to do so — as it is obvious an organized opposition originating at Washington, is getting up — and as little time as possible must be allowed for it to operate upon the Senate — So soon as the bill is printed, a copy will be sent you. . . .

JOHN B. WALLACE TO BIDDLE

Harrisburg — January 19. 1836

Dear Sir

As you are well informed by others of the state of things here, I do not trouble you with a recital of what you know. I may however add my decided opinion that the bill [1] is safe — unless something entirely unexpected occur — Washington influence, county meetings etc will not prevent it — . . . If the government of the U.S. had had as able a chargé at Paris as you have in McIlvaine here, our relations with France [2] would have been in a very different situation from what they are.

BIDDLE TO JOSEPH McILVAINE

Phil[a]. Jany 31. 1836

Dear Sir,

Since writing to you this afternoon, I have heard some matters about the Bill which have changed my views of its actual position — and produced a corresponding alteration

[1] The bill was introduced on this date. The title of the act of incorporation was unique. It was styled "An Act to Repeal the State Tax on Real & Personal Property and to continue & extend the improvements of the State by Railroads & Canals, and to charter a State Bank to be called the United States Bank." In other words, the re-charter articles, drawn up with consummate skill by those perfectly conversant with the subject, appeared as clauses in a general appropriation measure. But this did not deceive the citizens of the state nor the nation at large. On January 5, the *Richmond Enquirer* had called the attention of the people of Pennsylvania to the need of stability in the legislature on account of the devious maneuvers of the old Bank. The Bank papers might remain silent on the topic, but the presence of lobbyists at Harrisburg and the fact that the stock had risen from 110 to 118 in a few days were signs that could not be mistaken. Public meetings had been held for the purpose of proclaiming that the people had "no principles to barter for gold"; and everything had been done to arouse the people to a sense of their duties. Cf. *American Sentinel*, January 21, 25, 1836; *Pennsylvanian*, January 9, 15, 18, 22, 1836.

[2] The subject of President Jackson's relations with France are discussed in MacDonald, William, *Jacksonian Democracy* (New York, 1907), pp. 204–209; Sumner, W. G., *Andrew Jackson* (Boston, 1898), pp. 402–439.

in the intentions announced in my letter. The interests depending on the event are too important to omit any proper opportunity of promoting it — and I therefore strengthen your hands with the inclosed which you will use discreetly & only in case it should be necessary.[1]

CHARLES S. BAKER [2] TO BIDDLE

Harrisburgh Friday evening
February 5th 1836

Dear Sir

Yesterday and to day has been spent in Skirmishing — the troops being raw thay could not be brought to close action — a counsel of war has been held and it has been resolved to force the matter to-morrow. Burden [3] is to lead on and I assure you he is in a happy state of mind to perform that service. M[r] Penrose is now all confidence and in conjunction with D[r] Burden & M[r] Stevens is now engaged in arraigning every thing for to morrow. A test vote will be brought to beare upon the matter to-morrow and I think will evidence we are Strong, very strong, in the Senate — success I consider certain.

[1] This letter refers to the chief difficulty encountered by the friends of the bill in the committee stage in the Senate. Senator Dickey stated his determination to have a branch in Beaver County. This the noble Senator declared was his *sine qua non*, as it was the only possible excuse he could offer his constituents for his vote. McIlvaine acknowledged the justice of the Senator's contention, expecially as the latter threatened to vote against the bill and carry two votes with him. Biddle, in reply to a request for advice from his *chargé*, stated that he was not opposed to a branch at Beaver, but to the naming of a branch anywhere which might lead to the naming of others. Still, if the Senator insisted upon it, Biddle was willing to agree and wrote the above letter to McIlvaine. For a careful discussion of this subject, cf. *Report of the Select Committee Relative to the United States Bank together with the Testimony taken in Relation thereto* (Paterson, 1837), p. 5.

[2] A Whig member later voted against the passage of the bill. A defense of his position is given in the *Pennsylvanian*, February 26, 1836.

[3] Representatives from the County of Philadelphia in the Senate.

JOHN McKIM JR. TO BIDDLE

Baltimore Feby 6th 1836

Dear Sir

As I wrote to you on the 3ᵈ Inst. that a favourable Charter for the Bank of the United States could be obtained in this State, I have since Indeavoured to find out what could be done at Annapolis, as our Legislature our much in favour of the Bank of the United States and the following is the Result of my Enquire

A Charter could it is Believed be obtained on the following terms,

1st Individual Stock to the Amt. of 28 Millions

2ᵈ A State Subscription for 7 Millions, Payable in 5 pr cᵗ State Stock, Redeemable at the time of the Expiration of the Charter.

3ᵈ. The Charter to continue for 30 years

4th. The Company to have Liberty, to Establish Branches or Agencies, in A State or Territory of the United States, Who Will give Liberty to them to do so.

5th. The Corporation, Will annualy Pay to the State the sum of one Hundred Thousand Dollars during the Existance of its Charter. . . .

SAMUEL R. WOOD TO BIDDLE

Harrisburg 2mo 10th 1836

My dear friend

I wrote to thee yesterday by Jacob Louder who left at Midnight and who was to leave my letter & others at Smith & Hodgson's store and I hope thee got it early in evening.

A strange scene has been played off in Senate this day. After the usual morning business Mr Fullerton of Franklin Co. rose in his place and said, that the Reporter & Journal of yesterday contained a direct charge of an offer made to bribe an honourable senator, & that he was unwilling to proceed untill an investigation was entered into; & moved that the Sergant of Arms be directed to bring forthwith to the bar of the Senate Samuel D. Patterson & O. Barrett the editors of said paper — this resolution was adopted with very little debate, and in about half an hour these two gentlemen were at the Bar. Patterson had not written the article or Knew any thing about it, but the other avowed having written it & stated that Jacob Krebs, the Senator from Schuylkill County was his informant. That he heard from another person that such an offer had been made to Krebs about ten days ago. That he called on him, asked him if the report was true & was informed by him that it was, but that he would not tell the name of the individual who made the offer of the bribe. The evidence of Barrett was not concluded untill dinner time when the Senate adjourned untill half past 3 o'clock. Mr Krebs was then called upon & he read from his place a statement of the offer. I did hope to have been able to have got a copy of this, but the committee are not willing to let it go out. The substance of it is that James L. Dunn of Reading came to him in the Senate Chamber on the 28th of last month and stated that if this Bank Bill should pass that his (Dunns) coal lands in Schuylkill County would very much advance in price, and wished Krebs to vote for the Bill. That if he would, he (Dunn) would give Krebs one half of the amount of the rise which he estimated at 4,000 dollars but that should the lands raise in value ten thousand dollars which they might, that he would in that case give him five thousand dollars. Krebs gave him no answer on that evening. Dunn called next morning and pressed it on him but he declined and afterwards avoided Dunn.

That on the 30th of January or first of March Henry W. Conrad a member of the House of Representatives from Schuylkill County told Krebs that he would insure him twenty thousand dollars if he would vote for the Bank Bill, and that if he agreed to it Bird Patterson would make the arrangement and that he should have the money in two weeks after the Bill passed — after the Senator had read his statement a motion was made to appoint a committee with power to send for persons & papers — which was agreed to & Baker, Toland, Leet, Strohm & Langston named as the Committee when the Senate adjourned.

How Dunn will get out of it is doubtful but all believe that Conrad was only in jest and that the old man was weak enough to take it for earnest — for there was two or three persons present when Conrad made the offer. Conrad has been one of the most violent and determined opposers of the Bill in the House. The violent opposers here have endeavoured to produce an excitement out of this matter & are woefully disappointed. They have evidently weakened themselves by it and look discouraged & ashamed. The friends of it bore them much and are in high spirits as to the result. They will take up the Bill to-morrow and I hope nothing will interrupt its passage.[1]

---

[1] The "Krebs affair," mentioned in the above letter became the main issue in the latter part of the passage of the Bank Bill. Committees were appointed in both the Senate and the House. The Senate Report disclosed the fact that Patterson had not approached Krebs directly, but indirectly through Conrad; that the former had authorized Conrad to request Krebs to offer an amendment to the bill

J. R. Ingersoll to Biddle

House of representatives
Washington March 17th 1836

My Dear Sir

Mr Evans of Maine has exhibited to me a letter from certain Gentlemen to the East who are anxious to know the views of your Bank with regard to the establishment of branches or agencies, in other states. They have in view a branch or agency in Bangor: and desire to know whether they

to get an appropriation to the Danville & Pottsville Railroad; but Patterson denied that Krebs had been told "he might retire to private life independent if he voted for the measure." Therefore the committee reported that they were perfectly convinced that neither the Bank of the United States nor any agent of it were either implicated in the charge of bribery or had improperly interfered to promote its passage. The House Report was along the same lines and reached the same conclusion. Cf. *American Sentinel*, February 15, 1836; *National Gazette*, February 18, 1836; *Pennsylvanian*, February 18, 1836; *New York Journal of Commerce*, February 16, 1836; Niles, April 9, 1836.

Throughout the whole episode the correspondence of the agents of the bank to Biddle had taken about the same stand as that of the House Committee. McIlvaine, writing on February 5, stigmatized the affair of old Krebs as a "humbug"; Todd described the case as "all smoke"; while Wallace wrote he was unable to determine whether Krebs was "so utterly stupid as not to understand the meaning & nature of a bribe or so wicked as to pervert perfectly innocent conversations to political profit."

The bill re-chartering the old Bank was signed February 18. From all sides Nicholas Biddle received the congratulations and plaudits of his friends. The stock of the Bank rose from 125 to 129 in less than a week, and property in Erie, Pennsylvania, doubled in value. (Cf. Russell to Buchler, February 28, 1836, in Wolf MSS. in Pennsylvania Historical Society Library.) In the United States Senate Ewing of Ohio triumphantly proclaimed the re-charter, while Calhoun renewed his attacks on the Administration. But the opponents of the old United States Bank did not falter in their opposition. The Ohio Legislature passed a bill prohibiting the establishment of agencies or branches in that state, much to the surprise and alarm of Biddle and his friends (cf. Pennsylvania, March 25, 1836). Rumors were likewise circulated regarding the supposed antagonism of Virginia and New York (*ibid.*, February 24, 1836). Even President Jackson contemplated action against the bill when drafting the Specie Circular. This is disclosed in the Jackson MSS. in a memorandum containing an addition to the Treasury Circular. This is endorsed by Jackson "to be considered as to the present or future time."

could arrange the appointment of individuals by whom it would be conducted subject of course to the parental direction of the Bank. They wish to commence with a capital of $500,000 with the right to increase it from time to time as the business may warrant. . . .

While I have been writing at my desk a neighbour of mine has asked me whether it was the design of the Bank to establish an agency at Erie. He resides at Buffalo and thinks that the business which has heretofore been conducted at that place may be without difficulty transferred to Erie.

STEPHEN F. AUSTIN [1] TO BIDDLE

Philadelphia April 9. 1836.

Sir,

As the enclosed memorandum embraces the outlines of the Loan for Texas on which I conversed with you this morning, I take the liberty of handing it to you.

I should esteem it as a favor, if I could be informed within a short time, whether you think any thing could be effected in this matter.

I consider the cause of Texas is the cause of freemen, and of mankind, but more emphatically of the people of the United States than any other. I flatter myself that you view it in the same light, and that the security we offer is good, and therefore have no doubt you will give to it the attention which its importance merits.

The leading men of all parties in Washington are favorably disposed towards Texas. A reference to them will, I think, satisfy all persons as to this fact.

---

[1] Son of Moses Austin, pioneer of Texas. Sent as commissioner of state to secure recognition of the United States.

(enclosed memorandum)

It is proposed to negociate a Loan for the Government of Texas, on the following basis.

The Commissioners of Texas shall assign to the Bank of the United States at Philadelphia, the Bonds of the Government of Texas, which they hold, for the sum of 500,000 payable in not less than 5 years, and redeemable thereafter at the pleasure of the State at the rate of 20% per annum, and if not so redeemed at the end of ten years, to be wholly redeemable at 6 months notice thereafter, and bearing an interest of 8% per annum to be held in Trust by said Bank, for the benefit of the holders of a scrip to be issued by the Commissioners, based on said Bonds.

Books of Subscription shall be opened in the cities of Boston, New York, Philadelphia and Baltimore, for a scrip to be issued by the Commissioners in shares of $100, which said scrip shall entitle the holder to an interest in said Bonds equal to the amount of Scrip thus held by him, and said Scrip shall be payable as follows;

Of all purchases of land at the land offices in Texas, 20% of the sums due, may be paid and shall be receivable in said scrip.

Of all customs due at the Custom Houses of Texas 20% of the sums due, may be paid, and shall be receivable in said Scrip.

The holder shall be entitled to an interest of 8% per annum, payable at the Bank of the United States in Philadelphia, on all portions of said Scrip unpaid, and the Government of Texas shall have the privilege of paying the whole amount of said scrip, and redeeming their said Bonds, by paying 20% of the principal annually, after the expiration of 5 years, or the whole payable at 6 months notice after the expiration of 10 years.

The payments of the Subscribers to said Scrip shall be made, 25% at the time of subscription, and the remainder in 3 equal payments at 60, 90 & 120 days there after, to be secured at the time of subscription, by the notes of the subscribers, endorsed to the satisfaction of the Directors of the Bank of the United States, or persons appointed by them, & payable at such place as said Directors shall designate, provided the same be in the cities when said stock is subscribed.

The Bank of the United States shall discount the notes thus paid in, and pay over the whole amount of the proceeds thereof, and the amount of the first instalment thus paid in, to the Commissioners of Texas, and hold said Bonds as an additional guarantee for the payment of said notes.

BIDDLE (?) TO EDWARD R. BIDDLE [1]

Phil^a March 20, 1837

My dear Sir,

. . . I have made up my mind to two things — which I give to you as elements in your calculations — 1st That it is not our interest to prop people who must fall — and therefore I shall not be inclined to advance a dollar further for any body unless under very peculiar circumstances. and 2. That the Treasury Circular will not be immediately repealed. Such at least is the present intension of the Chief who is already discovered to be weak & vacillating. How this will affect your money market you can best judge . . .

---

[1] Engaged in the brokerage business in New York City; the second or third cousin of Nicholas Biddle.

THOMAS COOPER TO BIDDLE

Columbia South Carolina
private   April 29. 1837
Dear Sir

I wrote a letter to you some time ago on behalf of our Iron company: subsequent events have furnished a sufficient reply.

I enter upon my 79th Year, next October. By the time Mr Van Beuren's first period has expired, I shall be superannuated. I can have therefore no selfish motive in my present proposal. The tide is turning strongly agst the measures of the last and present Administration. The poor now groan under the financial follies of Gen. Jackson as well as the rich. To be sure, over trading and gambling speculation will account for three fourths of the present distress, but no one can be blind to the effects produced by the desperate ignorance of the last President.

At this moment your judicious conduct has placed you prominent as a wise and temperate man, and a public benefactor. You can go on pursuing cautiously the same course of conduct, and earning on all hands golden opinions.

Why not look to the Presidency?

Can your name be brought forward at a time more advantageous than the present? You are rising, your opponents are falling: strike the ball on the rebound, and I think this is the moment.

Is there any chance of success for such imbecilles as Benton, Harrison, or even White? Men without preliminary study, without knowledge patiently and laboriously acquired, without the business tact of experience, and floating on the bubbles of popular clamour. Think of this: and if needful command my services, such as they may be. I am, and so may you be, in the odour of political sanctity in this State: and this State is the South; for we have earned the character of honesty & energy. We have here two men of plausible & fair pretensions: of those pretensions I say nothing at present; the subject may be discussed, if needful, by and by.

The present suggestion is my own: received from and communicated to no one but yourself: & so it shall remain till you decide. . . .

JOEL R. POINSETT [1] TO BIDDLE

Washington
6th. May 1837

My dear Sir

I read with great interest M[r] Coxe's letter, which I now return. It confirms the melancholy state of things you explained to me as existing in the West, and for which I see no present remedy. The suspension of the distribution [2] presents the most substantial relief: but although we may have some legal excuse to suspend that of October, the instalment due the states in July will I understand be paid.

Can you not in your financial knowledge and experience devise some plan by which a wholesome control may be exercised over bank issues and exchanges be brought back to which they were before the destruction of the Bank — Some measure apart from a national bank even although it might be connected with the operations of a great state institu-

---

[1] Secretary of War under Van Buren.
[2] The best work on this topic is Bourne, E. G., *The History of the Surplus Revenue of 1837* (New York, 1885).

tion. I see obstacles to the charter of a national bank that are insuperable in the present state of things, and would gladly avail myself of your skill to support some measure which might save us the repetition of the evils we are now suffering.

BIDDLE TO JOEL R. POINSETT

Phil^a May 8. 1837

My dear Sir —

I have always thought that the best thing which Mr Van Buren could do in reference to himself personally, as well as to his political party, would be to make peace with the Bank — and the present state of things furnishes an admirable opportunity of accomplishing that object. Why indeed should he not? To all the members of the Cabinet except one,[1] I personally have always stood in a friendly relation, and in regard to the President himself there is no sort of personal difference. The way therefore would be open for a general amnesty — which for the sake of the country I am willing to consent to — and I do believe that just now the effect would be electric & decisive.

BIDDLE TO JOEL R. POINSETT

Phil^a May 8. 1837

Dear Sir —

I received last evening your favor of the 6th inst. The course of the Gov^t. being I presume settled as according to the newspapers, it now remains only to do what we can to diminish the sufferings of the country, and for this I shall certainly work as hard as if I had caused them.

[1] This evidently refers to Woodbury.

You ask whether some plan could not be devised by which the issues of the banks & the exchanges could be regulated as formerly, by a connection with some large state Bank. I have no doubt of it. I have no doubt that at this moment the simplest & easiest form of relief would be to make the present Bank of the U.S. the depositors of the public revenue. It would be only necessary —

1ˢᵗ. To let the Treasury & the Bank agree that the Bank should take charge of the public revenue — collect and distribute it — relieve the Treasury from all trouble about it.

2ᵈ. To let the Treasury — without disturbing or formally repealing the specie circular [1] — direct the receivers to take the notes of the Bank of the U.S.

3ᵈ. The Bank would then appoint its own agents — or affiliate with it other State Banks — being of course responsible for them all — & the whole system of the public revenue as it was in 1830 — which, now we may speak of it historically, was an admirable one — would be all restored.

The Western State Banks have mostly officers of the late Bank — the whole country asks nothing better than its notes which are now every where at a premium, and both at home & abroad the Bank has a reputation which it can put at the service of the Government.

I sincerely believe that in a week's time such an arrangement would restore confidence & credit.

The very prospect of it would stop many of the evils which are impending.

And why should it not be? If the thing promises well, why should we be deterred from attempting it? Why should Mʳ

---

[1] For a discussion of the Specie Circular, consult MacDonald, *Jacksonian Democracy*, pp. 286–291.

Van Buren & Mr Forsyth & Mr Dickerson & Mr Woodbury & yourself not agree to any project which promises relief, even tho' the name of the Bank be connected with it. I am sure you are all above the indulgence of any feeling on that score — and for myself, I am perfectly willing to forget all the quarrels with the last administration, which neither party would desire to have perpetuated.

Politically the effect would undoubtedly be good. Pennsylvania would be pleased, and the whole country would regard it as a proof of returning peace.

It would require a little time to mount again the machinery, but it could be done without much delay, & in the mean time the very knowledge that it was intended, would be infinitely soothing in the present initated condition of things.

Now, my dear sir, there is a project for you. If you can bring it to bear, you will have done great good to the country — a work in which you will always find a ready cooperation.

BIDDLE TO GENERAL ROBERT PATTERSON [1]

Phil^a May 8. 1837

Dear Sir —

In a letter which I have written by this mail to Mr Poinsett, I have suggested a measure which I think would be a brilliant stroke of policy, & give immediate confidence to the country. It is simply this, that the Gov^t. should make the Bank of the U.S. the depository of the public funds, and without repealing the specie circular, authorize the reciept of the paper of the Bank for dues to the Government. You will see at a glance the advantages of such a movement. . . .

[1] In 1836 Patterson was the President of the electoral college that cast the vote of Pennsylvania for Martin Van Buren. One of the largest mill-owners in the United States.

What prevents this? Some old feeling of party? Certainly not. We have fought out the battle with the last administration — with what success it is not for me to say — but at least we fought it fairly, and we do not wish to fight it over with this administration.

I submit all these matters to you, and if, as I trust, you will see them in the same light, I would ask your immediate concurrence in carrying it into effect. I care not how it begins, or who proposes it, but if it be necessary for me to commence, I am agreed. I am too proud to think my step humiliating which may benefit this poor bleeding country of ours.

GENERAL ROBERT PATTERSON TO BIDDLE

Confidential   Washington 8 May 1837
My dear Sir

I called this morning on Mr Van Buren and had nearly an Hours conversation with him — going over the whole ground — he is evidently in an unpleasant position [1] — conscious of the impending danger — and yet anxious to avoid doing anything which might appear to be a departure from the policy of his predecessor . . .

BIDDLE TO THOMAS COOPER

Phil^a. May 8. 1837
My dear Sir,

I have had the pleasure of receiving your favor of the 29th ult°, and rejoice to see in it the same vigor of mind & of style which I have admired for five & twenty years. I hope it may carry you through many Presidential Olympiads.

---

[1] The Van Buren MSS. in the Library of Congress show clearly that Van Buren thought he ought to follow in the footsteps of President Jackson.

I thank you for your approbation of my public conduct, which, whatever may be the result, has been dictated by a very honest desire to protect the great interests of the country.

In relation to the friendly suggestion which forms the purpose of your letter, I have received from various quarters intimations of a disposition to connect my name with the next election of President. These I have never considered seriously, nor indeed noticed at all: but to you I will speak for the first time & without reserve.

I believe that the prosperity & the character of the country require that those who now govern it should be removed and that all true men should unite to expel them — each taking the position, either of chief or subaltern, which the general voice assigns to him. I am quite sure that I have not the least affectation in saying, that to myself personally, the office has not the slightest attraction. Its dignity has been degraded by the elevation to it of unworthy men — and as to mere power, I have been for years in the daily exercise of more personal authority than any President habitually enjoys. But I stand ready for the country's service. If therefore you think that my name can be productive of good, I am content to place it — as I now do, at your disposal — under a conviction of the friendly & discreet manner in which alone it will be employed.

THOMAS COOPER TO BIDDLE

Private   Columbia May 14. 1837
Dear Sir

My friend the Governor of this State, a man of no brilliant talents, of no acquirement, but a great worldly tact and resource, and extremely popular, will not be here for some days. He is at Charleston where our State Bank have acceded to our request to the loan I wrote to you about. I shall sound him when he returns, cautiously but I think successfully: till then I make no move. Hitherto, he and I have acted with no variance of opinion.

I could write to Noah: but Altho' I have no doubt about his inclinations, I know not enough how his interest points. The Iron is quite hot enough in that furnace, to strike; but you have it under your own controul. In that field of battle you must trace the line of March. Movements of great danger & irritation seem to me probable in that quarter, that may furnish a favourable occasion for your prudent interference.

We have two aspirants here: both able, & both honest men: both regarded throughout the State, rather as looking steadily at the central Government, than as guided by a purely South Carolinian spirit. They are therefore not popular. Calhoun is rather borne with, than supported. He has talent, but without tact or Judgement. Remember, I am giving you, what leading and thinking men say.

Preston has more talent, more tact, more judgement, & is as honest as Calhoun. They are on the field of political competition. Preston is more approved. But he is too much of a diplomat: too much non committal; too Van Beurenish, but much superior to V. Beuren. People distrust him from his manner, more than they ought. But he is not popular. He has not the leading mark of a great man, he cannot attach to himself a corps of personal thorough-going friends. Gen¹ Hamilton of our State could do that. So does our present Governor Butler. Preston moreover is a Virginian. He would make a good minister at a foreign Court.

Both these Gentlemen are like me, Nullifiers. They could not be sustained out of the State, even if they could command South Carolina. It is an unfashionable Garb. It sticks like the shirt of Nesus. I am content however to wear it as my winding sheet.

You will have no opponents of equal talent, energy, & honesty with these two Gentlemen, whom I regard as hors de combat.

Strange times are approaching. Arrangements ought to be made to introduce the Subject; when, where, and how? For by the time Congress meets, the pressure will be at its acme, and the lower classes will feel it severely.

I trouble you with these preliminary hints, for the plan of the Campain must be thought about.

Webster will be set up as your Opponent: the South will not go for him; & they will go for you in preference. Webster has a character for talent, but he is not qualified for a leader. He has no personal friends. He is a good partizan parliamentary debater, but he cannot trace out the plan of a political Campain, nor is he fit to be at the head of it. I see no fearful competitor at present, or in prospect. . . . Adieu.

THOMAS COOPER TO BIDDLE

Private   May 24. 1837 Columbia
Dear Sir

. . . All to whom I have guardedly spoken, agree with me in opinion, decidedly. My friend the Governor has settled with to set up a new paper here; for we cannot make use of the Telescope, or the other paper of our town; and the strange infatuation of Mr Calhoun as to the presidency must be counteracted. I believe M'Duffie would go with us strenuously, if it were not for personal regard to Mr Calhoun. You have gained over Calcock of Charleston.

Among *our* people in Congress, White of Tennessee has friends; but White & Clay have been started on the course, and are broken down. Neither can succeed if entered again.

Mr Van Beuren, whom I like personally (for he is a Gentleman) will I think carry the next Congress with him. I have taken full and effectual care both to him & Mr Poinsett, to render mistake impossible as to my opinions. I have stated expressly and decidedly that I am a friend to State interposition agst an unconstitutional Law, by Nullification. That I disapprove of Genl. Jackson's exprints[?] on the finances of the Country, and that I consider the treasury circular as tending in its results to degrade the national credit and character. I have found this distinct explanation on my part, necessary.

If the Congress called in September should resolve on a national Bank, (which I doubt, for a majority as yet are Van Beurenists) it will be, either the readoption of yours, or a new establishment at New York, over which you will probably be invited to preside. But the measure of misfortune is not yet full enough, to drive the friends of General Jackson from their insane attempts. I think Mr Van Beuren has committed himself to the old man too far; and the call of Congress *may be* intended to introduce a little welcome force before he yields. . . .

THOMAS COOPER TO BIDDLE

S. Car^l. Columbia July 1: 1837

Dear Sir

. . . The time has not yet arrived for the *direct* nomination of any man as future president. But all secondary means and appliances may be usefully brought forward, and should be so: cast thy bread on the waters, it will be found again after many days.

Webster is a dexterous debater, but he has no judgement, no energy, or boldness of character. The man has no personal courage & cannot succeed: he is made to be governed. Here, we should decidedly prefer Van Beuren to Webster. But the battle is coming on (may be, literally) between the ultra radicalists and the Constitutionalists: if Mr Van Beuren has desperate courage enough, we shall have a monarchical government of no liberal character. If not, I see no serious obstacle to the success of my proposal. . . . Adieu. I wish you good success

BIDDLE TO JOHN RATHBONE JR

(*private*)   Phil^a. July 14. 1837

My dear Sir

You ask my views about the mode in which the Bank of the U.S. could assist in restoring the currency. I will tell you in a few words.

The present design of those who govern the Government at Washington is, I understand, to draw all the funds out of the Banks — then cut all connection with them — and establish subtreasuries where each receiver is to sit upon his small heap of gold & silver. This is the newest, & therefore the favorite, foolery. Congress, I think will not agree to this, or to any other experiment and will incline to either a real downright Bank of the U.S. chartered by the Genl Gov^t or to the present Pennsylv^a. Bank. . . .

If the Treasury & the Bank could come to an understanding as to the terms on which the Bank would do this business — everything would soon come right.

But I can do nothing at present which would not work more harm than good. This very proposition I made before the suspension. Had it been adopted the Suspension would have been I believe, averted. I cannot now renew it. My purpose now is to be perfectly quiet — to be ready — but not impatient & wait the action of Congress. If that body adopts any measure which promises relief I shall cordially concur in it — If not, having done my duty I remain where I was. My great object is to heal the wounds inflicted upon the country. I will spare no effort for that purpose. No misguided feeling of pride, no remembrance of past injustice to myself shall prevent me from a sincere & cordial cooperation with any public men who will honestly labor in the public service. These are the simple views — and the frank opinion of

B. W. LEIGH TO BIDDLE

Richmond, Aug. 21. 1837.

My dear sir

I am informed, that the hon^e William Smith, formerly of South Carolina, now of Alabama, has recently, in a public speech to the people of Huntsville, and on other occasions, stated that the late chief justice Marshall[1] owned seventeen shares of stock of the Bank of the U.States, at the time he decided, in the case of McCullock against the State of Maryland, that the charter of the Bank was constitutional. The argument of that cause was opened on the 22nd February 1819, and the chief justice delivered the opinion of the court on the 7th March; 4 Wheat. 316, 322, 400.

---

[1] For a discussion of the Marshall affair, cf. Niles, September 23, 1837, pp. 50–51; *ibid.*, December 2, 1837, p. 218; *ibid.*, June 2, 1838, pp. 210–211.

The most innocent purpose for which such a statement could have been made, was to detract from the weight of the chief justice's authority on the point of constitutional law; which Mr Smith, it seems, was willing to accomplish, by imputing to him a personal interest in the controversy. I say nothing about the motive or the candor of such an imputation, or of the evidence it affords of Mr Smith's scale of moral sentiment and honor.

I find upon examination of the Dividend Books of the office of the Bank at this place, that Mr Marshall received the dividend of July 1817 on 12 shares; and the dividends on 17 shares, of January 1818, July 1818, and January 1819; and that his receipt for this last dividend is dated Jany 23, 1819, just before he left home to attend the supreme court, the term of which then commenced on the 1st February. From thenceforth he never received any dividend (because, I infer, he never owned any stock) in his own right — tho' there was some stock standing *in his name and mine* as joint exōrs of G. K. Taylor of Petersburg, which *I* bought and always drew the dividends of — and, at a later period, some stock standing in his name as trustee for the widow and children of his brother William Marshall. It follows, that he must have sold his own 17 shares of stock, after the dividend of January 1819 was declared; but we cannot ascertain *here* the precise date when he parted with it. I have not the least doubt, that he sold this stock before he left home in January or February 1819.

Now I must beg the favor of you to ascertain the date of the transfer of that stock, on the the transfer book* at Philadelphia, the person to whom he transferred it, and (as he must have transferred by attorney) the date of the letter of attorney; and to give me the precise dates, and a copy of the letter of attorney and of the authentication subjoined to it. Have the goodness also, to have the facts stated in the form of a certificate signed by the proper officer of the Bank.

You may perhaps think I am taking over unnecessary trouble about this affair — but I do so at the request of a friend at Huntsville — and besides, I am persuaded, that if a grave charge of forgery, or perjury, or sheep stealing, were made against the most honest and honorable man in the country, it would do him some harm; so general is the belief of the universal corruption of the nation. I am, sir, with hearty respect & esteem

* 1819 [1]

Feb. 8th   12 shl to Thos Marshall
Mar (?) 26th   5 "   " Thos P. Cope & for

BIDDLE TO B. W. LEIGH

Phil[a] Augt. 24. 1837.

My Dear Sir,

I had last evening the pleasure of receiving your letter of the 21st inst. and immediately hasten to perform the sacred duty of defending the character of an honest man from the reptiles who avenge themselves for his superiority while living, by crawling over his dead body. I think we shall be perfectly successful in presenting the following results.

The argument in the case of McCullock & the State of Maryland began, according to your statement on the 22d of Feby 1819, & the decision of the court was pronounced on the 17th of March 1819.

Now of the 17 shares owned by the Judge Marshall on the

---

1 This is in pencil in manuscript.

1st of Jany. 1819, 12 were transferred on the 8th of Feby. 1819, under a power given by Judge Marshall on the 5th of Feby. 1819.

For the remaining 5 he gave a power to transfer them on the *21st of Jany.* 1819, though the transfer was not actually made on the Books until the 26th of March 1819.

So that in point of fact he was ostensibly the owner of five shares at the time of the decision.

Finding this I sent for Mr Cope, one of the Director's of the Bank of the U.S. and nephew of the Mr Thomas V. Cope named in the power of Atty. & requested him to examine the books of the House & endeavored to find the evidences of what I have no doubt was the fact, that Judge Marshall sold the Stock at the time of giving the power of Attorney on the 21st of January, and that the purchaser neglected to send it on till March to be transferred.

I have kept my letter open in order to give the result of Mr Cope's enquiries, but as the period is so remote he has not been able to complete his examination, & promises to let me know further tomorrow. He thinks however that he has ascertained that this stock was sent to the House by some person in Virga with other parcels of stock to be transferred, & that the probility is that the correspondent in Virga had purchased these five shares & paid for them.

I will postpone till tomorrow therefore the further examination, & in the meantime send inclosed a certificate from the Transfer Office & certified copies of the powers of Attorney on file. It may be well to add, that in the power of Atty of the 21st of Jany. 1819, there is a blank for the name of the Atty. and that the blank is filled up with the name of Thomas P Cope *in the handwriting of Thos P Cope himself*, whence I infer that the power was given in blank by Judge Marshall with the certificate & sent to M^r Th^os P Cope by his correspondent in Virg^a . . .

BIDDLE TO B. W. LEIGH

Phil^a Augt. 25. 1837.

My Dear Sir,

Referring to my letter of yesterday's date, I now inclose a memorandum furnished by Mr Caleb Cope by which it will appear that the Stock in the name of Judge Marshall was received from Mr John V. Wilcox of Petersburg V^a. That gentleman is still living, & could probably explain the terms on which he received it from the Judge. I have now furnished all the materials within my reach, but I shall follow the subject with great interest, and will be much gratified at hearing from you the result of your enquiries, the fame of that upright man being the common property of us all.

B. W. LEIGH TO BIDDLE

Richmond, Aug. 28. 1837

My Dear Sir

I write to acknowledge your letter of the 24th and 25th, and to thank you for them.

The letter of attorney for the transfer of Mr Marshall's five shares of stock in which Mr Cope was the attorney, was luckily attested by the James H. Lynch of this town; and I immediately resorted to him for information as to the date at which Mr M. parted with his property in that stock. Mr L. has furnished me conclusive proof, that that stock was sold to him at par, and paid for, on the 21st January 1819, the date of the letter of attorney; and he says, moreover, that he advised Mr. Marshall, at the time, not to sell his stock, but he assigned as his reason for selling it, that he did not choose to remain a stock holder, as questions might be brought before the supreme court in which the Bank might be concerned. M^r. L. does not remember certainly to whom he sold these shares of stock; but the scrip and the letter of attorney probably passed thro' several hands before they came to those of Mr Wilcox, who sent them to Mr Cope. But this is wholly immaterial, and I shall not take the trouble to write to Mr W. about it.

You shall be informed what I do in this affair. Do not doubt that I will give the Hon William Smith such a rap over the knuckles as he deserves. But that is not all I have to do — the gentleman who informed me of this mean and base slander on Mr Marshall's memory, said, that Mr Smith "made the statement upon the authority of a U.States Senator now representing Virginia." I cannot believe that he had any such authority; and I suspect he has slandered our Senators as well as Mr Marshall. But if it shall turn out that he vouched any such authority, and that either of our present Senators made any such communication to him, that Senator shall hear of it, and that in such a manner that he shall not forget it for the remainder of his days.

B. W. Leigh to Biddle

Richmond, Sept. 4. 1837.

Dear Sir —

You must pardon me for giving you a little more trouble.

I find from the dividend book of the office of the bank of U.States at Richmond, that Gen. J. B. Harvie of this town, the son-in-law of the late chief justice Marshall, received the dividends on ten shares of stock, of July 1817, January and July 1818, and January 1819, and thenceforth afterwards he never received any dividend on any of the stock. From a conversation I have had with Gen. H. this morning, I apprehend that these shares were originally purchased by Mrs Marshall the wife of the chief justice, but the transfer of it was made to Gen. H. and the stock stood in his name, tho' in fact as trustee for her — she had a sort of separate property,* which she managed for herself and disposed of the profits of it, or the principal, among her children, at her own pleasure. Gen. H. says this stock was given to him; Mr Marshall telling him at the time, that he wished to divest himself of all manner of interest in the bank, because there was suits pending (or might be such suits) in the supreme court in which the bank was concerned. But Gen. H. does not remember the precise date of the gift to him.

I beg you to get the transfer clerk to give me the precise date when, and the person to whom, Gen. H. transferred these ten shares of stock, and to send me a copy of his power of attorney for the transfer of it — and oblige

You will soon see in print my correspondence with my friend in Huntsville on the subject of Mr Smith's speech
* tho' not under any settlement

BIDDLE TO B. W. LEIGH

Phil^a Septr. 7. 1837

My Dear Sir,

I had last night the pleasure of receiving your favor of the 4th inst. & now inclose

1. A certificate from the Transfer Dep^t. of the Bank of the U.S. as to transfers from & to M^r. J. B. Harvie, &

2. Copies of the powers of Attorney by with which these transfers were effected.

I shall look with great interest for the correspondence which you promise — & remain meanwhile,

SILAS M. STILWELL [1] TO BIDDLE

New York Sept 9th 1837

D^r. Sir

    ... I am very much pleased with the message,[2] and the evident breaking up, to a sufficient extent, of party usages.

I think I see in the "conservitive 22" of the hour, a body of men who must be united, ultimately, to the Whigs. However we may look with more *confidence* to the result of their deliberations. I think there is no hope of the "Sub treasury" plan — the "conservatives"[3] will kill that. The "Pet Banks" are denounced by "the administration." A National Bank Mr Van Beuren is *pledged* to Veto. So what is there left to hang hope upon — except a *Contract* to releive the "government" — assist the people? — "To this complextion we must come at last." ...

CHARLES AUGUST DAVIS TO BIDDLE

New York 9 Sept^t. 1837

My D^r. Sir

    ... M^r. Van B—— has made a mistake in fixing on

---

[1] Lawyer and author of the general bankrupt law of New York; and in 1863 of the national banking act and system of organizing credits. Cf. *National Encyclopedia of American Biography*, vol. XI, p. 251.

[2] Richardson, *op. cit.*, vol. III, pp. 324–346.

[3] Party opposed to Sub-Treasury and led by Nathaniel P. Tallmadge of New York. For a good discussion of the conservative party in New York consult Hammond, J. D., *The History of Political Parties in New York* (Buffalo, 1850); or Alexander, D. S., *A Political History of New York* (New York, 1909).

the loco-foco portion of the *party* — and every day hundreds of his old friends drop off and openly denounce his doctrines — . . .

B. W. Leigh to Biddle

Richmond, Sep^t. 13. 1837.

Dear Sir —

I send you by the same mail with this, a copy of the Richmond Whig of this morning, containing my correspondence with D^r. Watkins of Alabama on the subject of Mr Smiths calumny on Chief justice Marshall. Pray, see that it is republished in the Philadelphia papers; and if you can, that it shall be also republished in the New York American. I hope you will think that I have struck the slanderer hard enough and not too hard.

Biddle to B. W. Leigh

Phil^a Septr. 15, 1837

Dear Sir,

I have this evening received your favor of the 13th inst. with the accompanying correspondence which I have read with sincere pleasure. I have already written to Mr King requesting its publication in the American, & shall see that it is widely circulated here.

Biddle to Charles King

Phila Septr. 15, 1837.

Dear Sir,

In a letter received this evening from Mr. Leigh of Richmond, he expressed a wish that his correspondence on the subject of Chief Justice Marshall which you will find in the Richmond Whig should be republished in the American. You will I am sure gladly contribute to vindicate the reputation of such a man from assailants who avenge themselves for his superiority while living by calumniating his memory. In doing this you will gratify Mr Leigh & oblige

E. R. BIDDLE TO BIDDLE

Septem^r 19^h 1837 —

My Dear Sir

I *must* have 5,000$ to accomplish some great good in my native state. I will give I hope a good account of it — at a proper time.

Do send it by return of mail.

BIDDLE TO E. R. BIDDLE

Phil^a. Sepr 20. 1837

My dear Sir,

Your note of yesterday is received & I would endeavor to comply with it at once but for this reason — From the phrasology of it I infer that it is not anything of personal interest to yourself — nor anything pecuniary — but merely political. Now the events that are passing satisfy me that it is not worth while to do anything in that line. I have renounced it altogether. Nothing would induce me to engage in it. Let me know if I am right & believe me

CHARLES AUGUST DAVIS TO BIDDLE

New York 27 Sep^t. 1837

My Dr Sir

. . . I have just return'd from "up the Hudson" after a few days absence. I found all the folks up there sour & sad

the Banks contracting & all suffering — the doctrine of the
Message dont suit them at all — & as the crops are good &
prices declining I suspect the farmers by Nov. will begin to
feel it too — & all the towns large & small desire they sh'd.
Every thing is working for good or I am sadly mistaken.
I Scarcely met a man of M^r. Van B. *late* party who does not
blame him & his "loco foco" [1] doctrines — the horror the
people have of the very name of loco foco is death to any
mans hopes who hinges on them, they think in the Country —
"loco foco" means flour rioters &c &c they are not far out.

The whole secrete of M^r. Van B. policy is to keep on the
side of democracy & when driven to extremities or compeld to
Show his hand — or take ground — it is then he strikes so
that none shall cut under him — feeling that democracy is
like a grass crop always springing up afresh & in good time
going to seed & when it reaches this point it is call'd aristoc-
racy & new crops follow but in boring his hold this time in
the great "Barrel politic" — he has evidently for the present
bored too low & will get dregs only — but his system is simply
this — whilst others adopt measures that divide society per-
pendicularly — he cuts horizontally — & always thus cuts that
no one shall cut under him — hence you may see him adopt
any measure that is likely to win with great maxim & rule. . . .

THOMAS COOPER TO BIDDLE

Columbia 20 Octr. 1837
Dear Sir
    The whole delegation of S. Carolina, save Calhoun and
his relative Pickens, voted against the Sub treasury bill. The

---

[1] For a brief account of the rise and activities of the Loco Foco Party consult
Byrdsall, F., *History of the Loco Foco or Equal Rights Party* (New York, 1842).

opinions of influential men here are divided about your bank. Preston and Hamilton are quietly in your favour. Quietly: for the day has not yet arrived to speak out plainly & boldly. Three fourths of the business men in our State are with you, but I think the time has not come in which we can call them out. If I augur rightly from the signs of the Times, a motion to reinstate your bank will be made in about 2 years; hardly sooner. But the expedients proposed & to be proposed as substitutes will all fail. I think even the 10 million bill will fail to relieve the New York merchants; and in that case, I dare not risk prognosticating the result.

The other proposal I made, in an early letter to you, must go on gently. It will work its own way, & has probability on its side. . . .

BIDDLE TO E. R. BIDDLE

(*private and confidential*)   Philᵃ. Novʳ. 6. 1837

My dear Sir

As you asked my opinion, I deem it right to Say that I think that neither your Bank nor any other Bank Should take the loan — and that it would be very hazardous for an individual since he would have to prove to the purchaser in Europe that it had not been originally purchased by a Bank. I believe that the best thing to do for you therefore both officially & individually is to abstain from it altogether, & so apprize the parties at once.

I had a long conversation to day with Mʳ Hunt the Minister from Texas — and suggested to him various changes which I thought useful in the Texas loan and which I have no doubt will be made unless some premature action takes place in regard to it. This you had better prevent.

E. R. Biddle to Biddle

New York Novem^r. 7th 1837 —

Dear Sir —

Your favor of yesterdays date is before me — Yesterday I declined making any proposition to the Comers from Texas, but I told them that if they would leave their address with me I would try and arrange to procure them a bid from a combination of individuals for 200,000$ provided the option of taking the whole amount should be given to the takers for 6 months, on their assuming an option of 300,000$ more in 90 days. This I think *can be* accomplished *by me* so as to pay me a handsome remuneration for my trouble. As however your letter induces me to stand aloof — I do so. Dont forget me however or *my Institution*, whenever you decide we are ready to unite with you.

E. R. Biddle to Biddle

New York Nov 11th 1837

My Dear Sir

The result of the elections [1] in this state is such as to

[1] The New York election was viewed with great interest during these months of distress, and it was evident that the outcome would be closely associated with the panic in the money market. The symptoms of a division in the Democratic Party in relation to banks and banking was early exhibited in New York. (Hammond, J. D., *The History of Political Parties in New York*, Buffalo, 1850, vol. II, pp. 462, 463.) The spring elections in the city of New York resulted in the choice of a Whig Mayor, and coming as they did in the midst of hard times "prepared the way for the avalanche in the fall." A little later the Sub-Treasury issue began to assume prominence in the politics of the state. Nathaniel P. Tallmadge, a Democratic United States Senator, openly opposed Van Buren's policy and endorsed Seward for governor of the state. Van Buren's message in September created a stir in Democratic ranks and was received with much displeasure by the Tammany men. The Whig papers rejoiced in the discomfiture of their enemies while the Democratic papers predicted a gloomy outlook for the Albany Régime. (*New York Times* quoted in the *National Intelligencer*, October 3, 1837; *New York Spectator*,

ensure a renewed confidence in our securities in the European market.

This will warrant are thinking *now* of the Texian Loan. Rest assured a large sum is to be made by it and we are ready to father it, if you will unite with us. . . .

E. R. BIDDLE TO BIDDLE

Nov: 24th 1837 New York

My Dear Sir

. . . I will take no steps as to the Loan, believing I can in no way better serve you, than keeping it at your command. I might I think realize a commission on it of 2 or 4 pr. ct. by some exertion on my part. . . .

THOMAS COOPER TO BIDDLE

Columbia S.C. 16 Decr 1837

Dear Sir

. . . Very many think as I do, that a sound general

October 12, 1837.) The returns verified their forecasts. The Whigs carried the Assembly by 101 to 27 and 10 of the 22 Senators, showing a gain of 144 on the preceding year. (Niles, November 25, 1837.) Great was the rejoicing in the Whig strongholds over the victory. (Niles, November 18, 1837; Adams, J. Q., *Memoirs*, vol. IX, pp. 431, 432.)

The Democratic papers set to work explaining the cause of their defeat. "To our mind," said the *Worcester Republican*, "there is no mystery to explain in order to solve the reasons of the change in the state as well as in the city of New York. The city and state are a highly commercial people. They have felt severely the pressure in the money market for the last two months and upwards. And this is the strongest argument that can be urged to men in their wants. . . . It has been urged against the administration that its course of policy has been the cause of the difficulties and pressure in the money market. This has been too successfully urged." (*Worcester Republican*, November 22, 1837.) "The late elections," reiterated the *Globe*, "have been carried under the influence of a panic excited by a false issue." (*Globe*, quoted in *Wooster (Ohio) Republican Advocate*, November 23, 1837.) To Jackson the political tornado was caused by the apostasy of the Conservatives, but to all it was evident the cry of "hard times" raised so efficiently by the Whigs, had worked like magic. (Moore, J. B., *Works of James Buchanan*, Philadelphia, 1908, vol. III, p. 338.)

currency will not take place among us unless by returning into the beaten road we have unwisely quitted. But the necessity must be felt, 'ere it is adopted. Of course your friends & the friends of your institution must permit the course of events to guide their course. Van Beuren cannot make head agst Clay, unless he goes in good earnest for the South, which I think he will do. Strange to say, I hear no objection to your talents or your integrity, among those whom I have cautiously sounded, but they all object to you as being in want of the necessary knowledge and experience as a party politician. To be sure, like the modest girl in Magdalen, who was advised to go out and qualify herself for admittance, you might go for a session into that house of ill fame the H. of Rep. in Congress, with political morals sufficiently debauched to become a president; but I sh^d. not recommend this course of education as indispensible. My own opinion is, that the regular course of events will ere long point out the course you might be able to adopt. . . .

M. NEWKIRK [1] TO BIDDLE

Washington Jany 20th 1838

My Dear Sir,

    . . . I have had a good deal of Conversations with different individuals about the passage of the Sub-Treasury Bill. Mr Clay is very Confident they can defeat them in both houses — in the Senate by a Majority of three. Mr. Kendall is Very Confident they can carry it by a Small Majority alltho he thinks it will be a Close Vote Hon. Frank Thomas thinks it Can not be Carried at this time. Our Own friends appear very much divided in their opinion about its passage. . . .

[1] A director of the Bank, 1836–1840.

D. A. Smith to Biddle

Washington 28ᵗʰ January 1838

Dear Sir,

... The sub Treasury Bill is a subject of much conversation here, and its fate in the Senate is very doubtful; and it is believed by some of our friends, that the failure of the Common wealth Bank of Boston will operate in favour of its adoption. Mʳ Grundy [1] will receive instructions to vote against it and will obey; Mʳ Rives [2] is firmly opposed to the bill in its present shape, and Mʳ. Talmadge will make a great effort to defeat it. Morris [3] of Ohio will obey instructions if they should be received in time, but Allen [4] it is said will not. Mʳ Cambrelling is confident of the passage of the Bill in the Senate, but thinks it will meet with more difficulty in the House; He says the present Congress will not consent to discuss any project for a National Bank of Discount, and says that the administration is firmly determined to try the experiment of collecting and disbursing the revenues of the Government without the use of Banks. I have

[1] Felix Grundy of Virginia, served as Attorney-General under Van Buren, September, 1838, to December, 1839, when he resigned to sit in the Senate in the place of Ephraim H. Foster. In 1838 he was instructed to vote against the Sub-Treasury system, which he did even though favoring it.

[2] Appointed by Jackson Minister to France, but later filled the place of Tazewell in the Senate. In 1834 Mr. Rives resigned in "consequence of his unwillingness to participate in the Senate's vote of censure on President Jackson's removal of the United States Bank deposits, of which he approved, but which the Virginia Legislature reprobated." He was returned again to the Senate in 1835 where he remained until 1845. In January, 1837, he voted for Thomas H. Benton's "expunging resolution."

[3] Thomas Morris was nominated for Vice-President by the Liberty Party at the Buffalo Convention in 1844, but died one month later.

[4] William Allen of Ohio, elected to the House in 1833, in 1837 was elected a United States Senator. When in the Senate he was nicknamed "Earthquake Allen."

been upon terms of intimacy with Mr Cambrelling for many years, and am very certain that He has given me his views in perfect sincerity, and that there is no one in Congress who is better acquainted with the sentiments of the President and his Cabinet.[1] . . .

BIDDLE TO HENRY CLAY

(*confidential*)   Phil^a Feby. 3. 1838
                                              12 o'clock Saturday night

My dear Sir,

You may readily suppose that we are not idle while this insane Sub Treasury scheme is urged forward to break down all the great interests of the country — and preparations are made to obtain from our legislature at Harrisburgh instructions to our representatives in Congress to oppose it. I learn from a friend who has just left me on his arrival from Harrisburgh to night, that the resolutions for that purpose were to be introduced into the House of Rep^s *this day.* If so, they will be taken up on *Monday* — & if then passed will be sent to the Senate & passed finally on *Tuesday.*

I lose no time therefore in suggesting that you would keep up the debate in the Senate for a few days until the resolutions can reach you. I attach great importance to this measure as separating our State from these desperadoes, and the country looks to you eminently to exert your great powers as they have been so often before displayed for its protection.

---

[1] On January 29, 1838, Webster wrote to Benjamin D. Lilliman as follows: "We begin the proceeding on the S.T. Bill tomorrow. It will probably pass this House, without amendment, by 2 or 3 votes. Its fate in the other House is greatly doubtful. The decision on the Mississippi election is expected to day or to morrow. The Sub Treasury Bill may, perhaps, be a good (deal) dependent on the decision." Van Tyne, C. H., *Letters of Daniel Webster* (New York, 1902), p. 211.

Henry Clay to Biddle

Sunday night 10 O'clock
(Feb. 5. 1838)

My Dear Sir

I have this moment rec^d. your letter, and rejoice at the movement which it states to be in contemplation. Buchanan told me that he would obey instructions. I hope they will come. They may [be] decisive of the fate of the atrocious measure.

The final question shall *not* be taken this week.[1]

Henry Clay to Biddle

Washington, Feb. 6. 1838.

My dear Sir

I received your favor of the 4th. & met Mr. B. last night at a small party given at the house at which I board. I rallied him on the subject of instructions, & he remarked to me, as he had done once or twice before, that if they came, he would obey or resign, intimating, I thought, a preference for the latter alternative.

We are now in the midst of the debate on the Treasury Bank, the denomination which should be given to it upon every occasion. Rives began a very good speech, yesterday, which he will finish to-day. I do not know that an occasion will present itself, but if it does, I will embrace it, to draw from Mr. B. a more explicit declaration. We will run them to the girt in the Senate. If they carry their abominable measure, it will not be by a majority of more than two votes.

---

[1] For Clay's opposition to the Sub-Treasury Bill, cf. Schurz, *Henry Clay* (Boston, 1898), vol. II, pp. 139–142.

I am worked almost to death, & to relieve myself, I have to engage the good offices of a young friend as an amanuensis.

C. S. BAKER TO BIDDLE

Harrisburg Thursday Feby 7ᵗʰ 1838

My dear Sir

Your favor of yesterday came duly to hand. The Sub Treasury Resolutions will be disposed of to-morrow. Thay could have been carried today but Mʳ Johnson would not bring them up. The philᵃ Delegation having taken a stand against Stevens on the Improvement bill and the Improvement bill being so intimately connected with Johnsons Interest he feels that he ought not to be treated by the Whigs as they have treated him because Stevens has been pleased to trifle with our Interests. . . .

DANIEL WEBSTER TO BIDDLE

Washington, Saturday noon
(Feb. or May, 1838?)

Dear Sir

. . . The Sub Treasury bill remains *in status quo*. Calhoun is moving heaven, earth, & — to obtain Southern votes for the measure. He labors to convince his Southern neighbors that its success will relieve them from their commercial dependence on the North. His plausibility, & endless perserverance, have really effected a good deal. Even your relative Mr. C. Sheppard has been, & indeed now is, in a state of doubt. Still, I think the Bill cannot pass; but the majority will be Small. The labors of Mr Calhoun, & the power & patronage of the Executive, have accomplished more than I have thought possible.

CHARLES S. BAKER TO BIDDLE

Thursday evening Febry 8/38

My Dear Sir

This day has been one of no ordinary Character in Harrisburg. The Sub Treasury Resolutions were the orders of this day — we forced it through Committee of the whole at the point of the Bayonet. The Van Buren men are in a State of excitement I never saw surpassed — we have a vote of 49 for 43 against, one of our Members Absent. It is impossible for them to bring *all* theire members *into* the House. If no screws gives way we shall have them through to morrow but it will be a hard contest. The Van Buren Men called the Yeas & Nays on us 17 different times on the Vote to adjourne — every man stood firm but we had to submit to an adjournment on acct of our friends it being nearly 1/2 past 3 OClock. . . .

CHARLES S. BAKER TO BIDDLE

Harrisburg Feby 9th 1838

My dear Sir

We are still in the field of Battle. This morning we expected to have carried our Resolutions but were disappointed by 3 of our men deserting to the enemy. I had examined every part and found all apparently safe. The danger Sprung upon us like a Tigers coming as it did from our own Ranks — but it would not answer — we contested the ground until 1 OClock when we moved to Adjourn the vote being 48 for 48 against — the Motion lost. We then Immediately renewed the Motion intending to continue until we succeeded — our opponents then yielded us the field. All the Concentrated powers of Washington appear to be here and the operations of this day have perfectly dismayed them — every thing was prepared by them to defeate us and they were certain of success. I feel we are in danger but nothing like defeated — it all turns upon the absent members and the disposition we shall be enabled to make of the 3 that deserted. I think we can get 2 at least back — you may Rest assured I shall not give up the field as easily as Napoleon gave up Waterloo. The Banks are lost sight of — but we consider on this (The Sub Treasury) depends greatly the Kind of bill we can get for our Banks. Our position is greatly strengthened by what we have all Ready done. We have broken assunder the majority in the House. We defeated without difficulty a proposition or amendment to *Instruct our Senators* to vote for the Sub Treasury. . . .

CHARLES S. BAKER TO BIDDLE

Harrisburg February 14th 1838

My Dear Sir

The Resolutions are Slumbering in the Senate, the reason this — one of our men thinking the Matter closed immediately left for home — we must now watch to avail ourselves of the first Moment one of theire men is absent to get the last Resolution Stricken off. We have suffered much for want of a person in the house who fully understood all the trick of the trade — the Slightest effort in the house would have defeated it had there been some one present to prompt to action — three of our men again voted by mistake. It can pass any moment in the form it now is before the Senate. . . .

please say if we can do no better must we pass the Resolutions as thay are —

CHARLES S. BAKER TO BIDDLE

Harrisburg February 16ᵗʰ 1838
Friday evening

My dear Sir

Your favor of the 15ᵗʰ Insᵗ came duly to hand and I am truly happy that this days acts in the Senate will meet with your Kindest favour. This day I determined to pass the Resolutions and made Known my wishes to Dʳ Burden who accordingly took the floor and called them up. The War Hoop was immediately raised but it would not do. Dʳ Burden foiled them at every point and forced them through at the point of the Bayonet truly. The Resolutions [1] are now on there way to Washington and to morrow we shall endeavour to pass an explanation of what we mean by the compliment to Martin Van Buren — This is of course Humbug — The explanation will only pass as the views of the Senate. . . .

HENRY CLAY TO BIDDLE

Washⁿ 20ᵗʰ. Feb. 1838

My Dear Sir

I have recᵈ. your favor of the 18ᵗʰ. The Resolutions from Harrisburg have produced the effect of securing another vote in that of Mr. Buchanan agᵗ. the Govᵗ. Bank. He presented them yesterday morning and gave in his adhesion before I reached the Senate, from which I was detained half an hour, in consequence of a Speech which I had to deliver, and did deliver, against that measure. It was wise in your Senate to pass the resolutions [2] as they went from the House,

---

[1] *Cong. Globe*, 25th Cong., 2d Sess., vol. VI, p. 190.

[2] Van Buren was kept informed of conditions at Harrisburg as the following letter of Salisbury of February 17, 1838, illustrates: "It cannot be doubted for a

notwithstanding the two exceptionable paragraphs. The good in them more than counter balanced the bad, as the event has already proved. We now probably stand 26 against 26. One more vote would defeat the vile measure. We have a prospect of getting that by an instruction from Richmond to Mr. Roane but it is not certain. If it comes, he will obey it. Could it not be obtained from Trenton? Why could not a positive instruction (the Gen[1] Assembly *instructs* its Senators & requests its Representatives &c) emanate from that quarter? It would, I believe, decide Mr. Wall.[1] I think he would obey. And as he acknowledged such an obligation, it might be given without justly wounding the sensibility of Mr. Southard. . . .

JOHN SERGEANT TO BIDDLE

(*Private*)   Washington, April 28th. 1838.

My dear Sir,

Referring to what I wrote yesterday, I would now add, that there is a strong jealousy of New York rising in the South. You know the schemes of the Southrons [2] for get-

moment that motives most unworthy have induced seven members of the House of Representatives to forego the solemn and imposing duties which they owed their constituents. . . . Here then we have before us a practical illustration of the immense and alarming power of the banks, whose agents have been and now are as thick as bees prowling about the halls of both houses of our legislature." Van Buren MSS. in Library of Congress.

[1] Cf. Mr. Wall's speech on the Sub-Treasury setting forth his views on the measure in *Cong. Globe*, 25th Cong., 2d Sess., vol. VI, 1838, Appendix, pp. 230 *et seq.*

[2] The South fully appreciated the importance of their position and power during this struggle, as is evidenced in the following letter of Pickens to Hammond, February 9, 1838: "There is much doubt as to the passage. The vote will be close & much depends upon our delegation. . . . There never was such a time for the South to control as at present, if we would be united. The great struggle is whether cotton shall control exchange & importations or whether the Banks & the stock interest shall do it. The South will be more prosperous under cotton at 10c & no banks converted connected with the government lending its credit & power to the stock interest than we would be under cotton at 13c & the reverse of these things.

ting their own trade into their own hands. What support they have given to the Sub-Treasury has been to promote this view. The mass of them have been sincere. M[r]. Calhoun [1] has used it only to cloak his ambition. They are now alarmed at the prospect of a new union of the money power, with the political power by means of the free banking law of New York. The question is whether in this jealousy, (the present predominat feeling, whether well or ill founded) there is not a ground for an union of the Bank U.S. with the South. If you can make friends there, you will soon have Penns[a]., for she always goes with the South. I throw this out for your consideration. As you are to steer, of course you will observe where the wind is to come from. . . .

We will have a great contest & one which will fix our prosperity for 20 years, one way or the other." And as Pickens viewed the subject the South would be foolish to summit to cunning and fraud any longer. Hammond MSS. in Library of Congress.

However, a good explanation for the position of the South on the Sub-Treasury and the motives which impelled it to stand by the Administration in these days is given in a letter of Alfred Hager (?) to Poinsett, September 1, 1838: "As to the S.T. I really know very little about it . . . but surely, a very little reflection must teach every Southern man who is willing to be taught what our policy is. ' The Bank & the metallic basis ' — & the 'paper currency' are all debatable questions — but the *Black* Currency is *not*. How am I to be benefited by either 'Bank' or 'Sub. Treasury' without my land on Cooper River & the *Negroes* that work there? What signifies to *me* all the jargon *about* Whigs & Conservatives etc. etc. if the abolitionists stand between me & the White Gate at Longwood? these are the inquiries that make *me* an administration man — with me the very foundation of liberty is slavery & I go for Mr. Van Buren because Mr. Van Buren goes for me & it would be worse than hypocrisy in me to be hunting about for better reasons than this with a strong current sitting against us, with the whole world looking angrily at our institution & the prevailing feeling of mankind plainly developing a disposition to overthrow them, how can the South afford to talk about this man, or that man, with the message of the *President* & the actions conforming to his message staring us in the face?" Poinsett MSS. in Pennsylvania Historical Society Library.

[1] By this period Calhoun realized that his alliance with the Whig Party would absorb his followers and that a coalition with the party in power would better serve his purposes. Accordingly he broke his alliance with the Whig Party. For a careful and illuminating discussion of Calhoun's actions at this time, cf. Cole, *Whig Party in the South*, pp. 46–48.

BIDDLE TO JOHN FORSYTH [1]

(*confidential*) Phil^a. April 30, 1838 —

My dear Sir —

... The Bank of the U. States owes about six millions of dollars to the Gov^t. payable by instalments due in Sepr nxt — Sep. 1839–Sep. 1840. Now the Bank might anticipate these payments at once, and put the Gov^t. in funds for its pressing wants. In this Settlement, as it is the payment of a debt and does not come under the Same line as the ordinary revenue — there need be no operation of specie payment or any other payment, for the public creditor would be too happy to receive a draft on the Bank with the option of asking specie for it if he choose to demand it, just as the Secretary of the Navy last year paid the pensioners.

The first effect of such an arrangement would be to quiet the minds of the people as to what is regarded as the hostility of the Gov^t. to the Banks — the most serious obstacle at present to a general restoration of the Currency — and it would go further than any other measure I know to promote that object. An easy consequence of this would be a return to something like the ancient habits of inter course between the Bank & the Gov^t. which would lead to this result. I think that the Gov^t. may be satisfied that no System could work better than that of the late Bank of the U.S. Now the present Bank is only the late Bank with no change except in the origin of its charter. Its whole machinery can be remounted in twenty four hours — and thence forward it can, without difficulty, engage to receive & disburse the public funds in every part of the U.S. without any charge whatever, in specie or its equivalent,

---

[1] Secretary of State in Van Buren's Cabinet.

at the option of the public creditor. If therefore by a simple arrangement of that Kind with the Bank, you can restore the administration of the funds to its former footing, you accomplish several objects. The first of course is that the work of the Gov^t. is well done. The second is that you are relieved from all connection in detail with a multitude of banks, the fruitful source of trouble & political danger. Then you get rid of the debatable question of the National Bank — You avoid the embarrassment of retracting any fixed opinions — you restore in the most effectual way you can, at least you contribute as far as you can to restore, the currency.

Finally, you thus get peace — not a bad thing at any time — but a remarkably good thing at this time. For myself — this business of Texas, and a much more important matter which I project, make me desire to close up these old sources of discontent. I am therefore singularly pacific & amiable just now.

It seems to me then, that you have an opportunity of making a political movement — a coup d'état worth trying. I believe that at this moment a reconciliation between the Bank & the Gov^t. would do more both at home & abroad to settle our troubles than any other measure that could be adopted. Its influence here in disarming the hostility of those who consider the Gov^t. as indisposed to the credit system, you may estimate better than I can. This could be done simply by putting aside the Sub treasury bill, and all other projects, and leaving the whole matter on the footing of the resolution of 1816, which would make it the subject of treasury regulation.

Having thus unburdened my mind, I leave the rest to you, if you think the suggestion worth following out. If not, it of course rests between ourselves, as no one will be aware of the contents of this letter. The negociation for anticipating the first instalment is going on under the auspices of the gentleman who has had charge of it — but the occasion seems a good one to follow out the mere intended arrangement here suggested.

HENRY CLAY TO BIDDLE

Washⁿ. 30th May 1838

My Dear Sir

I rec^d. your favor of the 28th inst. You will have seen that the resolution, which had passed the Senate, rescinding the Specie Circular,[1] has also passed the House this morning in less than three hours after it was rec^d by a majority of more than five to one!

I sincerely hope that the condition of your Bank is such as to admit of your seizing this occurrence to make an early resumption. I am extremely anxious on *your* account as well as that of the public that your Bank shall continue to maintain its high character

You will have seen and *you* will comprehend the object and the benefits of the movement I made, in respect to a Bank of the U.S. It will turn public attention to the subject in the abstract. It will suspend or render harmless malignant attacks on your Bank. And it may even reconcile the public ultimately to the grant of a National Charter to your Bank. I should be satisfied with either.

---

[1] The Specie Circular was rescinded by a joint resolution of May 21, 1838, which forbade the Secretary of the Treasury "to make or to continue in force, any general order, which shall create any difference between the different branches of revenue, as to the money or medium of payment, in which debts or dues, accruing to the United States, may be paid." Cf. U.S. Statutes at Large, vol. v, p. 310.

Altho' I did not think it right to allude to our conversation on the few remarks I addressed to the Senate, I have to several friends said that *Mr. Biddle elevated patriotism made him look above the interests of the particular institution with which he is charged to* the welfare of his Country.

—— TO ROSWELL L. COLT [1]

May 30, 1838

My dear Sir,

Tonight my advices from Wash[n] are that the virtual repeal of the Specie Circular which has passed the Senate will pass the House in a day or two.

This will satisfy us — & I will make an immediate move for a general resumption in conjunction with the South & West — and a decision upon the New York application.

This will give an opportunity of repairing the losses of your friends which I have often heard you deplore

—— TO BIDDLE [2]

Private as murder (1838)

I will tell you a short story. I left W. for Boston, in April. I signified to my friends that on my return I should bring forward a measure, by itself, for repealing the Treasury order, & should put it in the same form, as my amendment, introduced for the same purpose, into the Sub-Tresury Bill. They all thought it would be a good move; & one of them said to me, as you have mentioned your purpose, and it will become known, lest you should be *anticipated*, you will do well to

[1] There is no signature to this letter, but it is in Biddle's handwriting.

[2] This letter, undated, was undoubtedly written in May, 1838, and throws an interesting side-light on politics in Washington at this period. It is in Webster's handwriting.

mention it to Mr. C. Accordingly, with that friend, I walked over to Mr C's lodgings, the Evening before I left Washington, explained my purpose to Mr C. & assured him that the first day after my return, I should bring forward the measure if, in the mean time, the H. of R. should not take up the Sub-Treasury Bill.

After I had been heard of, on my return, at New York, & one or two days before my arrival here, Mr C. *brought forward a Resolution himself* — and some considerable bruit ensued, about his promptitude to aid the mercantile interest & — — — — so the world goes!

Burn this — as it is libellous, in the extreme —

BIDDLE TO SAMUEL JAUDON

Phil^a. May 31, 1838

My dear Sir,

. . . The tide now has begun to turn, and the Bank has received to day a triumph such as it never enjoyed in any part of its career. You know that the stand taken by the Bank was, that it would not resume until the Gov^t. changed its course, as there could be no security for specie payments while the Gov^t. itself made the distinction between specie & notes. Accordingly the contest has literally been between the Bank & the Executive. With what result you will see by the proceedings of yesterday when on the *very same day* the Specie Circular was repealed in the Senate by a vote of 34 to 9, and in the House by 154 to 29. I have immediately endeavoured to justify the confidence of the country by issuing a note to Mr Adams [1] in which suppressing all feelings of

[1] Biddle's letters to Mr. Adams are reprinted in Niles, April 14, 1838, and May 31, 1838.

triumph, I merely announced the fact that we should now proceed to take measures for resumption. At the same time we resolved to yield to our New York friends who wished us to have a Branch there under the new Banking law. This application is itself one of the most extraordinary symptoms of the good feeling which pervades the commercial community of New York. I send you an extract from the newspaper of to-day containing a notice of it, as well as my letter to Mr. Adams — & I will inclose, if they can be prepared in time, copies of the correspondence with Mr Adams on the subject.

I now mean to turn my immediate attention to making a simultaneous movement in the South & West, so as to make the resumption really worth having — & I hope to be able to rally up the whole country to an efficient exertion.

The efforts made here to injure the Bank and which are echoed on your side, have ceased to have any effect here, & the Bank will probably be in a more desirable situation than it ever was.

I shall even not be very much surprized if some coquetting passes between our administration friends and the Bank, as we are in a singularly amiable humour.

You know that Woodbury is appointed Chief Justice of New Hampshire & leaves the Treasury, being in fact turned out in the shape of a resignation; so that according to European ideas, the President's ordinance being repealed, by both Houses of Congress, & the Minister who issued it being dismissed, it may be regarded as a civil revolution on the side of the Bank. . . .

BIDDLE TO SAMUEL JAUDON

Phil^a. June 9, 1838

My dear Sir,

We received yesterday your letter of the 5th ulto. I am not surprized that the echo in London of all the trash circulated here has annoyed you. But we have surmounted them on this side — and I think the Bank stands even better now than it ever did in the general estimation. You will have seen that we hailed the first glimpse of sunshine offered by the repeal of the Specie Circular. But as soon as it passed, the party of the Administration rallied upon the Sub Treasury Bill. That bill, as you know, passed the Senate, but is now in such a position in the House that it cannot be reached without a vote of two thirds. Accordingly Mr Cambreling has brought in a fresh bill which a majority can control, & which the Administration mean to push thro' the House. If this be the case, it will undo all that has hitherto been done. Mr Sergeant is here on a visit, and he thinks the matter so critical, & is so anxious to obtain even a single vote that we are about sending down some people to Washington to explain to the representatives from our State how extremely injurious to its interests such a bill would prove, and urging them to defeat it. With what success a week will determine. . . .

BIDDLE TO JOHN SERGEANT

Phil^a. June 15, 1838

My dear Sir,

We are doing some little matters about the Sub Treasury bill, which, from all I can understand, will not pass. At the same time I wish to omit nothing to prevent its passage — and therefore I will thank you to send me by return of mail if convenient, a list marked with all those who you are sure will vote against it, & let me know also *how many votes you want in addition*. Perhaps we may prove to some of our Penn^a members, that their course is injurious to the state & to themselves.

BIDDLE TO SAMUEL JAUDON

Phil^a. June 23, 1838

My dear Sir,

... I think now we are approaching the end of our war. The repeal of the Specie Circular was an actual surrender by the Administration — but since then, they have rallied in great force on the Sub-Treasury bill which was supposed to be dead & buried. The real political secret of this bill is that the most of the Admⁿ. party do not like it — that Mr Calhoun is driving them into it in order to promote his own advancement. I think however it will be defeated. Then we shall come to some modification of the deposit system. What I wish to establish is that the business of the country & the public revenue shall pass through Banks — & not thro' mere receivers — and this I think we shall establish at last. ...

BIDDLE TO SAMUEL JAUDON

Phil^a. June 29, 1838

My dear Sir,

I have but a moment, as usual, to write, as the Bank is closing, & the mail for the Sirius going.

The repeal of the Specie Circular has been followed by

a fresh defeat in the rejection of the Sub-Treasury.[1] Mr Buchanan has renewed the matter of the special deposit, but it will fail.

In England we should have seen an instant change of ministry. Here ministers are engaged on wages for a year — & however they may misbehave, will serve out their term. On the 9th of July, Congress will adjourn — and then the Administration, poor & dispirited, will be brought to reason as wild beasts are tamed by hunger.

Remember that whatever you may read to the contrary, the repeal of the Specie Circular & the defeat of the Sub Treasury are the results, exclusively, of the course pursued by the Bank of the U.S. If we had done as the New York Banks had, succumbed to the Gov^t. & resumed when they did, it would have been a surrender at discretion. I was willing to risk the temporary overshadowing to have a permanent sunshine; and I think we shall soon have it. . . .

BIDDLE TO THADDEUS STEVENS

Phil^a. July 3, 1838

My dear Sir

You are a magician greater than Van Buren, & with all your professions against Masonry, you are an absolute right worshipful Grand Master. I received yesterday your letter of the 27th ult^o. and to day I write the letter to the Gov^t. of which of which I annex a copy. This is worth to you a dozen resumptions. On that subject you will talk all the truth you dare, and if you can persuade our worthy friends that this is a matter to be decided exclusively by business & not politics you will do good service to the good cause.

[1] The vote to reconsider the measure was lost in the House, 205 to 21.

BIDDLE TO JOEL R. POINSETT

(*Private*)   Phil^a. July 11, 1838

Dear Sir

    Mr Kimble of the House of Representatives called upon me today and expressed to me a wish on your part to know whether the bonds of the Bank could be made available for the use of your Department. I hasten to say that from a desire to promote the public service, as well as from considerations personal to yourself, it will afford me great pleasure to do anything which may contribute to the successful administration of your Department.

    There are, as you are aware, three bonds payable on the 1st of October of 1838–39 & 40, respectively. The two which it is proposed to sell cannot be sold either in this country or in Europe, and the money can be furnished for them by the Bank only. But I should be disposed to advance the money on the first, second, and perhaps third of them, if it could be made the interest of both the Department and the Bank. If therefore you can in the first instance so arrange it as to have the bonds placed at your disposition to raise the money on them, and let me know how and where and when your disbursements are to be made, I will at once tell you what I can do.

BIDDLE TO THOMAS COOPER

                                 Phil^a. July 13, 1838

My dear Sir

    . . . You have seen that during this late tempest I took a deliberate stand against the administration determined to do nothing until they were defeated, and I *know* that this opposition caused their defeat. Now having triumphed, the resumption of specie payment will be speedy and effectual.

BIDDLE TO R. M. BLATCHFORD

Phil^a. July 31, 1838

My dear Sir

I will thank you to take charge of a little matter which may become important unless wisely managed. The Bank has just made a settlement, mutually advantageous to both parties, with the Gov^t. To you, who know all the bearings of such a measure, I need not say, that I regard it as the termination of the war, & therefore of great benefit alike to the Bank, and to the country. But if it be a matter of advantage to the Bank, or of triumph to its friends, like all triumphs it should be enjoyed with moderation. In noticing it therefore, by the press, I would specially avoid everything like exultation — everything like reproach to the administration as being forced, at last, to resort to the Bank. But on the contrary the administration should be treated as having done a good thing, and should have credit for a pacification which cannot fail to be useful to the country. It may be of some consequence to the Adm^n. to see that they do not expose themselves, by this step, to sneers and sarcasms from their political opponents.

Will you have the goodness to suggest this as the proper tone to be adopted by our friends in New York?

R. M. BLATCHFORD TO BIDDLE

New York Aug: 1, 1838

My dear Sir

I had the honor of receiving this morning Your letter of Yesterday.

The best answer I can give to it is the two extracts which I enclose — one from the Commercial — the other from the Star — they were prepared in haste but I believe they embody the spirit of Your Suggestions. I shall not approach the American on the subject — The Courier & Express I will take care of this afternoon.

I am heartily glad that the War is ended.

P.S. I have written to Albany in order that a proper tone will be assured by the Evening Journal which is after all the controlling Whig paper in this State.

BIDDLE TO SAMUEL JAUDON

Phil[a]. Aug[t]. 3, 1838

My dear Sir

Leaving to our friends Mess[rs]. Cowperthwait & Dunlap to give you all the details, I shall employ the only few moments of leisure I can command before the sailing of the Steamship, to say two or three things which may interest you.

1. We have settled with Gov[t]. for our bonds, and settled in a way particularly agreeable. You know my opinion, which I have never concealed, in regard to the individuals who have for the last ten years governed the country. These opinions are confirmed rather than changed. But looking, as I do, to what I deem the great interests of the country, & specially bound to protect the interests committed to my charge, my object has been to bring the existing Gov[t]. to such a course of measures as would remedy present evils, until some political revolution should restore wiser counsels at Washington. To bring this about, there was no safe course

but one of open and decided defiance, to show that the Bank was not at all afraid of the administration, and would not depart from its own policy until the Gov^t. had renounced the follies which it was laboring to propagate. Accordingly it became necessary to say that the Bank U.S. and the other banks would not resume specie payments until the Gov^t. had announced its own policy. The parties stood in that attitude, — the good cause weakened by the desertion & the weakness of those New York 2 1/2 per cent patriots — but still strong enough to face the enemy. Our efforts were of course directed to the repeal of the specie circular, & when that was done, and the adm^n. made a last rally on the sub treasury bill, by great exertion they were defeated on that point. This settled the matter. The real question, as you know perfectly well, was, whether the Gov^t. should carry on its finances by the instrumentality of banks, or of special receivers of Gold & Silver only; and the vote of the H. of Rep^s. decided that the sense of the country was for the old mode. The adjournment of Congress hastened the process of repentance, by leaving the Adm^n. without any means of carrying on the public business, unless by the sale of the Bonds. I had taken my own position in that narrow defile, thro' which I was sure they would have to pass, and where accordingly we met. What befel, you may imagine, — since we have come out good friends; — and after a little coquetry and a little flirtation, I think it not improbable that M^r (not M^{rs}) Woodbury & I will be tender & true, after the Douglass fashion.

The settlement is in this form:

The first bond due in September next, will be divided into three instalments, payable on the 15th. of August, September and October, respectively.

The second bond, due in September 1839, is immediately cashed on the 1ˢᵗ insᵗ.

The third; the Secʸ is not yet sufficiently pressed to sell — but when he does sell, we are to have the refusal.

The money is placed at once to the credit of the Treasurer of the United States, & remains *on deposit* with us — without interest — and the Secʸ gives a List, & the Secʸ of War gives another list, of the points where he wants the disbursements made, which embrace the whole West & South West, and the warrants of the Treasurer are drawn on the Bank of the United States, payable in Missouri, Arkansas &c &c.

The benefit of time and exchange are thus apparent — and the Bank is now actually a depository of the public money; — so that the result is, that, after all the nonsense of the last few years, the Govᵗ. takes in payment of a bond, a credit in a bank which does not pay specie yet, and which had declared that it did not mean to pay specie until that very Govᵗ had abandoned its course. Our Washington friends are scarcely aware of the concession which this involves, and I have taken pains, throughout the country, that the opposition should indulge in no exultation — no sarcasm — nothing which should startle the treasury and blight our budding loves; — for my present intention is to make the Bank a general depository of the funds of the Govᵗ. You know what a difficult and almost incredible work that will be, — but there is no room for despair after what has occurred, — for the partizans of the Govᵗ. are not yet recovered from the amazement caused by this recent inexplicable movement.

You see that we resume on the 13ᵗʰ of this month. We begin without having sacrificed any great interest. We begin with a wide circle of resumers, whom our delay has enabled to prepare; — and we begin after having fairly beaten down the Gov^t., and secured the ascendency of reason for the future. We arrive in port without having been under the necessity of throwing over any of our cargo. We arrive, for every useful purpose, just as soon as our neighbours, who lost over board a large part of the passengers; and we only stopped on the way to sink a pirate. So that, on the whole, I have no reason to be dissatisfied with our course.

2. Just as we were preparing our machinery for the New York concern, we found, to our great surprize, that under the law it was doubtful whether the Bank, as a corporation, could become an associate, and we were obliged to give up our plan. I think it very probable, however, that the object will be accomplished, even in a better form, if we make an arrangement with a small association to do our business in New York. We say nothing of this on our side of the water; but I think that the arrival after you receive this, will give you details. I mention it now, merely that you may know that we shall probably soon do the largest commercial business in New York. . . .

B——[1] TO BIDDLE

Phil^a Augt 11th 1838

My dear Sir

I have had quite an interesting interview with a Loco Foco friend who has returned last night from the South. He has been as far south as the Springs and has had very free conversations with the President relative to the *Party* and the future prospects of the greate Democratic family. The

---

[1] This letter is in the handwriting of C. S. Baker, who had maneuvered the Resolutions against the Sub-Treasury through the Pennsylvania Legislature.

result of my friends mission is very satisfactory. As He was commissioned by me for the purpose of ascertaining the views entertained by the President toward the Bank of the United States he turned his attention to that subject entirely. He urged upon the President the absolute necessity there was of abandoning the present policy and hinted that in his opinion the only way of defeating Mr Clay was by making Peace with the Bank of the U States. The President received his Hint in a very gracious manner and said he was in the Hands of the poeple and If thay resolved to have the Government connected with the Bank He the President would not oppose the will of the majority when it had been clearly expressed. The President agreed with him that if Mr Rives of Virg^a could be reconciled it would be accomplishing much towards a Reconcilliation of the differences that had recently existed in the party. This would be a death blow to the Conservative party and then remarked my friend would not the withdrawing of the Bank of the United States from the whig party produce the same effect upon them (the Whigs) as the loss of Mr Rives would be to the Conservative Interest. The president remarked, it is entitled to consideration, my impression is it would. To sum up my friend is impressed with the Idea that the President is personally very anxious for a Reconcilliation and If Mr Rives will consent to run as Vice president theire would be no difficulty in making the arrangements. All the best plans of getting back to the old Land marks of the party were discussed — the disposition to be made of Blaire & others conditioned an arraingement of this Kind were entered into was glanced at and considered perfectly feasible. The greatest difficulty appeared to be the consummation of the act. The disposition or feeling is Right —

... I have also a Letter from my Virginia friend. He remarks the President is quite wearied in fighting Banks and feels that he has been defeated by the monsters — to Speak more plainly The President attributes the defeate of the Sub Treasury to the Influence of the Bank of the U States — my friend Remarked to the President in the coarse of the conversation "I should think it bad policy to have in the field so formidable a foe." The President smiled and said Mr Biddle was a hard opponent—more when I have the honour of an interview.

THOMAS COOPER TO BIDDLE

Columbia 14 Aug. 1838. S. Car.

Dear Sir

I wish to state *why* I penned the communication I have lately sent. You need not write to me in reply, but reflect on my suggestions. 1. Webster, Clay, Van Beuren, are the next presidential Candidates. *Clay* goes for a national bank, *but not for yours*. Van Beuren wishes to be driven into the adoption of one *at Washington*, under his eye & control.

I think Clay looks to the same Site, for the same reason.

Whether *Webster* goes with you or not, I cannot tell: probably yes.

If Clay can get the votes of New York or Pennsylvania, his chances for election are good. Van Beuren will get *perhaps* a majority of the South: I greatly dislike the ultra federalism of Webster, but it is clear to me, your interest is allied to his; and that his success depends on overcoming the reasonable republican prejudices of New York & Pennsylvania against him.

Hence, it is of great importance, *if you wish a reinstatement,* to stand fair before the populace in a political point of view. Without this, you cannot counteract Clay: I should say, keep up the ball I have thrown up into the air by frequent discussions in the papers. You have honest, honourable, popular ground to place your foot on, firmly. . . . These are *my* notions; I have no desire to know yours: therefore you need not write to me on the subject. I send directions, to make up, the part of my communication which was omitted for want of documents. I remain with kind respects . . .

BIDDLE TO SAMUEL JAUDON

Philad^a. August 15, 1838

My dear Sir

I have little to add to what I wrote by the Royal William, of which I enclose a copy.

Our arrangements with the Gov^t. are in very satisfactory progress. We have placed to their credit the proceeds of the two first bonds, and they indicate the points of disbursements, which, being very remote and numerous, afford the advantages of circulation & exchange. But the greatest satisfaction of all is, that this arrangement brings back the Gov^t. to its old position of doing its business thro' Banks, and by means of Bank credits. So, the triumph, is, I think, complete. The two political parties, meanwhile, are confounded, and are not yet able to comprehend it. The Admⁿ people believe that I must have bought Mr Van Buren, — the opposition fearing that this will strengthen the ministry and work against the interests of Mr Clay. You know that my own course has reference merely to the service of the Country, and if these people are beaten into measures that are beneficial, I shall not permit myself to avoid co-operating with them, lest it should injure the prospects of our political party. The great power of the Bank lies in its total independence of all of them.

Our resumption on the 13th works very well, the demand for specie being very small.

BIDDLE TO DANIEL WEBSTER [1]

Phil^a. Septem 6, 1838

My dear Sir

I stated to you, last year, my views in regard to Texas; and you then thought that if the plan of annexation to the United States could be abandoned, every consideration of feeling & interest would conspire to make us desire its prosperity. That question is now settled. Mr Jones, the new Minister, arrived two days ago in Phil^a., and he is instructed to withdraw the proposal of union. This troublesome part of the question being thus disposed of, I am much inclined to think that if their loan of Five millions were taken in the United States, it would be far better than if they were obliged to seek it in England. I do not however wish to mix myself with the political contests of the day nor to interfere in matters which have been the subject of party warfare; and I should like to have the benefit of the opinions of judicious friends before doing something final in respect to it. Will you then say, whatever you feel at liberty to say, in the question, whether it would not be greatly for the interest of our common country that Texas should continue independent of all foreign nations, — that she should be protected by this country and not permitted, if possible, to owe her prosperity to any other aid than ours. Say, too, whether your opinion is

[1] Cf. letter on same topic reprinted in Van Tyne, *Webster*, p. 213.

that Texas can maintain its independence, or whether, in the last extremity, this country would permit her to be conquered, or reconquered; and, being free, whether you think a loan to her would be perfectly safe. You will readily understand, by the strain of these remarks, that I am predisposed to serve Texas, because I believe I should benefit our country by it; but, before taking any decisive step, I would wish to have your judgment, because I know that your opinion will be an impartial and a patriotic one. If any circumstance, public or private, indisposes you to answer, I request that you will not answer. But if you incline to speak, — speak — for I think the occasion worthy of you. and so speak that if, when I have decided, I should want the benefit of your judgment to sanction my course, I may have it and use it publicly or privately. I will only add that what you say I wish you to say quickly.

BIDDLE TO HENRY CLAY

Phil^a. Sept 7, 1838

My dear Sir

Your introduction of Mr Burnley, Commissioner of Texas, makes it not unnatural to confer with you on the subject of the loan which he is endeavoring to negotiate.

The subject of Texas is one familiar to me since my connection in Paris, thirty three years ago, with the treaty of Louisiana,[1] the execution of a great portion of which fell under my own personal inspection. On that subject I hold very decided opinions. But the question which now occupies my attention

[1] For Biddle's connection with the treaty of Louisiana, cf. Conrad, Robert T., *Sketch of Nicholas Biddle*, in *National Portrait Gallery of Distinguished Americans*, vol. III, pp. 12 *et seq.*

is this: The Minister of Texas, just arrived & in this city, means to withdraw, formally, the proposal to enter the Union. So far, the embarrassments and troubles which that measure threatened are, for the present at least, removed. The question then becomes an open one, and it offers for consideration this point: Whether, if we are to consider the revolution there as complete, — if this country will not permit Texas to be conquered by a new master, or reconquered by its old one, then it is not of great importance that her prosperity should be of our own creation, and that she should not be obliged to incur obligations to any other country? She now wants money to consolidate her power & fix her institutions. Is it not better — far better — that she should obtain it from us than from any other power? Now I am inclined to make the loan. At the same time I mean to do nothing rashly — nothing which shall not, in my judgment, be highly beneficial to our Country. But I do not wish to take any decided step without the opinion of some friends on whose judgment I rely. Allow me then to ask what you think of the question? Do you think that Texas will maintain its independence, or that the United States would permit any power to deprive her of it. Do you think it would be wise to take the loan and not suffer her to owe her success to England?

If you feel any the slightest reluctance to say anything about the matter, you will of course say nothing. But if you feel disposed to give any opinion, let it be such as, hereafter, if I deem it useful to use your authority as confirming my own views, I may quote, and if necessary, make public. I mention this that you may limit, precisely, the nature & extent of your communication.

DANIEL WEBSTER TO BIDDLE

Boston Sept[r] 10th 1838

My Dear Sir

I have rec[d]. your favor of the 8th instant. The decision
of the Gov[t] of Texas, to withdraw its application for a union
with the U. States, is, in my judgment, an event, eminently
favorable, to both countries. She now stands, as an independ-
ant state, looking to her own power, & her own resources, to
maintain her place among the nations of the earth, an attitude, vastly more respectable, than that which she held, while
solicitous to her own political character, & to become part
of a neighbouring country. Seeking, thus, no longer a union
with us, & assuming the ground of entire independence —
I think it highly important to the interests of the U. States,
that Texas should be found able to maintain her position.
Any connexion with a European State, so close as to make
her dependent on that State, or to identify her interests with
the interests of such State, I should regard as greatly unfortunate for us. I could not but regret, exceedingly, to see any
union between those parts of our continent, which have
broken the chain of European dependence & the Governments of Europe; whether those, from which they have been
disunited, or others. You Remember the strong opinion, expressed by M[r]. Monroe that the U.S. could not consent to
the recolonization of those portions of this Continent, which
had severed the ties, binding them to a European connexion,
& formed free & independent Governments for themselves; or
to the establishment of other European Colonies, in America
— The spirit, & reason, of these sentiments, would lead us to
regard with just fear, & therefore with just jealousy, any con-

nexions, between our near American neighbours, & the powerful states of Europe, except those of friendly & useful commercial intercourse. It is easy to forsee the evils with which
any other connexion, than that last mentioned, between
Texas & one of the great sovereignties of Europe, — might
threaten us. Not to avert to those of a high & political character, one, likely to have a direct bearing on our commerce, a
connexion on the great staple of our southern production.
Texas is destined, doubtless, to be a great cotton producing
country, & which we should cheerfully concede to her all the
advantages which her soil & climate afford to her, in sustaining a competition with ourselves, we could not behold,
with indifference, a surrender, by her, of her substantial independence, for the purchase of exclusive favors & privileges,
from the hands of a European Government.

The competency of Texas to maintain her Independence
depends, I think, altogether on the character of her Gov^t. &
its administration. I have no belief, at all, in the power of
Mexico to re-subjugate Texas, if the latter country shall be
well governed. The same consideration decides, also, the question, whether a loan to Texas would be safe. I have supposed,
that her new formed Gov^t was gradually strengthening, &
improving, in all the qualities requisite for the respectable
exercise of National power. That in institutions so recent,
there should be, for a time, some irregularity of action, is to
be expected. But if those to whose hands her destinies are
now committed, shall look steadily to two great objects, —
first, real & absolute, as well as nominal, National Independence, & second, the maintenance of a free & efficient Gov^t.,
of which good faith shall, from the beginning, be a marked
characteristic, I see nothing to render it less safe to regulate

money transactions with her, than with the Gov^{ts}. of other countries. On the other hand, if a spirit of speculation & project should appear to actuate her councils, & if she should trifle with her public domain, involve herself in contradictory obligations, — or seek to establish her prosperity on any other foundations, than those of justice & good faith, — there would, then, be little to be hoped, either in regard to punctuality in pecuniary engagements or to the probability of her maintaining an independent National character.

My opinion, on the whole, is, that the prospects of Texas are now far better & brighter than they have ever been before; that the interests of our own country require, that she should keep herself free from all particular European connexion; & that whatever aid can be furnished to her, by individuals, or corporations, in the U. States, in the present state of her affairs, to enable her to maintain a truly independent & national character, would tend to promote the welfare of the U States, as well as of Texas herself.

HENRY CLAY TO BIDDLE

Ashland 14th Sept. 1838

My Dear Sir

I received this morning your favor of the 7th instant communicating several inquiries, respecting Texas, on which you are desirous to obtain my opinion. This I have not the least objection to express; but without a strong necessity I should not wish it to be published. And my aversion to its publication arises solely out of the consideration that, at this time, I desire voluntarily to appear in the public prints as little as possible, lest I should be thought to be endeavoring to conciliate public support.

I am glad to learn from you that the Minister from Texas intends to withdraw the application from Texas to be incorporated in our Union. It is a wise step; for it is perfectly manifest that, whether it is expedient or not to annex it to the U. States, the public mind in this Country is not in a temper to sanction such a measure, at this period. The longer agitation of the question can do no possible good to our party, whilst it has a positively injurious tendency upon the domestic interests and relations of the other. If the question were to be prolonged, and a foreign attack, other than from Mexico, should be made on Texas, I think that a majority of the American Congress could not be got to succor Texas in warding off such an attack. Whereas, if the project of annexation be abandoned, and any European power were to attack the independence of the new Republic, I think it would be the inclination, as I am sure it would be the interest and the duty of the U.S. to prevent the success of the attack.

Whether Texas will be able to maintain the Independence which she has declared, or not, I have no means of judging which you do not possess, perhaps not so many. I am inclined to believe that she will, if the Government is administered with reasonable ability. Time is everything to Texas, whilst delay is ruinous to the Mexican reconquest. The French Blocade [1] operates most advantageously to Texas, by rendering her secure against attacks from the Gulph, which I have always thought her most vulnerable side. She ought to wish that this Blocade may be long continued. In the mean time emigrants are pouring into Texas, and daily adding strength to her. I do not see how Mexico, torn as she is by

---

[1] For the French blockade, cf. Yoakum, H., *History of Texas* (New York, 1836), vol. II, pp. 252–257.

factions, with her finances totally disordered, no efficient army nor commanders, and no good materials for an army to be sent on a distant conquest, can subjugate the revolted province. If France were out of the way, and Mexico *had* and could *keep* the preponderance at Sea, Texas might be in danger.

If Texas is to be an independent power, it is the obvious interest of the U.S. to cultivate her friendship, as their nearest neighbour, in that quarter; and it is consequently their interest that Texas should *feel* that she has been well treated by them. Hitherto she has had no just cause to complain of the U.S. whatever they may have given to any other power. This feeling of friendship towards the U.S. on the part of Texas, for one, I should be happy to see strengthened, by all the good offices that can be rendered, consistently with our neutrality. The loan, which she wishes to negociate, and which you are inclined to make, may unquestionably be effected, without any violation of any Neutral duty by which the people of this Country stand bound. Of course, I give no opinion as to terms, or the security which may be offered for its reimbursement. Assuming them to be satisfactory to the parties, I think it, in every respect, highly desirable that Texas should contract an obligation for the loan in this Country, and not in any European State.

I do not believe that the U.S. will or ought to interfere, so as to become a party to the contest, whilst it is confined to Mexico and Texas. But if any European power, and especially if G. Britain or France, were to attempt the conquest of Texas, or to aid Mexico in reconquering it, in my opinion the U.S. could not regard any such attempt with indifference.

I have thus, my dear sir, frankly expressed my opinions. I shall be happy if you should be able to derive any assistance from them; but for the reason already stated, to which I should add that I send the first draft of my reply, without correction, and without retaining any copy, I do not wish publicity given to them without an urgent reason.

THOMAS COOPER TO BIDDLE

Columbia S. Carolina
Octr 1. 1838

Private
Dear Sir.

To the following letter make no reply. If I say anything that has not occurred to you before, which is very unlikely, use it in your own way.

My original proposal met with the concurrence of every sensible man to whom I stated it, as a desirable event if it could be carried. But all doubted its present practicability, from the prevailing ignorance & prejudice about Banks. That prejudice is evanescing. But I think, the matter may be managed some years hence, if you take advantage of a stepping stone, which I am persuaded is likely to be placed for your accomodation. I see clearly that H. Clay is likely to be the successful candidate. Harrison is out of the question. So is that very able man Webster. I think, Clay does not mean to advocate your bank as the national Bank. In fact, *You* are that Bank. When you quit it, you carry with you its Character. All the good it does, and great good it has done, is not given as credit to the Bank, but to Nicholas Biddle. It is all imputed righteousness to yourself, and when it is managed by other heads, it will be difficult to support its present reputation.

Why not take Woodbury's place under Clay? Then the national bank will be your Bank — an appropriate field of usefulness and reputation will be open to you — you will have made a great step upwards — and it will be your own fault, if you do not make the next step into the chair which you ought to occupy.

Probably you and H. Clay may have come to an understanding about this; for I am not unaware that the opportunity has occured. Remember, I enter my 80th year this month; & I am talking of probabilities which cannot be realized till I am in the grave. In meantime, if any preliminary movements before the public should be needed, command me if I am living at the time. But I shall not last long. I have had my three warnings. Adieu.

BIDDLE TO E. C. BIDDLE [1]

Phil^a. Octo 31. 1838

My dear Son

. . . Everything goes on very comfortably here. You may judge of the relation in which the Gov^t. and the Bank stand when I tell you that a few minutes ago a gentleman left me having come directly from Washington charged with a communication from Mr Poinsett. Among other things he said Mr Poinsett took occasion to speak to Blair in the presence of Mr Van Beuren, about the Bank; and that the President desired Blair not to attack the Bank or myself any more. M^r. Poinsett himself moreover wrote an article for the Globe, explaining the late Circular issued by the Gover^t., directing the Officers to disburse the notes of the Bank. This article Blair was obliged to publish, adding some remarks of his own, just enough to save his own consistency. I will try to enclose the two articles. . . .

[1] Eldest son of Nicholas Biddle and at this time at Liverpool. Born, 1815.

BIDDLE TO JOHN FORSYTH [1]

(*Private*)   Phil[a]. Novem. 27th. 1838

My dear Sir

I have been wanting for some days past to go and talk with you; but I presume that I must pay the penalty of my notoriety by abstaining from being in Washington just now, and accordingly I write what I would much rather say. What I wanted to speak of was

1. Texas.

I mentioned when you were here, the intention of that Gov[t]. to withdraw its application for admission into the Union. That is now done, and it is very important that the President in his message should speak kindly and if possible cordially about that country, — intimating that this withdrawal does not abate any of our good feelings towards Texas, and that we wish her prosperity. One kind word might do her good; — and that word may now be hazzarded without much risk, for I have reason to know that it will be repeated and approved by some of the most prominent leaders of the opposition. I wish therefore you would see that the message is kindly on that point.

The other matter was

2. That part of the message which relates to money. I do hope that he will not vamp this worn out foolery of M[r] Calhoun, and say any more about the Sub Treasury. The country is disgusted with the subject, — It cannot possibly do any good to the country, — it will do great harm to M[r] Van Buren; — and if he will only say nothing about it we may get along very well; but if we are to have any more such

---

[1] Biddle wrote to Poinsett setting forth the same ideas as stated in this letter.

nauseous stuff, men now well disposed to the President will be alienated, and it will not be easy to forsee all the consequences.

Now upon these two matters I pray you to take order. You are politically responsible for the acts of this administration; — you may be personally responsible for the next administration, if you do not permit these experiments to be continued.

JOHN FORSYTH TO BIDDLE

private   Washington Nov 29 1838
My dear Sir

The Message [1] has received its last touches before your letter of the 27th reached my hands. I cannot therefore avail myself of your suggestions. But I must not suffer you to suppose I would have done so, had they been received in season. The times do not permit any specially favorable notice of Texas. You will find however nothing of unkindness in the simple statement of our relations with the Republick. Admitting, what I do not believe, that you are entirely correct in the other topick the Sub-Treasury, — as I know that M[r] V.B.'s opinions have undergone no change I could not advise him to omit taking notice of the Subject in the message. Under present circumstances such pressure would betray a *want* of firmness & consistency which no danger of consequences politically or personal should tempt any one to betray. . . .

[1] Richardson, *op. cit.*, vol. III, pp. 483–506. Poinsett sent word to Biddle that the President could not take up the Texas question in detail owing to the difficulties with Canada at this period arising from the Aroostook War.

CARD TO BIDDLE [1]

The President
requests the Honor of Mr Biddle's
Company at dinner Tuesday the 26ᵗʰ Feby at
6 Oclock
The favor of an answer is desired

BIDDLE TO DANIEL WEBSTER

(*confidential*)   Philª. Decr. 13. 1840
My dear Sir,

The impression which I have that the coming administration will be in fact your administration: one which I can
honorably support & be connected with has revived a project
in which I have for some time indulged — but which I have
never mentioned to any one even of my own family. You will
therefore receive it in the same confidence in which it is written.

I have retired as you know from all active affairs:[2] I do
not wish to return to them. Whatever share I may have had
in the war now happily ended — by the elevation of my
friends, I have no pretensions — and shall stand in no man's
way. It is a great wish of my family to travel in Europe, and
I should incline to indulge it. But as you know travelling in
Europe to a mere private gentleman is a dull business. If a
man had a high public station & a higher public fame, as you
had, he gets along well, but a private gentleman delivering
cold letters of introduction & making his way into what is

---

[1] This card is interesting in that it discloses the close relations existing at this
time between the President and Biddle after their long Bank war, for at the top
of this card is written in ink, "President — 1839."

[2] Nicholas Biddle had retired from the Bank Presidency in March, 1839, at
the age of fifty-four.

called society has a task extremely repugnant to his pride. I am too old for that & I am satisfied that the only way of being comfortable is to have some public character which at once settles your rank & places you above the necessity of groping your way. Of these stations some are troublesome from the business to be done & from the crowds of country-men with whom one comes into contact: others give less rank but less labor. Now my object being to travel I would not be willing to remain in London or Paris or Petersburgh — but I would prefer some position within striking distance of all the places on the continent, which would form the circle of travel and on the whole the place which seems best adapted for that purpose is Vienna. In regard to fitness, I have nothing to say — I began my career as Secretary in Paris & afterwards in London. I was to have been sent by Mr Madison as Minister to London at the close of the last war, & was not sent because I was not a member of Congress — the 'Far I have never made any suggestion about it, I did not know even of the design till some years afterwards, & as I should be "able" & able from my own private means to do all the external honors of a legation & have already been at Vienna. I think I might be not a very bad successor [1] to the recent incumbent. That place too happens to be vacant so that no one need be removed and it is moreover ought of the sphere of ordinary competition among political men. The great interest to be encouraged there is the introduction upon better terms of our own tobacco and this I think I could man-

[1] Van Buren had appointed Henry Muhlenberg of Pennsylvania Minister to Austria. In 1841 C. S. Todd was nominated, but was shortly afterward succeeded by Daniel Jenifer of Maryland. (*American Almanac, 1843*, p. 108.) Biddle, later, on several occasions wrote to Webster in regard to the post, but the correspondence shows no reply. The possible reason for his non-appointment may be found in the letter of Webster to Biddle, December 24, 1840.

age better, perhaps than any mere planter who would carry about him the odour of his "business in this state."

And now my story is told. I wish to travel & deeming some public character essential I have thought of one which might enable me to do some good, & to represent not unworthily the new administration & the new Secretary for foreign affairs both of which I suspect have been misrepresented in more sense than one abroad. To my objects position not salary is what I desire not so much a place as a passport. Now tell me what you think of all this? Is it a reasonable thing? Is it a probable thing?

DANIEL WEBSTER TO BIDDLE

Private   Dec. 24. '40
My Dear Sir

I duly rec^d your letter, on a certain subject, & have that subject "in all my thoughts." Nob'y could be better for the Country — & nothn would be more agreeable to me, than what you suggested. The difficulty will be with the *Tobacco* men. These Gentlemen got up the Austrian mission, some years ago, & expected a Marylander or a Virginian to fill it. Mr V. Buren disappointed that expectation, & appointed Mr. Muhlenberg, because he could talk German so well. Mr M. having returned, a new rally has been making, & two or three Tobacco raising candidates are in the field already....

BIDDLE TO DANIEL WEBSTER

(*private*)   Phil^a. Decr. 30. 1840
My dear Sir

...2. I have received a visit of many hours from a friend who has just returned after passing several weeks in the midst of the most confidential circle of the President Elect and his friends — a disinterested cool observer and I have no doubt of the truth of his observations. He says decidedly that in the opinion of all that circle Mr W. is the person who will have much more influence with the President than M^r. C. . . .

4. My friend came full of another idea. He says that the same knot are of great friends of mine — that the President himself when lately at Louisville made a very strong & decided eulogium upon me, and that this circle of friends believe that he wishes me to go into the Treasury. When I told him my determination on that head, he concluded with this declaration — Well I assure you, you can make the Secretary "of the Treasury." Now I would not go into the Treasury for all the money in it — but if I could help to put a good man there I would do so. But where is the man? If in this turmoil of Pennsylvania candidates, the President wants to get over a difficulty by naming a Penn^a man & wishes to name me I will refuse by return mail, and then we can find some competent person. I mention this, that you may understand exactly the footing on which M^r. H and I are . . .

R. M. BLATCHFORD TO BIDDLE

New York Jan: 21. 1841

My dear Sir

. . . The Sub Treasury bill cannot now be repealed too soon — it is believed at Washington that the House will repeal it if the Senate will, and it is thought there that with the Penn: Senators a majority of the Senate will vote its repeal. Buchanan I understand has said that if he is instructed to repeal it he will resign. Your Legislature is Whig

— is it not practicable to get them instructing your Senators. Such a movement would Come well & with great power from your State. We could instruct Mr Wright in our State but he does not give faith to the doctrine. It might not be amiss to get Mr Webster's views on the Subject. The Sub Treasury being out of the way The Bank *must* step in.

BIDDLE TO DANIEL WEBSTER

(*confidential*)   Feby 2. 1841
My dear Sir,

    I understand, tho' at second hand, that a gentleman has arrived from Cin^i who states that he heard the inaugural read — and that it speaks of the necessity of a national Bank, & almost recommends it. You may have heard this elsewhere but I mention it that you might be prepared to modify it if you think it should be modified. On the whole I should think the expediency of announcing that purpose so early was questionable. It does not seem to me necessary in the inaugural — however it may do in the message to the new Congress — and I should think it might rally at once the opposition on topics that might be turned to mischief against the new administration before it had time to strengthen itself.

DANIEL WEBSTER TO BIDDLE

Confidential   Feb. 4. '41
Dear Sir,

    Those of us who are here are quite united in opinion, that the Inaugural should be confined to *principles*, & not go into *measures;* or [at] least, with one exception, & that would be to suggest the necessity of early augmentation of *naval means.*

CHARLES AUGUST DAVIS TO BIDDLE

New York 10 April 1841

This steamer will take to you advices of an interesting nature. The death [1] of our Venerable President though sincerely lamented will produce no material change in the policy of our new Administration. The Vice President his successor is a Gentleman of great purity of mind and well calculated to assume the office and we shall probably see the measures originally proposed carried out with signal unanimity.

BIDDLE TO JOHN TYLER

(*private & confidential*)   Andalusia Augt 19. 1842

My dear sir,

In my quiet seclusion I watch with great anxiety the progress of things at Washington — and as lookers on at the game sometimes see a move which may escape the busy players, I venture to make a suggestion. It is prompted by an intense sensitiveness to the present state of the country — by my desire to see your administration prosper — and more especially by the instinctive wish to come to the aid of one [for] whom I have long entertained a sincere personal [2] regard at the moment when he is overcome by numbers.

It is manifest that your opponents are striving to make you odious as an enemy to the interests protected by the Tariff [3] which you are ready to sacrifice in order to gratify

[1] Harrison died April 4, 1841.

[2] Tyler had rendered good services to the Bank in the old war. Cf. Catterall, *op. cit.*, pp. 255, 267, 356.

[3] A full account of the struggle between President Tyler and the Whigs on the Tariff can be found in Von Holst, H., *The Constitutional History of the United States* (Chicago, 1888), vol. II, pp. 451–463; also brief accounts in Taussig, F. W., *The Tariff History of the United States* (New York, 1894), vol. II, pp. 434–439.

Biddle's Home at Andalusia

your personal dislike to Mr Clay and Mr Clay's favorite measure.

Now if I understand your last veto — You do not dislike the Tariff bill itself — & you would have signed it but for its connection with the Distribution clause. If this be so, you have a chance of striking one of those master strokes which decide instantly the fate of the campaigns. It is this:

To send immediately a message to Congress, urging, in consideration of the exhausted State of the Treasury a revenue bill exactly like that vetoed bill — word for word, or as near as you can to it — without saying anything about the Distribution clause. Look at the effect of it. If it succeeds, if your adversaries dare not vote against it — it is your triumph — your measure — a popular measure — for the country cares only for the Tariff & comparatively little for the Distribution. But if it fails — if your opponents vote against it, you will have done your duty. . . .

JOHN TYLER TO BIDDLE

Washington Aug 25th 1842.

Dear Sir,

I thank you most sincerely for your letter of the 19th. Before it reached me the House of Representatives as you have seen by the papers, had passed the Tariff Bill, which I had vetoed without the distribution clause. The Bill is now before the Senate, where it may undergo some amendments, in which event the probability is in favour of its passage. The suggestion you make had occurred to me, and I was strongly impelled to take the step, but upon informing myself with some degree of accuracy of the state of opinion which prevailed here, I abandoned it. A violent contest as I learned had arisen between the tariffites and the distributionists, which fully manifested itself in the final voting in the House, so that the tariffites were driven to look to the democrats for aid, in order to enable them to carry through any measure. The democrats looked to some measure more moderate in its provisions than those of the bill, which I had returned to the House, and being really anxious to have a good, sound and permanent measure passed, I feared evil rather than good. . . . I have therefore resolved to rest on my oft repeated recommendations to Congress, and leave it to assume all the responsibilities, growing out of and connected with that delicate but important question. . . .

BIDDLE TO DANIEL WEBSTER

Andª Feby 27. 1843

My dear Sir,

I beg you to listen to the following oracular sentences which if they have no other inspiration are dictated by a public regard for you & for the Country.

Do not leave your present position!

If you do, you descend —

You must hereafter be only a king or a king maker.

You can do nothing abroad which you cannot do better while you remain here & speak thro your agents — as Secretary you are the Govᵗ — as a Minister you are the Government's agent.

Then if you go who is to take your place?

Some transcendentalist — some cobweb spinner.

— So stay — stay —

Having delivered myself of these profundities I descend from my tripod & am

D.(ANIEL) W.(EBSTER) TO BIDDLE

Mar: 2. 1843

My Dear Sir;

I have not the least idea of going abroad, or of taking any appointment, whatever — But I do not expect to remain where I am, more than a month — This, *inter nos.*

D.(ANIEL) W.(EBSTER) TO BIDDLE

Strictly private & confidential   Mar: 11. 43

Dear Sir

I may as well tell you, in the strictest confidence, the whole truth, respecting the state of things here. The President is still resolved to try the chances of an *Election.* This object enters into every thing, & leads, & will lead, to movements in which I cannot concur. He is quite disposed to throw himself altogether into the arms of the loco foco party. This is just enough towards the Whigs — but it is not just to himself, or his own fame & character. He has altogether too high an opinion of the work which can be wrought by giving *offices* to hungry applicants. And he is surrounded by these, from morning to night. Every appointment, therefore, from the highest to the lowest, raises a question of *political affects.* This is terrible; especially in the Department where I am; & I fear the interest of the Country, & the dignity of the Gov^t. may both suffer from it. Before the Whigs quarreled with the President, I had no reason to complain of any want of proper influence, in regard to appointments connected with foreign affairs; altho the President had quite too many persons on hand to be provided for as chargés . . .

Since the formal abandonment of the President by the

Whigs, my position is entirely changed, as I can ask him for nothing. Between us, personally, there is entire good will; & if his object now was *only* to get thro his present term with credits, we should agree, in every thing. But I am expecting, every day, measures, which I cannot stand by, & face the Country. I must, therefore, leave my place. It seems inevitable. Who will take it; I know not; or what is to become of us all, I know not. I fear, a confused & unsatisfactory scene is before us. — When you have read this, burn it.

BIDDLE TO JOHN TYLER

Anda March 4, 1843

My dear Sir,

I wish to make a suggestion to you & as in all cases the plainest course is the best, I proceed at once to my purpose. How it may accord with your own views I do not know — but your conduct in 1834 has given me a very strong feeling towards yourself & your administration, and it is as the friend of both that I speak.

The subject most canvassed at present is the retirement of Mr Webster — a question of much importance to the country — & of great interest to yourself. Looking at it in both aspects, I have reached these conclusions

1st as regards the country

I take it for granted that there is no fitter man for the place.

This is settled by acclamation

His successor must be his inferior

Now his value lies in being precisely where he is. If he went to England he would be only a single minister — now he is the instructor of all your ministers. Even in England the strength of his name would be greater as Secretary of State giving your instructions to the resident minister in England, than if he were there in person — while to all other foreign governments that strength would be lost.

Then

2. as regards himself,

You could not find a successor who would be so valuable & faithful an assistant to you.

There is no man sufficient[ly] prominent to justify his selection who would not be liable to more personal and political objections, than he has. Yet he has now but shown them. He has run that gauntlet — He is seasoned — and is acknowledged on all hands to do honor to your choice. Besides — and this is the great matter for you personally — he is the Secretary of State — and nothing more. He has no political party, no body of political adherents. All these he has left for you. He has therefore no political aspirations. His strong hold on the country is that he can do the duties of the Department better than any one else — and he will do it. He must work cordially with you — without any cross purposes or intrigues having no political objects of his own. I remember well how my old friend M^r. Monroe was annoyed by having in his Cabinet three aspirants[1] for the Presidency.

I would therefore not let him go from the Department of State whether he wishes it or not.

Yet after all, these may be the thoughts of a retired person who is entirely wrong: for I do not sufficiently understand the personal footing upon which you are & which in

---

[1] J. Q. Adams, Secretary of State; William H. Crawford, Secretary of the Treasury; and John C. Calhoun, Secretary of War.

truth, must decide the question. But if there be no private reasons for your separation, all the public considerations are against it.

Allow me to request that you will not answer this note. It is a subject easy for one to write about — not easy for you — and my purpose is merely to convey the very sincere sentiment of a friend without troubling you with an increase of correspondence.[1]

MEMORANDUM [2] OF BIDDLE TO DANIEL WEBSTER

April 5, 1843

You are going to resign — that you think inevitable — well —

But the matter of resignation is less important than the manner.

In parting with the President the programme will of course be perfectly amiable. Nothing will be visible on either side but reciprocal good will and you are hereafter to be the object of a friendship much cemented by — separation. That settled, the next question is what do you retire to? and by what route?

You retire of course to absolute private life. Any thing else will be a fall obvious and incurable.

Then by what route do you retire?

If you have any political engagement with any one of the candidates, I have no more to say — you must of course abide his fortunes.

But if you are entirely uncommitted the three roads of

[1] On March 7, Biddle sent Webster a copy of this letter with the admonition to show it to no one; and asked Webster "whether You think it will do good."

[2] Memorandum sent by Biddle to Webster.

retreat are open — the route of Mr Tyler — the route of the Loco Focos, the route of the Whigs.

Now I take the route of Mr Tyler to be entirely impossible. The moment you leave him, you cease all political sympathy with his administration.

The route of the Locofocos is equally impracticable. They will never leave their own leaders — they will never move cordially under the banner of him against whom they have all their lives been fighting.

There remains only the route of the Whigs.

Now I have studied that part of the map — with less judgment of course but with more impartiality perhaps than you have done — because your own sensitiveness has made you more alive to the conduct of that party.

They have had jealousies and heart burnings with regard to you — they have treated you unkindly & unjustly. Coldness there has been — shyness, alienation, soreness at the injury done to them by your ceasing to act with them. But in my judgment there is no bitterness — no wound not easily healed and the prevailing sentiment is rather regret & sorrow than hostility.

Believing therefore that you must fix yourself somewhere, that seems to be the best place.

And I have imagined this course —

One of these days — and soon — before your motives are misinterpreted go to some public meeting — not apparently made for the purpose, and say

Six months ago I told you in Fanueil Hall that I was a Whig unchangeable. I repeat it now — you separated from me, not I from you, because I staid in power. But I did not so, because I thought I could do good. I think I did do good in making the English Treaty [1] and you agreed that I was right.

Well, I thought by staying a little longer I could do more good.

I told you so, and tried.

But I find that I cannot do the good I proposed — and therefore I would not remain in place a moment longer than I could serve the country.

And so I have come back to you.

I ask nothing — I want nothing — I take my stand in the ranks of the party willing to work with you, to support our measures, and our men.

Such a step will be decisive — it would be hailed with a shout throughout the country.

It would make a brilliant retreat — it would extricate you from your present awkward position and make your future path public & private as smooth as you could desire.

Think of this —

I offer it because I wish you to know my views before I know yours.

If you have decided or shall decide otherwise I will bring myself to think it best, but now:

this line of retreat both in a military & civil aspect is the best in my judgment.

You would think so too, if you studied the retreats of Lord Wellington in Spain.

If possible, I would say nothing or what is equivalent to nothing at parting.

The fear is that you may seem to approve too much of the past — which is much to be avoided.

[1] Webster — Ashburton Treaty.

—— TO C. B. PENROSE [1]

And^a Apr. 24. 1843

My dear Sir,

Knowing how anxious you are [to] serve the country it strikes me that you might be useful now.

I look with infinite regret at the prospect of a separation between Mr Tyler & Mr Webster. I think Mr Webster is not disinclined to stay if he were made to stay, & he ought to be made to stay. I believe moreover that all the expectations ascribed I trust unjustly to Mr Tyler of making the democratic party *his* party are wholly fallacious. No matter who thinks so such a belief will only mislead him. His patronage has not yet made him a single friend. No. He must take his own course — make his own party of the best men of the country — but not seek to win over any existing class of politicians. He has before him a noble career if he will make an administration of his own exclusively. But if Mr W. goes away I think he will lose the chief strength & the great ornament of his administration.

He spent 24 hours here last week — & seeing unbroken vigor of his understanding I could not avoid feeling it a public misfortune that he should be withdrawn from the public counsels.

Help to prevent it if you can. [2]

[1] C. B. Penrose was appointed by President Harrison as Solicitor of the Treasury, which office he held until the close of the Tyler Administration. He was also one of the editors of Penrose and Watts's Reports of Cases in the Supreme Court of Pennsylvania (1832–1833).

[2] In Biddle's handwriting.

BIDDLE TO JOSEPH GALES

Andalusia Jany 9 1844

My dear Sir

When I had the pleasure of seeing you here we conversed about the benefit which might accrue to the Country from the union of Mr Clay & Mr Webster & their respective friends so as to ensure their triumphant election & a strong & cordial administration of public affairs — I continue of the same mind — I believe that the thing most desirable now would be the nomination of Mr Clay for Pres^t & Mr Webster for Vice Pres^t & this rather because it would shew both in this country & in Europe the cordial union of these two American statesmen in whom the most confidence is placed in Europe than because of any adaptation of Mr Webster for that Station which is one of mere pagent.

Should however this union be impracticable, the next best thing in my judgment would be that Mr Webster should be wholly unconnected with Mr Clays administration, should not I mean be a member of his Cabinet — there is not room enough for two such men in so small place. In that event his proper place is the Senate where he would I have no doubt go & where he might occupy Mr Choats place.[1] ...

BIDDLE TO DANIEL WEBSTER

Andalusia 9 Jany 44 [2]

My dear Sir

I have written to day as I said I would to Mr Gales

[1] When Webster was appointed Secretary of State under Harrison, Rufus Choate was elected to his place in the United States Senate. He was opposed to the annexation of Texas. Cf. Appleton, *Cyclopædia*.

[2] Seven weeks before death. Nicholas Biddle died at Andalusia, February 27, 1844.

my present purpose as far as You are concerned is to avoid all scism between You & Mr Clay. I should for many reasons prefer in the first instance the union of the two names on the same ticket as an assurance both here & in Europe of your cordiality. If any reason should dissuade from that, the next thing is for You to be unconnected with Mr Clays administration & "bide your time" . . .

APPENDIX

Appendix I

AN incomplete "statement of the loans made by the Bank & its Branches to members of Congress (as far as is known), Editors of Newspapers & officers of the Gen¹ Gov^t. & the terms of such loans.

"There are no means in possession of the Bank of ascertaining all the loans made to these several classes of persons during the period of the charter, but as far as is known, the following list comprises the names of such persons who have been or are responsible to the Bank as drawers or endorsers of notes during the last f̶i̶v̶e̶ ̶o̶r̶ ̶s̶i̶x̶ ^few° years."*

New Hampshire	
Isaac Hill	3.800
Massachusetts	
W Appleton	10,000
Dan¹. Webster	17,782.86
N Silsbee	8,000
James Lloyd	8,000
New York	
D. D. Tompkins	40,000
Jas. W Webb	18,000
Sam¹. Beardsley	4,900
Pennsylvania	
Joseph Hemphill	10,500
W^m. Ramsay	8,000
Philander Stevens	3,500
Jno G. Watmough	1,700

° Change made in manuscript. * Manuscript in Biddle's own handwriting.

W^m. Wilkins	6,460
Henry Baldwin	35,819
Louis McLane	5,150
R Walsh	6,541.72
Edwd Livingston	1,000
George A Waggaman	4,800
H. A Bullard	9,050
Joseph R Chandler	2,000
Jasper Harding	37,434.81

Maryland

S Smith & Buchanan	1,540,000
Wm Graydon (?)	9,800

Washington

James Monroe	10,596
John C Calhoun	4,400
James Barbour	16,000
Thos. Hinds	6,000
W H Overton	6,000
Jno H Eaton	9,000
Jno Branch	5,100
J L Southard	1,000
W H Crawford	1,500
W. B Lewis	10,765
Henry Clay	7,500
Gales & Seaton	32,360
Duff Green	15,600
Josiah R Johnston	28,405
Jno McLean	6,733.30
Amos Kendall	5,375

Virginia

Andrew Stevenson	2,000
W^m. C Rives	5,500

W^m. L Archer	2,500
Hugh Nelson	1,000
Robt. S Garnett	1,500
Danl. Sheffey	5,000
Thomas Ritchie	10,900

North Carolina

W^m B Sheppard	5,000

South Carolina

Ja^s. Hamilton Jr	15,400
Joel R Poinsett	13,100
H Middleton	6,000

Georgia

R H Wilde	6,000
Jno Forsyth	20,000

Kentucky

R M Johnson	10,820
W^m J Barry	5,503
George M Bibb	7,500 §

§ In Biddle Papers; Vol. 73; 1837, in Library of Congress.

INDEX

Index of Proper Names

ABERDEEN, Lord, 60, 60 n.
Adams, J., 208 n.
Adams, J. Q., 48 n, 56 n, 63, 63 n, 64, 67, 70, 156, 169, 188 n, 190, 197, 311, 311 n, 312, 347 n.
Allen, W., 298, 298 n.
Angel, W. G., 161.
Appleton, W., 219, 219 n, 237.
Archer, W. S., 156.
Arnold, T. D., 150.
Austin, S. F., 269, 269 n.

Babcock, W., 161.
Baker, C. S., 264, 264 n, 267, 301, 302, 303, 304, 321 n.
Barbour, J. S., 207, 210, 210 n.
Barbour, P. P., 43, 43 n, 44, 45, 46, 47, 48, 90, 149.
Barnard, F., 147 n.
Barnard, Gen'l, 121, 121 n.
Barney, J. W., 45, 45 n, 46.
Barry, W. T., 87, 87 n, 139, 139 n, 140, 150.
Bell, J., 150, 156.
Benton, T. H., 105 n, 131, 272, 298 n.
Bevan, M. L., 81, 81 n.
Biddle, C. C., 9, 9 n.
Biddle, E. C., 334, 334 n.
Biddle, E. R., 267, 267 n, 292, 294, 295, 296.
Biddle, J. S., 197.
Binney, H., 170, 170 n, 172, 220, 220 n.
Blair, F. P., 127, 322, 334.
Blatchford, R. M., 233, 233 n, 317, 340.
Blatchford, S., 233 n.
Bonaparte, N., 7 n, 8, 9, 303.
Bowne, W., 37, 37 n.
Boyd, J. P., 40, 40 n.
Breck, S., 224, 224 n.
Brooke, F., 142 n.
Brown, B., 149, 157.
Buchanan, J., 304, 315, 340.
Buckner, A., 143, 149.
Bucknor, W. G., 194, 194 n.
Buel, J., 243.

Burden, Dr., 264, 304.
Burke, E., 60.
Burr, A., 5.

Cadwalader, G., 33, 33 n, 75, 146, 147, 147 n, 151, 152, 154, 155, 158, 160, 165, 191, 192, 193.
Calhoun, J. C., 28, 29, 105 n, 114, 122, 141, 141 n, 179, 203, 222, 223, 231, 231 n, 268 n, 279, 280, 281, 293, 301, 306, 306 n, 314, 335, 347 n.
Cambreleng, C. C., 44, 44 n, 46, 66, 298, 299, 313.
Cass, L., 150, 160, 160 n, 183 n.
Cheves, L., 27 n.
Choate, R., 352, 352 n.
Clarke, M. St. Clair, 85, 85 n, 86, 87 n, 246 n.
Clay, H., 48, 48 n, 50, 51 n, 61, 105, 105 n, 110, 114, 115, 122, 123, 135, 135 n, 142, 142 n, 143, 145, 149, 153, 154, 154 n, 156, 171, 179, 196, 197, 202, 202 n, 218, 220, 235, 281, 297, 299, 300, 300 n, 304, 309, 322, 323, 324, 326, 330, 333, 334, 342, 352, 353.
Clayton, J. M., 148, 187 n, 188 n, 189.
Clinton, DeW., 102, 160 n.
Colt, R. L., 13 n, 30, 30 n, 45, 46, 66, 87, 104, 122, 199, 245, 310, 310 n.
Connell, J., 169, 169 n.
Conrad, H. W., 267.
Cooke, B., 161.
Cooper, T., 208, 208 n, 209, 211, 213, 215, 230, 272, 277, 278, 280, 281, 293, 296, 316, 323, 333.
Cope, C., 287.
Cope, H., 255.
Cope, T. P., 285, 286, 287, 288.
Crawford, W. H., 347 n.
Creighton, W., 193.
Crommelieu, J., 41, 41 n.
Crowninshield, A., 33, 33 n.

Dallas, G. M., 148, 152, 156, 159, 172, 173, 174, 176, 177, 190.

Davis, C. A., 101, 101 n, 257, 290, 292, 342.
Dewart, L., 151.
Dickerson, M., 148, 152, 157, 276.
Dickins, A., 53, 53 n, 54, 59, 75, 76 n, 77, 128, 131, 146, 172.
Doddridge, P., 149.
Drayton, C., 46, 150, 156.
Duane, W. J., 15, 211, 213, 214, 215.
Dun, W., 73, 79.
Dunn, J. L., 266, 267.

Eaton, J. H., 75 n, 87.
Eaton, Mrs. J. H., 77 n.
Ellis, P., 149.
Ellmaker, A., 179, 179 n.
Erskine, D. M., 5, 5 n, 6.
Etting, S., 234, 234 n.
Evans, G., 156, 268.
Everett, E., 44, 44 n, 253.
Ewing, T., 197, 268 n.

Ferdinand VII, 8 n.
Fisher, M., 241 n.
Fisher, R., 241, 241 n.
Fogg, F. B., 97, 98.
Ford, J., 151.
Forman, J., 101 n.
Forsyth, J., 149, 152, 157, 223, 276, 307, 307 n., 335, 335 n, 336.
Foster, E. H., 97, 98, 298 n.
Fry, W., 4 n.

Gales, J., 46, 46 n, 55, 56 n, 58, 125, 190, 352.
Gallatin, A., 122, 123, 242.
Gibbes, R. W., 139, 205.
Gibbs, G., 34, 34 n.
Gorham, B., 44, 44 n.
Gouge, W. M., 211, 211 n.
Green, D., 61, 62, 96 n, 122, 124, 124 n.
Greene, G., 170.
Grundy, F., 105 n, 149, 157, 298, 298 n.

Hagan, J., 82, 83, 84.
Hamilton, A., Sr., 169 n.
Hamilton, A., Jr., 88, 88 n, 91, 244.
Hamilton, J., 171, 294.
Hammond, C., 225, 225 n, 305 n.
Hanna, R., 149.
Harding, J., 257.

Harper, J., 48, 67, 67 n, 74, 110, 110 n, 127.
Harrison, W. H., 253, 255, 256, 272, 333, 351 n.
Harvie, J. B., 288, 289.
Hayne, R. Y., 121, 121 n, 149.
Hemphill, J., 86, 86 n, 87 n, 116, 117, 118, 124.
Hendricks, W., 149, 153.
Hoffman, G., 61, 61 n, 62, 69 n, 87, 91.
Hogan, W., 161.
Holland, Lord, 5.
Hopkinson, J., 221, 221 n.
Horn, H., 151, 156.
Hunter, J., 114, 114 n, 116 n, 126.
Huske, J., 253.
Huskisson, W., 60, 60 n.

Ingersoll, C. J., 171, 171 n, 174, 179, 181, 183, 184, 185, 186, 187, 188, 188 n, 200, 268.
Ingham, S. D., 53 n, 76 n, 77, 77 n, 78, 86, 94, 105 n.

Jackson, A., 56 n, 62, 63, 70, 74, 77 n, 78, 79 n, 89, 92 n, 93, 93 n, 94, 105 n, 107, 108, 109, 109 n, 111, 113, 120, 121, 122, 131, 140, 141, 142, 143, 145, 150, 152, 153, 160 n, 172, 172 n, 175, 176, 179, 190, 194, 199, 201, 208, 209, 211, 212, 223, 230, 263 n, 268 n, 272, 277 n, 281, 298 n.
Jaudon, S., 81, 81 n, 82, 226, 253, 311, 313, 314, 318, 324.
Jefferson, T., 3 n.
Jenifer, D., 338 n.
Johnson, R. M., 63, 63 n.

Kane, E. K., 153.
Kendall, A., 139, 183, 205, 214, 215, 221, 297.
King, A., 151.
King, C., 291.
King, W. R., 149.
Krebs, J., 266, 267 n, 268 n.

Lansing, G. Y., 161.
Lawrence, I., 34, 34 n, 36, 153 n.
Lawrence, W. B., 123, 257.
Leigh, B. W., 283, 285, 287, 288, 289, 291, 292.
Lenox, R., 31, 31 n, 36, 72, 73, 73 n, 212, 215.

Lent, J. W., 161.
Letcher, R. P., 121, 121 n.
Lewis, M., 88 n.
Lewis, W. B., 72 n, 79, 79 n, 80, 82, 83, 84, 85, 87 n, 93, 97, 99, 103, 114, 117, 160 n, 183.
Livingston, E., 121, 121 n, 129, 150, 171, 174, 175, 176, 177, 178, 184, 187, 190, 191.
Livingston, P. R., 160, 160 n, 161.
Lloyd, J., 38.
Louder, J., 265.
Luchhesini, 185, 185 n.
Lynch, J. H., 287.

McDUFFIE, G., 44, 44 n, 46, 47, 114, 116, 119 n, 123, 130, 141, 150, 151, 152, 153, 154, 155, 156, 157, 158, 159, 176, 178, 188, 188 n, 189, 197, 280.
McIlvaine, J., 49, 49 n, 56 n, 261, 261 n, 263, 264 n, 268 n.
McKim, A., 13.
McKim, J., 13, 13 n, 39, 96, 265.
McLane, L., 128, 129, 130, 131, 138, 139, 140, 146, 147, 148, 149, 150, 151, 153, 157, 160, 161, 165, 169 n, 174, 176, 183 n, 191, 206.
McLean, J., 63, 63 n, 68, 69.
Madison, J., 3 n, 7, 176, 189, 207, 338.
Mangum, M. N., 139, 149, 152, 157.
Mann, J. K., 151, 156.
Marat, 196.
Marshall, J., 93, 283, 283 n, 284, 285, 286, 287, 288, 291.
Marshall, Mrs. J., 289.
Marshall, T., 285.
Marshall, W., 284.
Mason, J., 33, 33 n, 34, 52, 52 n, 53, 73, 73 n, 75.
Mercer, C. F., 140, 140 n, 149, 156.
Miller, S. D., 149.
Mitchell, G. E., 149.
Monroe, J., 3, 3 n, 4, 7, 7 n, 12, 13, 14, 15, 328, 347.
Montesquieu, 207.
Morris, T., 298, 298 n.
Muhlenberg, H., 338 n, 339.

NEWKIRK, M., 297, 297 n.
Newton, T., 149.
Nichol, J., 72, 72 n, 106, 107.

Norris, J., 256.
Norvall, J., 120, 120 n, 121.

OLIVER, R., 13 n, 206.
Overton, J., 97, 98, 109, 109 n.

PARSONS, E., 125, 125 n.
Patterson, R., 276, 276 n, 277.
Patterson, S. D., 266.
Peel, Sir R., 60, 60 n.
Penrose, C. B., 264, 351, 351 n.
Pickens, *F. W.*, 293, 305 n, 306 n.
Pierson, J., 161.
Pinkney, W., 3 n, 5, 5 n.
Poinsett, J. R., 104, 273, 273 n, 274, 276, 281, 306 n, 316, 334, 336 n.
Pointdexter, G., 149, 153, 157.
Porter, A., 97, 98, 235, 235 n.
Potter, J., 48, 48 n, 95.
Priestley, J., 208 n.

RANDOLPH, J., 208.
Rathbone, J., Jr., 198, 198 n, 215, 282.
Reed, E. C., 161.
Reed, W. B., 258, 258 n, 261.
Ritchie, T., 212, 212 n.
Ritner, J., 247 n, 251, 261 n.
Rives, W. C., 298, 298 n, 300, 322.
Robespierre, 196.
Robinson, J. McC., 153.
Root, E., 149.
Rush, R., 55, 55 n, 56, 59, 61, 62.

SEARS, D., 32, 32 n, 153 n.
Seaton, W., 95, 96.
Sergeant, J., 43, 43 n, 46, 78, 147 n, 154, 154 n, 200, 222, 260, 305, 313.
Seward, W. H., 160 n.
Shepard, W. B., 149, 149 n, 156.
Sheppard, C., 301.
Shippen, E., 136.
Silsbee, N., 92, 92 n, 135, 155.
Smith, D. A., 298.
Smith, J. S., 231.
Smith, R., 6 n, 53, 53 n, 117.
Smith, S., 54, 54 n, 62, 65, 87, 94, 121, 123, 138, 143, 148, 150, 151, 152, 153, 155, 157, 161, 177, 197.
Smith, S. H., 227, 227 n, 229.
Smith, W., 283, 284, 288, 289, 291.
Soule, N., 161.

Stein, Baron von, 186 n.
Stevens, T., 247 n, 261 n, 262, 264, 301, 315.
Stevenson, A., 151, 151 n.
Stewart, Commodore, 206.
Stilwell, S. M., 244, 290, 290 n.
Swartwout, S., 213, 213 n, 217.
Swift, Dean, 63.

Tacitus, 207.
Talleyrand, 185.
Tallmadge, N. P., 290 n, 295 n, 298.
Taney, R. B., 139, 139 n, 183 n, 206, 216 n, 223.
Taylor, G. K., 284.
Tazewell, L. W., 121, 121 n.
Thomas, F., 297.
Tilford, J., 73, 73 n, 74, 110, 135, 197.
Toland, H., 84, 85, 85 n, 86, 87 n, 267.
Tyler, J., 86 n, 342, 342 n, 343, 346, 349, 351, 351 n.

Van Buren, M., 63 n, 87, 89, 89 n, 101, 101 n, 102, 102 n, 104, 104 n, 105 n, 111, 122, 141, 141 n, 160 n, 171, 172, 173, 176, 179, 193, 201, 202, 202 n, 208, 209, 250, 251, 276, 276 n, 277, 277 n, 279, 281, 282, 290, 293, 295 n, 297, 298 n, 302, 304, 304 n, 306 n, 315, 323, 324, 334, 335, 336, 338 n, 339.

Van Lier, B., 97, 98.
Vaux, J., 97, 98.

Wallace, J. B., 262, 263.
Walsh, R., 4 n, 6, 51.
Watmough, J. G., 190, 190 n, 202, 221.
Webb, J. W., 194, 194 n, 227, 243.
Webster, D., 38, 41, 52, 58, 85, 145, 147 n, 155, 158, 169, 170 n, 193, 197, 202, 203 n, 205, 214, 216, 218, 220, 231, 231 n, 250, 251, 251 n, 255, 280, 282, 299 n, 301, 310 n, 323, 325, 325 n, 328, 333, 337, 338 n, 339, 344, 345, 346, 348, 348 n, 351, 352, 352 n.
Wellington, Duke of, 60 n, 88 n, 350.
White, C. P., 30, 30 n, 42, 149, 153 n.
White, H. L., 98, 250, 255, 272, 281.
Wilcox, J. V., 287, 288.
Wilde, R. H., 150.
Wilkins, W., 86, 86 n, 148, 152, 159, 183.
Williams, L., 172, 172 n.
Williamson, B., 147 n.
Wirt, W., 3 n, 179, 179 n.
Wolf, G., 175, 224 n.
Wood, S. R., 265.
Woodbury, L., 73 n, 79, 139, 140, 150, 183 n, 215, 274 n, 276, 312, 319, 333.
Woodworth, J., 244, 244 n.
Wright, S., 341.

The Riverside Press

CAMBRIDGE . MASSACHUSETTS

U . S . A